the
dream of
a common
movement

the dream of a common movement

SELECTED WRITINGS
OF URVASHI VAID

EDITED BY
JYOTSNA VAID &
AMY HOFFMAN

Foreword by
Tony Kushner

Duke University Press   *Durham and London*   2025

Printed in the United States of America on acid-free paper ∞
Project Editor: Bird Williams
Designed by Courtney Leigh Richardson
Typeset in Warnock Pro by Copperline Book Services

Library of Congress Cataloging-in-Publication Data
Names: Vaid, Urvashi, author. | Vaid, Jyotsna, editor. |
Hoffman, Amy, editor. | Kushner, Tony, writer of foreword.
Title: The dream of a common movement / selected writings
of Urvashi Vaid ; edited by Jyotsna Vaid and Amy Hoffman ;
foreword by Tony Kushner.
Other titles: Selected writings of Urvashi Vaid
Description: Durham : Duke University Press, 2025. |
Includes bibliographical references and index.
Identifiers: LCCN 2024035210 (print)
LCCN 2024035211 (ebook)
ISBN 9781478031628 (paperback)
ISBN 9781478028444 (hardcover)
ISBN 9781478060659 (ebook)
Subjects: LCSH: Vaid, Urvashi. | Gay activists—United States. |
Gay liberation movement—United States. | LGBT activism—
United States. | Gay rights—United States. | Homosexuality—
United States.
Classification: LCC HQ76.8. U5 V34 2025) (print)
LCC HQ76.8.U5 (ebook)
DDC 306.73/30973—dc23/eng/20241122
LC record available at https://lccn.loc.gov/2024035210
LC ebook record available at https://lccn.loc.gov/2024035211

COVER ART: Urvashi at Dyke March, 2011. © Donna Aceto.
Courtesy the photographer.

For Urvashi

CONTENTS

PART 3. TAKING STOCK

FOREWORD

Tony Kushner

I believe fairly conventional things, among them—that power yields nothing without a demand and without some kind of countervailing power to win that demand; that organizing to more democratically redistribute power and access is how we will win change; that sex is as central to human beings as food, and as potent a motivator in our lives; and that the biggest job of intellectuals, be they in activist realms or in academic realms, is to disturb power and challenge tradition. — URVASHI VAID

Some people shouldn't die.

Urvashi Vaid succumbed to cancer at sixty-three years old, in May 2022. Those of us who knew and loved her are and aren't surprised at how keen our grief remains.

Urvashi was an activist. She was a leader of the LGBTQ+ community. She was a builder of bridges and a repairer of breaches; she was a restorer and a revolutionary. She was a pragmatist and a visionary. She was also a luminous human being, delightful, loving, loyal, compassionate, passionate, a sensual intellectual, an intellectual sensualist, a straddler and examiner of contradictions. She deeply enjoyed her renown, she relished her partner Kate Clinton's fame, she attracted a glittering array of semi-celebrities and full-blown celebrities, the great and the good, all of whom adored her. When her protean contributions weren't recognized or understood, as sometimes happened, it troubled her—but not very much, or at any rate, she seemed able to shrug off narcissistic injury. The work always mattered more to her than any acclaim and the work was always political and always collective. Urvashi knew that solipsism and self-promotion are destructive of community; she knew, with more certainty than most of the rest of us, that nothing is lovelier or more thrilling or more sexy or more meaningful than the experiences of communal building and belonging, of actively participating in the efflorescence of power from within a community seeking liberation.

Urvashi Vaid was an activist, a political woman in whom anger and hope cohabited with remarkable, dynamic comity. Her rage against past injustices would explode, accompanied by horror and despair, and then, fed by some mysterious, powerful, eternal spring deep within, rage would surrender to a reasonably confident anticipation of justice being realized on earth in real time. One of her soul's principal leavening agents was an impatient patience; she knew that progress takes time and its paths are almost always corkscrew. But maybe those of us who depended so much on her wisdom, wit, prodigious energy, and courage shared a secret assumption that justice wouldn't dare not to arrive while Urvashi was alive.

So to repeat: Some people shouldn't die.

It'll be obvious to those who read the essays in this book that, in an important sense, in every sense other than the merely physical, Urvashi is very much alive. Anyone who makes a list of organizations she created or helped to create; the organizers, scholars, artists, politicians, lawyers, rich people, poor people, teachers and students with whose lives her life intersected; the journalism, advocacy, and protest alluded to in her writings—which form only part of the picture—will see that the sheer quantity of good she contributed to the world will ripple outward, uninterrupted by the tragedy of her death, building in strength, creating kinds of change Urvashi dreamed about and kinds of change she couldn't imagine. That's the tragedy: when progress happens, Urvashi ought to be there, to see it, to join it its shaping, to worry over its preservation and expansion, to dance in celebration. She loved to dance. She will be there, of course, in memory. This book will help progressive people remember who she was and why she mattered.

It will also help anyone who cares to understand what really went on in the tumultuous, excruciatingly painful, hideously reactionary, and electrifyingly revolutionary times through which Urvashi lived. She kept careful account of how exactly the LGBTQ+ movement coalesced after Stonewall. She paid rigorous attention when the nightmare of the AIDS epidemic overwhelmed us; she participated in the heroic refusal to surrender the forward momentum of liberation to a biological catastrophe (made infinitely more lethal by state and social hatred of queer people). She was equally rigorous in reporting the epidemic's revelations of vulnerability and interconnectedness, of the costs of class and race and gender, lessons circumscribed by failures of empathy, solidarity, and vision. In common with other great historians, Urvashi is true to the truth of what happened; the facts, scrupulously recorded, analyzed as dispassionately as possible, render the profoundest judgments.

And yet Urvashi was not a historian. There's very little in this book written purely for the purposes of remembering or memorializing. All of these essays were intended to map out paths of political action. From fastidious observation, Urvashi in these speeches and articles is always gleaning lessons to be learned, distilling complicated experience to its practicable core, identifying from each of the several historical epochs through which she lived and in which she was an active participant and often a major figure, a handful of usable, workable, memorable tenets to take with us as we continue on with the fight. Even when she declares it her intention to remember, to write history, the activist can be discerned, fidgeting impatiently in the back seat, while the historian tells her story. Eventually, the backseat activist will clamber into the driver's seat, gently nudging the historian away from the steering wheel. Urvashi's interest in the past, serious as it is, always gives over in her writing to her immense passion for a better, more just, more humane future. Every sentence she writes inclines toward that future, every sentence urges her readers to understand and then act.

Urvashi is never, ever disdainful of thinking. The process that leads to effective political action, she tells us over and over, involves understanding, comprehending, even contemplating—as long as pensive inaction is genuinely a means toward answering the immemorial, central question: What is to be done? Unwilling to privilege economics over race and identity, and unwilling to subscribe or submit to any single theory, Urvashi wasn't a Marxist—or at least I don't think she was. I'm realizing now that I don't think I ever asked her if she was. But her sense of praxis, of the dialectical interplay of thought and action, is absolutely consonant with Marx's famous declaration at the conclusion of his *Theses on Feuerbach*: "Philosophers have hitherto only interpreted the world in various ways; the point is to change it."

This is, therefore, a book of essays of practical politics. Rhetoric is steadfastly avoided.

Even religion is subject to vigorous, precise language and hardheaded thinking. Urvashi recognizes the role of faith in progressive political struggle, both historically and personally. She acknowledges religion and spirituality, like cultural tradition, cultural difference, and identity, as forms of human energy indispensable to the fight for justice, which demands so much human energy. She recognizes the value of faith in making self-sacrifice possible—something else justice demands. Faith, she insists, is deserving of respect. But, ever the lawyer, she avoids theology and its attendant thickets. She never puts on prophet's robes. When Urvashi calls for vision in the struggle for the good—critically necessary, as she never neglects to remind us—she never lapses into the incantatory or the vatic. Vision for Urvashi is not ooky-spooky immaterial; it's the creative application of intellect, passion, generosity, and daring ambition to concrete circumstance. Political energy and effectiveness are strengthened, not weakened, by aiming at large targets, by building coalitions, not just single-purpose movements, by attacking the roots of injustice rather than snipping off a few of its thorny tendrils and prematurely declaring victory.

If a philosophical construct can assist in clarifying or concentrating a point, Urvashi doesn't hesitate to employ it. She doesn't abuse theory, theorists, academics, or scholars, as some activists do; she's fully aware that effective action requires consciousness, conscientiousness, and intellectual as well as physical struggle. But it is an article of faith with Urvashi that no degree of complexity with which action is confronted in the abstract ever legitimately paralyzes the imperative to act. There's a statue of Giuseppe Mazzini in Central Park that rests on a plinth on which are inscribed the words "Pensiero ed azione"— thought and action. Activism is the only means to achieving synthesis.

And even when engaging in theoretics, Urvashi is allergic to language that excludes people who lack access to specialized vocabularies or knowledge. Her words are as deeply democratic as her politics. In what might be his last poem, Bertolt Brecht wrote:

> And I always thought: The very simplest words
> Must be enough. When I say what things are like
> Everyone's heart must be torn to shreds.
> That you'll go down if you don't stand up for yourself—
> Surely you see that.

Any writer's work describes three things simultaneously: the writer's times, the writer herself, and her imagined audience. As her work conjures up her audience, the writer reveals what she believes people are made of, what we're capable of—both for good and for evil—how capable we are, or aren't, of tolerating and creating change.

Chief among Urvashi's articles of activist faith, chief among the articles of faith of those who think that democracy is a good and workable way for people to attempt to live together, is an unbudgeable certitude in the demos, in the people. Urvashi's life and work are an affirmation of Brecht's prayerful poem. Our hearts will be torn by an awareness of injustice inflicted on others. We understand that unless we stand up for ourselves, we'll be destroyed. We are able to identify our own subjectivities, our own selves, our inalienable rights, and we are able to extend that self-awareness to an awareness of the Other. Elizabeth Alexander concludes her poem "Ars Poetica: I Believe" by asking her reader, "and are we not of interest to each other?" Beyond doubt, Urvashi's answer to that all-important question would be a full-hearted and full-throated "YES."

That conviction in the fundamental reasonableness and goodness of people is today being challenged by local and global eruptions of malevolence unlike anything people of my generation have lived through, whipping our heads around to gaze with horrorstruck recognition at old forms of barbarism, long ago relegated to history's garbage heap, back now with and for a vengeance, fueled by an uncanny, insatiable, devouring energy, a determination to destroy that's a nightmare, mirror-reversal of progressive activism. In our present moment, the expectation of governance appears to have been abandoned by millions of people, for whom the political has become mainly a platform for gruesome public enactments of what's worst in us, of our most antisocial, anti-intellectual, xenophobic, sadistic, death-driven fantasies.

Are these essays, in this awful moment, of use? The years to which they bear witness were felt, by those who lived and struggled through them, to be very tough years, filled with many dangers and hardships; but there was an undergirding sense of the possibility of progress. In today's floods of calamity and cruelty, we're faced daily with the temptation to despair. Do we now read Urvashi's patient parsing of actual, discernible, empirical reality, her hope for change and her faith in human beings with (Goddess help us) nostalgia? Would it not be better to counter the right's kakotopia bacchanalia with, I dunno, performance art of our own?

I'm pretty sure Urvashi, after she'd finished rolling her eyes at "kakotopia bacchanalia," would be first in line for any festival of progressive performance art. But then she'd return to her work, which was an articulated and by-example insistence on the irreducible value of working as the only legitimate answer to the anti-politics of reaction and recidivism, as the only true means of refusing despair.

In the pages of this book we're given a great blessing: the privilege and joy of watching one of the best of us in her passages through the labyrinth, winding up in her deliberate way the threads that connect causes and consequences. Travel with her, and your understanding will grow, the ground beneath your feet will regain some of the solidity you'd felt it had lost. Despair is defeated by meaning. Engage with the life and work of Urvashi Vaid, and you'll feel less lost, and braver and smarter about where to go, how to live, how to build resistance, how to move and how to build movements.

FIGURE I.1. Urvashi interrupts a speech by President George Bush at the National Leadership Coalition on AIDS Conference in Arlington, Virginia. She was escorted from the hall by Arlington police. March 29, 1990. AP Photo/Dennis Cook.

INTRODUCTION

Jyotsna Vaid and Amy Hoffman

On March 29, 1990, President George H. W. Bush was to give his first major policy speech on AIDS at the National Leadership Coalition on AIDS Conference. Among the five hundred invited attendees gathered to hear what initiatives the Bush administration would announce to address the crisis that had already taken 180,000 lives was a thirty-one-year-old woman of Indian origin, an out lesbian since college, and the executive director of the oldest and largest organization on LGBTQ rights, the National Gay and Lesbian Task Force. When it became clear that no new policy or funding initiatives were forthcoming in the president's speech, the young leader quietly opened her briefcase, stood to face the president, and held up a sign that said, "TALK IS CHEAP, AIDS FUNDING IS NOT." She was immediately escorted out by security. Her protest, captured in an image that was prominently featured in news coverage across the country, catapulted Urvashi Vaid onto the national stage as the face of peaceful but forceful resistance, and of personal courage and integrity.

Although that moment brought her national attention, Urvashi was already well known by then as a powerful advocate for social justice and a skilled strategist who was as adept at writing policy briefs as she was at delivering rousing speeches. Lit from within, politics infused her life. Her favorite saying was "Praxis makes perfect." (She was so identified with the phrase that her friends later emblazoned it on T-shirts they created for her fiftieth birthday bash.) Urvashi came to that AIDS conference in 1990 with two decades of political activism already behind her. She had protested the war in Vietnam at the age of eleven, delivered her first political speech for a progressive candidate for president at the age of thirteen, organized in college at Vassar a divestment campaign against the apartheid regime of South Africa, and written for the influential Boston weekly *Gay Community News* while earning a law degree from Northeastern University.

Trained in gender and sexuality law, Urvashi started her career in the mid-1980s as a staff attorney for the American Civil Liberties Union. She then joined the National Gay and Lesbian Task Force, the youngest person and first person of color to assume the role of its executive director. She left the task force in 1993 to work on her first book, and later returned as director of the Task Force Policy Institute, commissioning several research reports and surveys. From her years in advocacy, she moved to philanthropy where, as deputy director of the governance and civil society unit at the Ford Foundation, executive director at the Arcus Foundation, and board member of the Gill Foundation, she helped shape funding policy and gave millions to support social justice projects. She was a visiting scholar at the City University of New York and a senior fellow and director of the Engaging Tradition project at Columbia University School of Law. From 2015 until 2022, she was CEO of the Vaid Group, LLC, a social-innovation consultancy firm, and its associated think tank, Justice Work, launching several important initiatives and networks. In a career that would span four decades, Urvashi became known, in the words of the *New Yorker* columnist and author Masha Gessen, as the "most prolific" organizer in the LGBTQ movement's history, sought after for her incisive analyses and political acumen.

The years between 1987 and 1993, when Urvashi was working at the Task Force, were a particularly significant period in the LGBTQ movement. As historian John D'Emilio observed, at a 2023 symposium held at Emory Law to commemorate Urvashi's legacy:

> The combination of the AIDS crisis and the transforming impact of the 1987 March on Washington created more rapid growth and an upsurge in militancy that dwarfed what emerged from the Stonewall uprising two decades earlier. Massive numbers of people were coming

out; funding for organizations expanded; more organizations had paid staff rather than simply volunteers; and LGBTQ-positive legislation was getting passed by Congress for the first time. So—the point is that Urvashi found herself in a critically important role at a critically important historic moment.

As D'Emilio further notes, under her leadership, the work that the Task Force was already doing with Congress and the executive branch of the government expanded, with the passage of the Hate Crimes Statistics Act, a large AIDS care and prevention funding appropriation, and the inclusion of HIV-positive status as a protected category in the Americans with Disabilities Act. Urvashi brought a new approach to the Task Force, returning it to its roots as a grassroots organization. Under her leadership, the Task Force trained activists to "organize, organize, organize, and connect, connect, connect." Urvashi strongly believed that, to be effective, the LGBTQ movement had to build the movement at the local and state level. To facilitate these efforts, she and Sue Hyde, director of the Task Force's Privacy Project, co-founded the Creating Change Conference, as an initiative of the Task Force. This annual conference, launched in 1988, has become the largest national gathering of supporters of LGBTQ rights, drawing several thousand participants each year.

On April 25, 1993, at the third March on Washington for Lesbian, Gay, and Bi Equal Rights and Liberation, Urvashi again captured national attention with a powerful speech, which was heard by the estimated one million people in attendance. Millions more have viewed and heard the live video of it on C-SPAN in the thirty years since. The speech, which wove together a call for coalition-building with an identification of the religious Right as a resurgent opponent of LGBTQ rights, ends with these words:

— Well, perhaps the religious Right is right about something.
— We call for the end of the world as we know it.
— We call for the end of racism and sexism and bigotry as we know it.
— For the end of violence and discrimination and homophobia as we know it.
— For the end of sexism as we know it.
— We stand for freedom as we have yet to know it.
— And we will not be denied.

These words ring through the decades as the core of Urvashi's vision; they toll now with her untimely passing from breast cancer in 2022, at the age of sixty-three. Urvashi leaves behind a vast body of writing; several organizations, policy initiatives, and networks she launched; and generations of activists and scholars inspired by her example. For those who knew her life's work, Urvashi was an icon. For those who knew her personally, she was an icon and a treasure.

From her earliest days, Urvashi was passionate about righting wrongs. She was eloquent in articulating her progressive vision of LGBTQ liberation and controversial because of it. Often the only woman of color in the room in gatherings of movement leaders, funders, and activists, she demonstrated in her very being that identity is multi-dimensional and that the LGBTQ movement, if it is truly working for social justice, must be as well. In her outspokenness, so prominently on display that day during President Bush's speech, and in her speech at the March on Washington, she inspired both people to whom her perspective was brand new as well as those who shared it.

As part of her life-long involvement in movements for social, economic, and racial justice as a strategist, organizer, and scholar-activist, Urvashi was highly sought after as a speaker. Her speeches offer lessons for activists and scholars alike on how to build and sustain a movement for social justice. Her vision was intersectional and inclusive, from the beginning.

She would invariably begin her analysis of the status quo or, as she put it, the "status queer," by laying out the broader political, economic, or racial landscape within which to understand the issues at hand, and she would invariably conclude with a set of concrete recommendations for action. There were always things to do.

In addition to public speaking, Urvashi was a prolific writer, publishing articles, essays, legal briefs, invited columns and opinion pieces, policy-oriented surveys and research reports, and three books. Her first book, *Virtual Equality: The Mainstreaming of Gay and Lesbian Liberation* (Anchor/Doubleday Books, 1995), made the case that the goal of the LGBTQ movement should not be assimilating into mainstream institutions, which gives only the appearance of equality; the goal should be liberation by transforming those institutions. The book won two awards and has garnered over a thousand citations. It became a classic in progressive circles, energizing a generation of younger activists who went on to become leaders in various social justice organizations.

Urvashi's second book, *Creating Change: Sexuality, Public Policy, and Civil Rights* (St. Martin's Press, 2000), coedited with John D'Emilio and William B. Turner, brings together twenty-three essays by scholars and activists on how LGBTQ individuals and organizations were able to mobilize after Stonewall to bring about significant changes in public policy across a range of issues.

Her third book, *Irresistible Revolution: Confronting Race, Class and the Assumptions of LGBT Politics* (Magnus, 2012), is a collection of nine speeches. The book, as Urvashi notes in the introduction, "joins a lively, ongoing and decades-long conversation about the agenda, composition, and imagination of the LGBT movement," and argues that "an innovative LGBT movement must move beyond seeking the reform of laws to maximizing the life-chances, freedom, and self-determination of all LGBT people."

In her work and in her personal life, Urvashi had a unique talent for bringing people together from all kinds of backgrounds—professional, ideological, cultural, and racial. Her ever-expanding circle of friends included artists, musicians, athletes, policymakers, scholars, community organizers, philanthropists, faith leaders, and political leaders. By her own example, she inspired others to do more, and to bridge differences to build a better world together. Rooted in a pragmatic approach to movement strategy that emphasized coalition-building, her thinking was forward looking for its time and anticipated many of the key problems in progressive politics that we are still grappling with.

The insights and analyses Urvashi offered throughout her life remain startlingly relevant. As D'Emilio says, they came at a formative time in American civil rights history. Mobilized by the AIDS crisis, the movement for LGBTQ rights had grown into a national movement. At the time, the religious Right had not yet coalesced to become the dominant force it is today within conservative (and, increasingly, Republican Party) politics. The prescience of her 1993 speech, with its warning against the religious Right as the enemy of any movement for freedom and dignity, is all the more striking. Urvashi was not content with marriage equality as the goal of the LGBTQ movement, nor confident that the passage of laws granting protections to people on the basis of sexual orientation or gender expression meant LGBTQ people had achieved liberation: laws could always be repealed. Without a movement that saw the interconnection between racial justice, economic equality, and civil rights, and that actively sought to address the vast power of the Right, she felt that progress was doomed to unravel.

Themes of Urvashi Vaid's Movement-Building Work

Four themes of Urvashi's work are particularly relevant in the present moment.

LGBTQ Rights Are Human Rights

Urvashi believed that lesbian, gay, bisexual, and transgender people are human beings who deserve to be treated with dignity and respect. She adamantly rejected the stigmatizing view of LGBTQ people as sinful, immoral, criminal, or dangerous. Beyond this belief, shared with others in the movement, Urvashi took issue with the view that the goal of the LGBTQ movement should simply be acceptance into the mainstream. Allied with the liberationist wing of the LGBTQ movement, she argued that assimilation into the "crumbling" mainstream world was not a model to aspire to and that the goal should be transforming existing structures. She pointed to forms of intimacy and resilience in queer culture that could serve as a model to emulate. As she wrote in her essay, "Assume the Position":

> Our subcultures turn pain into caring; our institutions deliver services, resilience, and humor instead of bitterness and violence; our extended kinship structures deliver emotional and material support, independent of blood ties. Our community is full of exceptional acts of generosity and affiliation with those who are social and political outcasts. (140)

Influenced by liberation theology ideas that political organizing must be guided by a moral vision, Urvashi reached out to others who were inspired by the same vision. She was among the first leaders of secular gay rights organizations to build relationships with progressive, faith-based organizations. In making these connections, she helped frame the struggle for LGBTQ rights as a civil rights struggle.

Single-Issue Organizing Has Limited Utility

Urvashi strongly believed that identity-based organizing (such as organizing around sexual identity or ethnic identity), although often necessary as a first step, is limited in its effectiveness and can actually forestall progress. To build and sustain a movement, connections beyond identity need to be drawn and coalitions formed. For example, in her analysis, the struggle to repeal abortion restrictions and reproductive rights more generally is an LGBTQ issue; it is the same struggle as repealing laws banning sodomy or, more recently, laws banning gender-affirming care. In all these cases, the issue is one of the state encroaching on an individual's right to make decisions about their body.

Liberation Has to Be for All, Not Just for Some

That liberation can only be achieved when the most vulnerable members of society are liberated is the third theme of Urvashi's work. She viewed liberation only for some as a hollow victory. As she pointed out in a 2016 talk, "Marriage = Virtual Equality":

6 · Jyotsna Vaid and Amy Hoffman

But marriage fails for the reasons that formal legal equality as an end goal fails: it does not deliver justice, transform family or culture, or expand queer freedom for all. It does not touch, much less end, structural racism; it does not change the enforcement of the gender binary; it does not deliver reproductive justice nor end familial homophobia. It has nothing to offer about ending mass incarceration and the systemic deployment of state violence against Black and brown communities. (142)

Know What You Are Fighting for, and Whose Vision You Are Fighting Against

Last, Urvashi believed it was imperative for a movement to articulate its vision of a better world, to know what it is fighting for. This also means knowing whose vision it is fighting against. In her view, the real enemies of the LGBTQ movement were not individuals who were prejudiced against gay people out of ignorance. The real enemy was the highly organized and well-funded Christian right-wing movement, with its close ties to authoritarian, white supremacist nationalism. This was a focus of Urvashi's organizing from her beginning days at the Task Force, when she launched a five-year campaign called Fight the Right, and it continued right up to the final months of her life, when she cofounded the 22nd Century Initiative to Counter Authoritarianism. Urvashi saw early on the existential threat the highly organized right-wing, autocratic movement in the United States and globally posed to individuals, to progressive movements, and to democracy itself, and devoted a good part of her efforts to organizing a broad-based movement on the Left that affirmed and protected democratic institutions and civil liberties.

To make change happen, Urvashi believed in—and used—a plurality of tactics. She recognized the value of direct action and grassroots protests, while also recognizing that elections matter, at all levels of government. She believed that protests can put needed pressure on those holding elected positions to effect change, while also recognizing the importance of voting progressive candidates into government.

The Dream of a Common Movement

This book brings together a representative selection of Urvashi Vaid's extensive body of work and includes both previously published essays and unpublished writings spanning thirty years that, collectively, articulate her "dream of a common movement" (a turn of phrase inspired by the poet Adrienne Rich's phrase, "the dream of a common language"). Our intention is to introduce Urvashi's writings to those who did not know her and to deepen the understanding of those who did. The collection presents Urvashi's vision for achieving the dream of a common movement from a queer lens, which focuses on the dimensions she believed were critical for lasting revolutionary change.

The writings cover issues that Urvashi cared deeply about: the importance of political organizing; AIDS activism; gender and sexuality law; the state of the LGBTQ movement at different points of time; the power of money in shaping social justice movements; the need to center race, gender, and class equity in the LGBTQ movement's mission; the threats posed to democracy by the religious Right and white supremacy; and lessons learned from a lifetime in activism.

We structured the book into four parts, each highlighting a different aspect or phase of movement building. The pieces within and across sections are arranged roughly chronologically.

Part 1. Building a Movement

In the selections in this part, which comprise some of Urvashi's earliest writings, she describes her political philosophy and vision for building a progressive movement, rooted in her experiences directing the Task Force in the late 1980s and early 1990s.

The first chapter, "Formative Influences," sketches the development of Urvashi's political identity and activism in her own words. The first half of the chapter contains an autobiographical essay that Urvashi included as the preface to *Virtual Equality* (1995). In it, she reflects on her arrival in the United States at the age of eight, the development of her political consciousness, her professional trajectory as an activist and leader, and her thoughts on the status and future of the gay rights movement in the United States. She noted in later interviews that her immigrant history—moving to the United States from a poor country at a young age—gave her a kind of "double consciousness," an early awareness of cultural difference that opened her up to differences in perspective. Similarly, she observed that the experience of being the only woman, out lesbian, or person of color in many of the circles in which she moved in her career often made her feel like an outsider, and speculated that the feeling of not belonging anywhere may well have shaped her focus on transforming existing structures rather than conforming to them. The second half of "Formative Influences" consists of excerpts from letters Urvashi wrote to her family between 1979 and 1994, a period in which she moved to Boston after graduating from Vassar, plunged into grassroots activism while attending law school at Northeastern University, started her professional career in Washington, DC (at the ACLU and then at the Task Force), and then moved to Provincetown, MA, to work on *Virtual Equality*. The letters offer a window into the pace and texture of Urvashi's life as a rapidly emerging public figure in the LGBTQ movement.

Chapter 2, "A National Lesbian Agenda," is a keynote speech Urvashi gave at the 1991 National Lesbian Conference in Atlanta, Georgia. In the speech, she outlines her vision of a national lesbian agenda in which lesbians bring radical social change for the benefit of all people.

Chapter 3, "We Stand for Freedom as We Have Yet to Know It," is the full text of Urvashi's passionate 1993 keynote address at the third March on Washington for Lesbian, Gay, and Bi Equal Rights and Liberation, in which she lays out why the religious "Right" is fundamentally "wrong"—morally, spiritually, and politically.

Chapter 4, "A Shared Politics of Social Justice," presents a wide-ranging 1998 interview with Alternative Radio host David Barsamian, which was subsequently published in an edited collection by South End Press titled, *Talking about a Revolution*, which also included essays by Howard Zinn and Noam Chomsky, among others. In the interview, Urvashi discusses many aspects of her politics, including the relationship between the LGBTQ movement and a larger American Left, which often denigrated identity-based movements such as those of women and queer folk, as "divisive." In later essays, she delves more deeply into the importance but also the limitations of identity-based organizing.

Chapter 5, "Awakened Activism: AIDS and Transformation," is a lengthy discussion of the impact of the AIDS epidemic on gay rights activism. It is taken from *Virtual Equality*. The piece begins with a poignant portrait of a gay couple, close friends of Urvashi, as one of them cares for the other, who is very ill. The essay goes on to discuss the successes of the LGBTQ and AIDS movements in confronting the epidemic, as they cared for the sick and protested the indifference of government. The essay also points out the movement's failures, as it "de-gayed" the AIDS crisis.

Many in the national LGBTQ movement have implicitly constructed the LGBTQ community as white, male, and economically privileged. In this section, Urvashi makes the case that the only ethical and pragmatic way forward for the movement is to broaden its view of whom the movement stands for and to make racial, class, and gender equity a core commitment. This section highlights the development of Urvashi's politics. In *Virtual Equality*, she argued that obtaining legal rights was a necessary part of the LGBTQ agenda. She begins to explore the idea that fighting for formal legal rights is not enough, because queer people who are poor, of color, disabled, or marginalized in other ways will not be able to access legal rights unless the movement also fights for justice for everyone.

Chapter 6, "Inclusion, Exclusion, and Occlusion: The Queer Idea of Asian-Pacific Americanness," was the lead article in a special issue on South Asia in 2000 of the journal *Amerasia*. In it, Urvashi provides a thorough discussion of identity politics and its (limited) place in progressive social movements. She argues that people must understand their histories, traditions, and social contexts, but they must also unite with others beyond their particular community. Along the way, she discusses the evolution of her own Indian American, immigrant, queer identity.

Chapter 7 features Urvashi's unpublished remarks delivered at a historic conference in 2008, called Race, Sex, Power: New Movements in Black and Latino/a Sexualities, at the University of Illinois. In the essay, she focuses on the ways that race is muted and ignored both by progressives and in the mainstream, as they wish for a "post-racial, post-gender, post-gay" world. She notes that, for many prominent leaders of color, "the erasure of racial identity is the price of admission to the inner circles of power."

Chapter 8, "What Can Brown Do for You? Race, Sexuality, and the Future of LGBT Politics," was first presented as the 2010 Kessler Lecture at the Center for Lesbian and Gay Studies, City University of New York, and is one of Urvashi's most important and nuanced essays. In the essay, Urvashi calls out the racism she and other people of color experienced in the LGBTQ movement and argues, as always, that a substantive treatment of racial equity has to be integral to the mission of the LGBTQ movement for the movement to progress. The essay documents the pervasiveness of a white racial frame in the LGBTQ movement, and notes that the movement has become ever-narrower and more normative as it seeks acceptance and legitimacy by the mainstream, moving "from its anti-militarist, anti-racist, and feminist origins in the late 1960s to its present patriotic, patriarchy-accepting nationalism."

Chapter 9, "Assume the Position: Class and the LGBT Movement," is based on a 2011 invited talk at Vassar College. Finding herself at her alma mater, Urvashi reflects on how attending an elite college changed her class position, both economically and socially. She presents a detailed exposition of how class status affects how we see, want, and transform our conditions. In particular, she reminds us that our class position—the way we see and are seen—is raced and gendered, an observation that she illustrates in the context of the failure of the mainstream LGBTQ movement to grapple with class and economic inequality.

Chapter 10 presents unpublished remarks Urvashi delivered at the 2016 After Marriage Conference hosted by the Center for Lesbian and Gay Studies in New York. In her talk, "After Marriage = Virtual Equality," she explains why gaining the right to marry does not at all mean that the work of the LGBTQ movement is over, as some marriage-equality activists believed.

Part 3. Taking Stock

In these later essays, almost all of which are unpublished, Urvashi used her experiences in philanthropy and academia to offer insights about how funding can shape a movement's focus. She also analyzed threats faced by the LGBTQ movement by the rise of authoritarianism.

In Chapter 11, "Queer Dreams and Nonprofit Blues: The Context in Which Nonprofits Operate," Urvashi presents a history of philanthropy and nonprofit organizations, arguing—in opening remarks at a 2013 conference that she convened with legal scholar and trans activist Dean Spade—that funding priorities must be set by the communities engaged in the work of making change, not by funding agencies.

Chapter 12, "Homo/mentum of the 'Status Queer': A Critical Look at the LGBT Movement," is taken from an invited lecture Urvashi delivered in 2015 at Rice University. She begins by noting the "astonishment" that activists feel as they look back on the movement's progress between the 1970s and 2015. Queer people are covered in the media and portrayed in films and television, they have gained the right to marry, and sodomy laws have been overturned. However, she warns that these gains are not enough. She envisions an "LGBT movement thinking beyond marriage and toward social justice . . . [in which] its organizations would not just be LGBT centered but would instead be progressive with an LGBT focus."

In Chapter 13, "Irresistible Revolution: Understanding the LGBT Movement," based on an unpublished talk delivered at a Global Women's Conference at Middle State Tennessee University, Urvashi concentrates on the threat the right wing, and the Trump administration in particular, poses not only to LGBTQ rights but to democracy itself. She discusses the growth of modern conservatism from the 1960s to the present, and explains that it is essential that the LGBTQ movement take up the challenge of confronting this dangerous trend.

One of the last initiatives Urvashi cofounded, along with racial justice activist Scot Nakagawa, was the 22nd Century Initiative to counter authoritarianism. Chapter 14, "The 22nd Century Initiative to Counter Authoritarianism," concludes this section, presenting their 2021 position paper on the initiative. The initiative's first action was a national conference organized by Nakagawa, in collaboration with Sue Hyde, in July 2023 in Minneapolis, which brought together more than three hundred progressive activists from around the country to talk goals and develop strategy.

Part 4. The Promise—And Precarity—Of Justice

In the final section, we gathered pieces that point to themes that preoccupied Urvashi in her later years: the faith required of activists, a global perspective, queer radicalism, and her own struggle with cancer. Although seemingly disparate, they are united by an overarching concern for justice and love.

In Chapter 15, "Politics as an Act of Faith—Ten Lessons from LGBT Activism," based on a 2009 talk to a faith-based organization and condensed from an essay published in *Irresistible Revolution*, Urvashi outlines her view of politics at its most inspired and shares ten lessons she has learned from a life in activism.

Chapter 16 is an invited op-ed piece from 2018 that was first published in the *Times of India*. In "Forward-Looking 377 Order Holds Lessons for the World," she celebrates the Indian Supreme Court's overturning of the country's colonial-era anti-sodomy law. At the same time, she cautions that while "court decisions declare what is lawful, ... extra-judicial organizing, education, and political engagement will be needed to extend rights and realize equality for all LGBTQ people, not just a privileged few." (Her warning became even more relevant in 2023, when, instead of legalizing marriage equality, as LGBTQ activists had hoped, the Indian Supreme Court tossed the question back to the Hindu nationalist-dominated parliament.)

In 2019, at the fiftieth anniversary of the LGBTQ Stonewall Rebellion, *The Nation* magazine published a series assessing the movement. Chapter 17, "It's Time to Re-embrace a Politics of Radical, Queer, Outsider Activism," is Urvashi's hard-hitting contribution to that series.

Chapter 18, "Chemo Killed the Small-Talk Gene," is a reprint of a highly personal 2014 article that Urvashi wrote for a special issue of the *Journal of Lesbian Studies*. It gives a devastating account of her "journey through diagnosis, treatment, and recovery" from thyroid and then breast cancer. It's worth remembering that she took this journey while at the same time doing much of the writing, teaching, and activist work depicted in this book. The story she tells is both personal and political: an account of personal stamina, community support, and the depredations of the US health care system.

Chapter 19, "Longevity Is a Precarious Dream," concludes this section. It is Urvashi's final public talk, delivered virtually in 2022, while she was undergoing treatment for a recurrence of her earlier bout with breast cancer. It was a speech given at the Creating Change Conference, accepting the 2022 Sue Hyde Award for Longevity in the Movement from the National LGBTQ Task Force. Urvashi ends it with a reflection on the precarious longevity of a movement, and of her life.

The final chapters of the book provide a brief early history and professional biography of Urvashi followed by an extensive bibliography of writings by her and about her.

As Urvashi noted in "Race, Power, Sex, and Citizenship," the goal of liberation should be "a fundamental redefinition of what is good and what is defined as evil," and "gayness is a moral good, . . . sexuality is good, and . . . sexual freedom—defined as the cultural transformation and opening up of ideas of sex and gender—must also be an integral outcome of our struggle for full human rights." Taken together, the compilation of her writings in this collection showcase the inclusive vision that undergirded Urvashi's dream of a common movement and motivated her persistence in pursuing it.

How This Book Came Be

To provide a context for how this book came into being, we first offer a brief account of who Urvashi was to us, individually.

JYOTSNA: Urvashi (or "Urvash" as she was known in our family) was my sister, the youngest of three girls. We attended the same schools—in India and in America—and even the same college, and thus had many shared experiences. I was the shy and serious one, while Urvashi had a magnetic exuberance of spirit that drew people to her. She was generous, loving, and fun to be around. To her niblings—Alka, Alok, Kaveri, and Shantanu—she was an anchor, a cool *masi*, who took an active interest in their lives. In caring for our parents in their final years, Urvashi was all in, even as it clearly took a toll.

Over the years Urvash and I had many long conversations about our professional and personal lives. She was always interested in what I was doing, writing, or worrying about, and would tell me what she was thinking about, politically and personally. In the last few years, she was on a campaign to have me move to the East Coast, to be closer to her and our other sister. Undeterred by my objections that I could not afford to live in New York, she would send me real estate notices of apartments in her neighborhood. At some point I stopped raising objections. After all, moving to New York would mean being near her; being able to share meals, discuss books, movies, and politics; play Scrabble, dance, and argue, in the best Vaid tradition. But that was not to be.

I am grateful that I was able to spend meaningful time with Urvash in New York just before the pandemic, and to visit her and Kate in Provincetown just after, when she was undergoing treatment in the summer of 2021, and to see her again in New York a year later and be by her side in her final days. Losing my brave and beautiful younger sister has been the hardest of losses. We were going to grow old together. Putting this book of her writings together has helped keep her close. And to know—and love—her in a deeper way.

AMY: I met Urvashi when I was twenty-eight. I had just become the managing editor of *Gay Community News*, and she was twenty-two, in her first year of law school at Northeastern University. She and I were introduced by Richard Burns, GCN's previous managing editor and my best friend, who had encountered Urvashi on their first day of law school, as Urvashi positioned herself in the middle of the student lounge and ostentatiously read a copy of GCN, advertising her sexuality and politics to all and sundry.

Urvashi and I were lovers for two years, and after we broke up we stayed close, as lesbians do. When love comes around, we don't let it go. We were part of each other's queer family (Richard Burns, too) for the next forty years. She and I shared a politics of an expansive, feminist, anti-racist, joyous queer movement, but after those early years, we didn't do our political work together. She was on the national stage, while I stayed local, in Boston, and became a writer. Our relationship was simply personal.

Everyone who encountered Urvashi experienced her generosity. She donated lavishly to all sorts of progressive organizations and candidates. And there is more than one person whom she supported financially during a hard time. But even more important was her emotional generosity. She listened to you, and then she told you what to do. Or sometimes she told you what to do and then listened! She was a great giver of advice, and a lot of it was pretty good. Because she saw you. She knew you. She praised you at every opportunity—to your face, to anyone within earshot. She shared her opinions and ideas—and she wanted to hear yours, even when you disagreed with her—or maybe especially then. She kept no lid on her feelings. She laughed out loud. She blew up at you and then let it blow away. She put on a record and grabbed your hand and pulled you into a dance. She told you she loved you, always.

After Urv died, a friend—someone I'd met through Urvashi, of course; she was always bringing people together—said to me, "This must be so hard for you, since you were part of Urv's inner circle." And she was right, it is hard. And then she said, "But, *everyone* was part of Urv's inner circle." That too.

Which brings us to this book.

Amy and Jyotsna had been introduced to each other by Urvashi but we had never worked together. The idea to put together a collection of Urvashi's writings came to us independently around the same time. Within weeks after Urvashi's passing, Jyotsna had begun to informally archive Urvashi's writings for posterity. Urvashi's life-partner Kate Clinton had generously given Jyotsna access to Urvashi's electronic files, which contained a near complete record of her talks and writings. It became clear to us that Urvashi's powerful and prescient writings, some of which had previously only appeared in specialized outlets, deserved a wider readership. With Kate's support and the encouragement of Urvashi's close friends, Susan Allee and Richard Burns, and her former editor, Charles Flowers, Jyotsna and Amy decided to team up on this project, bringing to it our different perspectives, networks, and experiences, but also a shared commitment to keeping Urvashi's voice alive. It has turned out to be a wonderful partnership. The project has been both meaningful and comforting.

Perhaps it is fitting that this first book after her passing has a personal genesis; we know of no one who better embodied the feminist maxim that the personal is political than Urvashi. Urvashi brought out the best in others, inspiring them to act with courage. Her generosity to causes and individuals, her unease with money and marriage as property, all came together as a commitment to showing up, being present. Seeing firsthand how the government and families of origin failed to show up for LGBTQ people dying of AIDS led her to see that there was an inseparable connection between personal and political action. Navigating simultaneously between contradictory worlds, wealth and poverty, Indian and American cultural expectations, straight and queer, theory and practice, participating from her hospital room or her home in events that she could no longer attend in person, all sketch an outline of what Urvashi was like.

As relentlessly as Urvashi worked, and as much passion as she poured into her work, her activism was not the only important thing in her life. Her energy for relationship was boundless. She never failed to attend to the people in her life, to her much beloved Kate, above all.

The determination, persistence, and "realistic optimism" that Urvashi showed as she sought to build and sustain her "dream of a common movement" were qualities that she applied to her own struggle for survival in her final two years.

Conclusion

Urvashi Vaid was guided by a moral vision that gave her the strength to undertake the long and hard struggle to bring about social change. She persuasively argued for forging connections between seemingly disparate issues and groups in order to build strong movements. And she was clear-eyed that this work is difficult and that longevity—of a movement or of a life—is by no means guaranteed and cannot be taken for granted. She understood that hard-fought legal gains can be taken away—as, for example, in the US Supreme Court's *Dobbs* decision, which overturned settled law on reproductive rights. As a veteran activist, she also understood that setbacks and derailments are part of the process and that, rather than feel defeated, we must "keep our eyes on the prize," in the words of the civil rights movement's freedom song, and look to each other for support, pick up the pieces, and build anew. Her writings are a living legacy, a reminder that the work continues.

The Hebrew poet and World War II martyr Hannah Senesh wrote, "There are stars whose radiance is visible on earth even though they themselves have disintegrated. And there are people whose memory continues to light the world after they have passed from it. These lights shine brightest in the darkest night. They light the path for us."

We are again living through the darkest of nights, and Urvashi explains cogently and in great detail in her writings what makes this night so dark. Antidemocratic forces are becoming bolder, seizing power, marauding over the earth. Still, she finds light and hope—in our human capacities for love and for creativity, in our determination to bend that proverbial arc, hanging onto it with everything we've got, to keep it pointing the way toward justice. Let us hold onto that light and that hope.

PART 1. BUILDING A MOVEMENT

1

Urvashi rarely wrote autobiographically, but she did so in her engaging preface to her book Virtual Equality: The Mainstreaming of Gay & Lesbian Liberation. *It provides some useful background information about her life, the origins of her politics, and her thought process.*

Preface to *Virtual Equality: The Mainstreaming of Gay & Lesbian Liberation*

On June 28, 1969, as gay people took to the streets outside the Stonewall Inn, I was ten years old. Three years earlier, my family had emigrated from India to America, and I still remember the drive from Kennedy Airport to Upstate New York, where I would grow up, not only for its twelve-hour length, but for my excitement at seeing snow. My father, Krishna Baldev Vaid, an accomplished novelist, taught English literature and writing at the State University of New York at Potsdam, while my mother, Champa Rani Vaid, an equally accomplished teacher and poet, tried for many years to get a job in that little town. I was the youngest of three daughters. We were part of the second large wave of Indian migration to the United States. Questions of assimilation, of crossing cultural borders, and of developing an authentic identity marked my coming of age.

My first overtly political act was to write a letter, when I was ten years old, to President Richard Nixon, urging him to sign the Anti-Ballistic Missile (ABM) Treaty. I never got an answer. In the spring of 1972, when I was thirteen, I gave my first political speech—a pro-McGovern valedictory talk at my junior high school graduation. As the San Francisco gay leader Jim Foster

became the first openly gay person to address the Democratic Convention, that same summer, I got ready for high school. I had not heard about gay liberation, but I was already pro–civil rights, antiwar, and a feminist. Still, my passion was rock-and-roll more than politics, and my first true love was Mick Jagger of the Rolling Stones.

In the summer of 1975, as the Washington gay activist Frank Kameney battled the US Civil Service commission to allow gay federal employment, I graduated from high school and got ready for Vassar. College taught me, without intending to, how to organize. In protests over admissions and financial aid, through the women's group on campus, and through the anti-apartheid group that I helped establish there, I learned all the tools of activism. As I organized, I studied and fell in love with the Romantic poets, Patti Smith, the Frankfurt School, the Situationist Movement, Shulamith Firestone, a number of my women professors, and all my best girlfriends.

The most formative influences of my college life were the four feminist conferences I helped organize on campus. In 1977, my friends Susan Allee and Betsy Ringel met Amy Horowitz of Roadwork and decided to produce a women's music concert. The result was Olivia Records' Varied Voices of Black Women Tour, which we brought to Poughkeepsie in 1978. Our encounters with the women on the tour—notably with the late poet Pat Parker and the musicians Linda Tillery, Mary Watkins, and Gwen Avery—changed us in profound ways: we discovered a lesbian culture. Producing a Holly Near concert in 1979, and going to the Michigan Womyn's Music Festival that same year further exposed me to the national community of lesbians and feminists.

By the end of college, I was sure that I was a lesbian. For me, coming out happened when I first fell in love with a woman—but I should have known when my rock-and-roll idol changed from Mick Jagger to Patti Smith. I told my sisters immediately, and we worried about how to break the news to our parents. Despite my hesitation about dealing with their reaction, I kept up my political work.

At the time of the first National March on Washington for Lesbian and Gay Rights, on October 14, 1979, I had just turned twenty-one. I had moved to Boston that same month with my best friend in order to "join the women's movement." I opted to look for work instead of taking a bus to the march, and I am still mad at myself for not going. Working as a part-time secretary for two lawyers, I threw myself into Boston's feminist, lesbian, and gay communities. In my lesbian group, Lesbians United in Non-Nuclear Action (LUNA), I worked on a civil disobedience action at the Seabrook nuclear plant in New Hampshire. I joined the most important political group in my life in

FIGURE 1.2. At the US Out of El Salvador March on the Pentagon (left to right): George Chauncy, unidentified person, Amy Hoffman, Richard Burns, Urvashi, Kevin Cathcart, and Tom Huth (holding sign), May 2, 1981. © Ellen Shub, courtesy of the Estate of Ellen Shub.

1980—the nonprofit weekly *Gay Community News* (GCN). Volunteering every Friday night to stuff and mail papers, and later interning on the GCN staff, I formed friendships that would last me a lifetime.

As I moved through law school at Northeastern University in the early 1980s, I realized that the lifetime of many of my friends was to be shorter than we had imagined. AIDS entered my life through my closest gay male friends. Today, as AIDS overwhelms so many of the men and women I love with its relentless horror, I remember the incredulity and paranoia we felt in those early years as the epidemic emerged. We had no idea then of the devastation that awaited us. And we still do not have adequate ways to explain to unaffected straight people the terror turned into anger, the anger turned into numbness, the numbness turned into unrelenting despair, as the traumatic experience of mass death unfolds and shrouds our lives.

In 1980, I went home to Potsdam to come out. I wanted my parents to hear it from me, not read about my activism in the paper. But I could not get the words out of my mouth. That night I returned to Boston, and my sister called with the news that as soon as I left, my father had asked her if I was gay. She had said yes. My dread of this disclosure proved worse than my parents' reaction. Over the years, my parents moved from disapproval to incomprehension to acceptance to tremendous support. In some ways, my choice to leave mainstream work for full-time gay political activism was harder for them to accept than my sexual orientation.

By the time HIV was identified in 1983, I was living in Washington, DC, working as an attorney for the National Prison Project of the American Civil Liberties Union. I still worked with Roadwork to produce women's culture, and when Ronald Reagan was reelected, in 1984, I cofounded a lesbian direct-action group, LIPS. In 1985, with the encouragement of Mike Riegle, who founded GCN's Prisoner Support Project, I began the National Prison Project's work to bring more attention to the treatment of prisoners with HIV and AIDS. (Mike died of AIDS in 1991.) Living in Washington led me to meet the National Gay Task Force's (now NGLTF) lobbyist Jeff Levi and its exciting executive director, Ginny Apuzzo, and I began to consider gay rights work as something to do full time.

When the Second National March on Washington for Lesbian and Gay Rights was held, on October 11, 1987, I had quit my legal job at the ACLU and had been working at NGLTF as its public information director for more than a year. Over the next several years, I threw myself into media organizing, developing relationships with grassroots activists, organizing direct actions, devising strategy and policy positions, and eventually, when I became NGLTF's director, trying to raise the money to do all this work. I was a speaker at the March on Washington for Lesbian, Gay, and Bi Equal Rights and Liberation, on April 25, 1993, but by that time I had left NGLTF after six and a half years on its staff, and had begun to work on the book that became *Virtual Equality*.

I left NGLTF for personal and political reasons. Personally, I grew tired of juggling the pressure of national work with my desire for a personal life. I loved the movement, yet I wanted a fuller life. I wanted time to develop my relationship with Kate [Clinton], with whom I had maintained a long-distance relationship for five years; and I wanted the time to think and feel, something that the pace of national organizing precluded. On a political level, I left NGLTF because I was not sure that it could do what I felt needed to be done by the movement. At the time I made the decision to leave, in early 1992, I was clear about the importance of the mainstream civil rights work done by the organization and others like it. Yet I was not clear that this was the work I wanted to do. I was not sure that I had the ability to steer the group further in the progressive direction I believed was necessary. A national organization is a cumbersome load; the demands for it to represent a wide array of people are real and legitimate. I felt increasingly stifled in acting on the politics of social justice and liberation that I hold dear. Leaving to write was a decision that respected my needs as well as the realities of the organization.

My reasons for writing *Virtual Equality* were not literary or scholarly, but activist and also personal: to gain a better understanding of the problems the gay political movement faces and, in part, to figure out how best to use my own energies. This time of reflection became a chance to assess my political work over the past fifteen years of involvement in gay communities.

In its first incarnation, the book was a consideration of what happened in 1992, why it was such an unusual year for gay politics, and what the election of President Bill Clinton meant. I vividly recall the night Clinton won, because I walked around in such shock. The candidate we had supported, who had openly embraced us, had won! At the national level, I had seen the gay movement move from the margin of political life during the Reagan and Bush years to the center of the policy-development process. I had seen gay men, in particular, live with the complete destruction and reconstruction of their communities and gay families as a result of AIDS. After my involvement in crafting the national gay and lesbian movement's strategies for several years, I wanted to understand and explain how this could have happened.

As I wrote, however, the book came to be a document of self-criticism more than a history of the movement's accomplishments. I saw the shattering of my own illusions of change, as Clinton did to gay people what most politicians have done, and as our movement experienced the paradox of unprecedented cultural possibility accompanied by the persistence of the prejudice and stigmatization gay people had challenged for decades.

Out of these observations came my concept of "virtual equality"—a state of conditional equality based more on the appearance of acceptance by straight America than on genuine civic parity. New leaps in gay access, visibility, and power have not transformed the second-class status of gay, lesbian, bisexual, and transgender people. The political access some have gained has translated poorly to genuine clout, and the lack of an organized grassroots base remains the gay movement's Achilles' heel.

My book begins with an examination of where we stand and ends with a series of specific tasks to be tackled by those interested in doing more. My hope is to bring about a rethinking of our movement's approach to the dilemmas we face. As Allen Ginsberg wrote, "America, I'm putting my queer shoulder to the wheel." Let us do just that.

Letters to the Family

The excerpts of letters from Urvashi to her sister, Jyotsna ("Jyody") and to her parents start from when she has just moved to Boston, after graduating from Vassar, in 1979, and end in 1994, when she is working on her book, Virtual Equality. *During this period, her family was in different places (her sister Jyotsna was in graduate school in Montreal and then started her academic career in Texas; her sister Rachna was living in Rochester, NY, and then started law school in San Diego). Urvashi's parents were in the process of relocating from Potsdam, NY, to India; in the early 1980s her father was a visiting professor of English at the Indian Institute of Technology Delhi (IIT-Delhi), and later a writer-in-residence at Bharat Bhavan, an arts complex and museum in Bhopal, and her mother—Champa Vaid—started writing and publishing poetry in Hindi. The letters have been condensed and edited.*

October 1979
Allston, MA

Dear Jyody,

As you may have heard, I've found a home—a co-op in a large Victorian house—and now begins the real ordeal of job-getting. I feel good about this place. It's exciting, manageable, plenty of opportunity. I feel somewhat dislocated and lonely, and sometimes overwhelmed by the reality of the things I am doing, the way I live my life, my ambitions, etc. But life's supposed to be upsetting.

Generally, I am very well and hoping to make this all work out well. You must come visit as soon as you can and want to!

Lots of love
Urvash

Feb. 19, 1980
Allston, MA

Dear Jyody,

Life in Boston is fast-moving, always changing, and pretty exciting in general. At the moment I'm working two part-time jobs—one as a secretary for a two-man law firm, the other with a typing service called Letter Perfect. It's pretty manic to go from one to the other but I sure do know the transit system by now. I have applied for this other part-time job at Redbook (a socialist radical bookstore in Cambridge). . . .

My main reason for coming to Boston was to be in an active, diverse, large community of feminists—which does really exist here. I mostly hang out with women—mostly lesbians—and actively associate with the gay community here. That whole question becomes less a question and more a lucid statement as I "grow up." I am a lesbian and that's a pretty important part of my life and politics.

Will hear from law schools in a few months. I actually find myself wanting to get in (given all my reservations about the idea of being in school again). . . .

> I think of you and send you all my love.
> Urvash

April 26, 1980
Allston, MA

My dear Jyody,
So, I can't believe I haven't talked to you about your Brazil conference. It sounds as exotic and "far out" as I had ever imagined. . . . Send me copies of any new writings. I do read them!

Life's fine here. Busy as always. Just your basic survival stuff (work, cook, clean, laundry, transport, enjoy, create etc.) takes almost full-time effort.

Am still intensely in the middle of the political fray. Can you believe me in law school??? I have some problems with that but am excited nonetheless. Will call you with details. Take care.

> Lots of love
> Urvash

January 3, 1981
Allston, MA

Dear Jyo,
School resumes tomorrow after a very fast vacation which I've enjoyed immensely. The less said about law the better. Suffice it to say that it is beginning to make sense to me (resistant though I am—you know me and my need to rebel at every step!).

Between anxiety (law and state-of-the-world-related), organizing (Green Light, and the new Study Action Group) and love affairs, life rushes by!... Green Light is a lot of work. We now have sixty-two safehouses, and a lot of related activity like radio shows, speaking before community groups, even developing legislation for a state senator—they approached us for help!

So all in all I'm happy and hard at work. What keeps me going ultimately are the surprises and twists of successive days, and the fact that I can't wait to find out [what] I end up doing!!

Keep in touch with any old and new ideas, developments, projects.

Lots of love,
Urvash

January 3, 1981
Allston, MA

Dear Mummy and Daddy,

Happy new year!

My New Year's Eve was low-key: a poetry reading, an early party, and asleep by 1 A.M. If I sound bland and tired it's this late Sunday night moment. It's also the atmosphere here in America these days—expectant, as if calamity is imminent. The war mongering spirit rages. Every reactionary is having her/his day. The newspapers breathe futility and corruption.

As a partial response, my housemates and I and some close friends have formed a biweekly study/action group that hopes to come up with new strategies, writings, ideas for the future, for us and for our largely feminist movement as well. There is such a need for new vision, new theory, and some comprehensible practice. We began by reading Lillian Hellman's *Scoundrel Time* and will meet to review some history of political repression in the US.

I see it much less as a diversion than as a necessity (for me at least). The demoralization and disorganization I see around me is in stark opposition to the smug faces of Reagan and his hatchet men as they plan destruction of all but their own vested interests.

Love
Urvash

February 18, 1981

Dearest Mummy and Daddy,

My life has slowed considerably since I last wrote you, simply because I have cut back on most of my activities—doing only what is necessary to law school and personal health.... It feels good to have some time to myself, instead of running from meetings to classes to events to demonstrations to meetings to the library!

My Torts exam is next Friday. I admit I'm nervous, this being my first one. But I'll do my best and expect to pass....

My health is much better. I've begun to eat meat again. I found I had lost too much weight and was unable with my busy life to have the time to eat like a careful vegetarian should....

Please write. I'm curious to hear what your routines are in Delhi.

Love
Urvash

April 1981
Allston, MA

Dearest Jyody,

Great news about that *Psychology Today* article ["The Multilingual Mind," featuring a 1979 study by Jyotsna Vaid and W. E. Lambert]! My sister—the famous psycholinguist!

Life shuffles along—legal boredom, bouts with cold...spring restlessness making me even more impatient than normal, alternating between loving what I'm doing and being overwhelmed by it. Political reality is very escalated these days...everyone talks politics and has opinions (thank you Reagan).

New romance in the air, old ones turning into friendships....

Sorry this is so short, just wanted to congratulate you, urge you on to the finish. Am vaguely thinking of coming up to Montreal later in the spring. Would that be OK with you?

Lots of love
UV

After Urvashi graduated from Northeastern Law School in 1983, she moved to Washington, DC, to work with the ACLU National Prison Project.

October 13, 1984
Washington, DC

Dearest Mummy and Daddy,

My job continues to intensify and challenge me. In an average day at the office I write anywhere from ten to twenty letters to prisoners, lawyers, etc.

I just returned from Austin, TX, where I took my first deposition. . . . I've gotten involved in a new case which we filed in Hawaii (!) and I'll be going out there in November. . . .

My adjustment to Washington remains uneasy although, as time passes, I get more comfortable with it. In Boston I had a whole circle of friends who talked and argued about ideas, book, art, grassroots politics. Here I find lots of people who talk only about what's happening on the Capitol. . . .

Love
Urvash

August 1985
Washington, DC

Dear Jyo,

All's well in the east, except that I am getting rather restless in my job! I'm feeling a need to work on issues that directly interest me politically (i.e., feminist and gay issues) rather than indirectly (like prisoners' rights, which I support politically but don't emote with). Does that make sense? So I'm beginning to keep my ears open for jobs that pay well and are in organizing. . . .

Love
Urvash

September 20, 1986
San Diego, CA

Dear Daddy,

I'm writing to you standing up in Rachna's study, with the baby [Shantanu] in my arm . . . I've been here all week to help out while Mummy regains her strength. . . .

I've just begun my new job. It's quite a change and I am enjoying it very much. The work as public information director [at the Task

Force] appeals to the journalist in me. I do a lot of work with the press—helping reporters with background material for stories, suggesting stories to cover, writing press releases. . . .

I'll also be responsible for writing or editing all the publications of the organization—from bibliographic compilations of antidiscrimination ordinances to pamphlets about gay people—all aimed at breaking down myths and promoting understanding. I have a lot of flexibility in deciding what new material to publish. . . .

I find my legal training very useful in two respects: first, so much of the Task Force work involves the reform of laws or the legislative process. As a lawyer, my knowledge is invaluable. Second, the skills I developed as a lawyer—writing clearly and argumentatively, analyzing problems, oral communication—are perfectly useful here.

I hope your planning of your seminar at Bharat Bhavan is going well.

Love
Urvash

December 1, 1986
Washington, DC

Dear Daddy and Mummy,

Since you left, I've been continuing the task of settling into my new job. I am enjoying it very much. Working with the media, writing lots—it's all very different from litigation, and it's a difference I'm enjoying.

As Al, my former prison project boss [at the ACLU] used to say to me, "Law is an imperfect tool for social change. It's one of the best we've got, but it's not immediate or adequate." I've always enjoyed politics on its own, unmediated, and I think this is why I like the Task Force job so much.

Even in my current job, I use my legal skills daily. Whether it's advising someone . . . or reviewing a contract or proposed legislation, I realize the wealth of knowledge I've acquired over the last six years. . . .

I talk regularly to Rachna (who is enjoying the baby and Kavoo). I'm also, of course, in close contact with Susan [Allee] and Betsy [Ringel]. I'll be going to Fort Wayne for Christmas, my first visit to Mary's family. . . .

In your letters you have seemed so . . . ambivalent about being this far from us all . . . I see that you are very happy to be in India, your life is so much more interesting (than Potsdam!), but you are very far away and I wish the distance were not so great.

I hope the next visit you will stay with me—this city is lively, and I'd enjoy having you visit, despite our inevitable arguments and annoyances!!

I love you both very, very much.
Urvash

November 13, 1988
Washington, DC

Dear Mummy and Daddy,

This year has been turbulent for me too [a relationship has ended]. . . .

One of my turning-thirty resolutions was to work less hours on my job and devote more time to creative projects of my own—writing, photography etc. The new apartment is a symbol of a new phase of my life here in Washington.

Work continues its urgent pace. I was just at a legal conference in San Francisco this weekend. I presented a couple of workshops. We are hosting our own conference [Creating Change] on political skill-building and organizational development next weekend in Washington. It's a great program . . . and promises to be an exciting conference.

The election of Bush has depressed many people here. He represents the continuation of such reactionary policies. Still, I feel optimistic that we can have influence in this administration.

The work of effecting political and social change is slow. Since I have chosen politics as my life's work, patience and resilience are good qualities to nourish in adverse times such as these.

Love
Urvash

April 14, 1989
Washington, DC

My dear Mummy and Daddy,

Hello! So much has happened since I last wrote—many, many wonderful things. . . .

Since I last wrote, I've been to Mexico! It was a wonderful trip. Mexico is so beautiful. I traveled with my friend Kate Clinton, who you don't yet know. She's a writer, a comedian, actually, and she lives in upstate New York, near Syracuse. . . .

We spent two weeks in a small village called Yelapa. No phone, roads, minimal electricity, no TV! I spent my time reading, writing, walking, and cooking. I actually took Indian spices with me and made gourmet Indian vegetarian meals almost every night, and fed all sorts of people whom we met at that place. The whole trip was full of sun and laughter and rest.

You are very much on my mind and in my heart.

Love
Urvash

May 17, 1989
Washington, DC

My dearest Mummy and Daddy,

Work has been absorbing and interesting. The main news is that I have decided to seek a management position in the organization. I've submitted a résumé, etc. and am actively pursuing the position.

I'm telling you this not to cause consternation but to tell you what I am working toward. Political change is my life's work—it is what I love and thrive in. . . . The Board decides by the end of June. I'm optimistic about the future, whatever happens.

Love
Urvash

July 17, 1989
Washington, DC

Dear Mummy and Daddy,

Last week I learned that I had gotten the job as Executive Director of the NGLTF (where I've been now for three years)! . . . The new role carries with it much more prestige, power, political clout, money, and, invariably, responsibility. It's exciting because it means I'll be in a major position of leadership in the gay movement. I got the job after a national search in which eighty-six people applied.

I'm thrilled at the new challenges being the head of the Task Force poses. I'm the youngest director of the organization in its sixteen-year history, and I'm the first minority (or should I say, non-white) person to head any major gay organization in this country! The Director's position gives me responsibility for staff supervision (eleven people in total), fundraising the one million dollar budget . . . and public representation in the media and in Congress, and building bridges with other social change movements and organizations (from the civil rights and civil liberties communities to the labor movement and the women's movement).

Mum, are you still writing poetry? Has anything been published? I wonder if I'd even be able to understand it, my Hindi has gotten so bad. Congratulations on finishing another novel, Daddy. It is so amazing how productive you are!

Love
Urvash

April 1990
Washington, DC

Dear Mummy and Daddy,

Things are going very well since I last wrote. This past week was a week of speech-making on the road. . . . My speeches are a combination of factual reporting on the status of gay rights legislation nationally, and a lot of rabble-rousing rhetoric and commentary designed to inspire people to be more active in political work.

I've been speaking a lot about the importance of our movement to define itself as a social change movement—with an agenda that reflects a commitment to securing economic justice and freedom for all people. It's a new message for the gay rights leadership to be pointing out.

I seem to be doing many uncharted things as executive director! Jyo's letter referred to my standing up to address President Bush during his speech on AIDS. It was a small act but it received enormous coverage because I actually interrupted him to ask him to do more on AIDS.

Love
Urvash

February 22, 1991
Washington, DC

Dear Mummy and Daddy,

It's unbelievable how rapidly my days pass....

This morning I am packing to go on a five-day business trip. To Bryn Mawr first, where I give a keynote speech at the Seven Sisters Annual Conference; the speech is titled "Legitimacy or Liberation—What Do We Want?" Then tomorrow on to NYC—where I meet with major donors to the task force, with foundation representatives and colleagues in other organizations. It's a fundraising and visibility-raising trip.

Next week, I give a speech at Ohio State University, participate in the opening ceremonies of a major health clinic in Boston (with the new governor of Massachusetts), and then go to San Francisco for the annual gay writers' conference.

Apart from work, my life is lived in a narrow sphere. I see a lot of Betsy [Ringel], Mary [Farmer], and a handful of other friends. Long distance, I see Kate. My primary commitment for now is this work—sometimes it is more than enough—at other times, it is not. But—I'm happy!

I'm looking forward to your visit. I'll be seeing Jyo in a few weeks in Texas (I'm going to give a speech there).

Lots of love
Urvash

March 17, 1993
Provincetown, MA

Dear Daddy and Mummy,

My book is proceeding well. It's a critical appraisal of the politics of the gay rights movement and a lot of original political theory. I'm enjoying the process of thinking and writing.

I'm off to Eugene, OR, tomorrow to meet with a group of academics planning an international conference on Supremacist Movements and the Right Wing Revival in the US.

Next week I go to U Penn to speak and then to Toronto to keynote at a South Asian cultural festival, Desh Pardesh, organized by a group of young South Asians who want to network progressive, politically active expatriates in the US, Canada, and England.

Then in early April I go to Swarthmore, New Jersey, and Bowdoin for talks and finally to the March on Washington, where I'm a speaker at the rally!

Travel slows down in the summer by which time I hope to have a book contract.

Living in Provincetown is lovely. Kate and I are doing very well.

Love
Urvash

March 29, 1993
Provincetown, MA

Dear Jyody,

Thought you'd enjoy seeing this opus I propose to write. It goes to publishers next week (via my agent) and I should know by mid-May if anyone is interested.

The Desh Pardesh conference was fantastic. I strongly recommend you go next year. . . . What was great was the mix of artists, activists, community organizers (great from my perspective), the presence of lots of gay South Asians who are out and comfortable with themselves as gay. It was the first South Asian context I've ever been in in which I felt completely comfortable and involved.

Radhika [Balakrishnan] was there and we ended up hanging out a lot. The SALGA group [South Asian Lesbian and Gay Alliance] from NYC was there. Dolores [Chew] from Montreal came but I didn't really get to hang out with her.

Hope you are well. Lots of love to you, Ram, and the kids [Alka and Alok].

Urvy

April 22, 1993
Provincetown, MA

Dear Mummy and Daddy,

It continues to be far too hectic during this sabbatical! The big March on Washington for gay rights takes place next weekend (I'm one of the speakers). One million people are expected. Every newspaper and magazine is covering it (unlike the last March in 1987, which received far less attention although we gathered 500,000 people).

Love
Urvash

July 1, 1993
Provincetown, MA

Dear Jyody,

How are you doing? I'm hard at work in the research phase of my book [*Virtual Equality*]. I'm doing interviews with a lot of folks around the country and reading a lot of historical material. Then I plan to spend the fall writing. The notion that all the ideas— directions will get pulled together into a coherent argument seems unbelievable right now.

I've enclosed a small donation for your COSAW [Committee on South Asian Women] *Bulletin* work—all these years I've never given you any funds for the mailings you've sent. I know how expensive it is (as a fellow organizer who still funds a number of groups out of my pocket!).

It was really nice to see you at Rachna's last month. The kids are terrific. . . .

Kate and I are doing well. We are getting through the inevitable bumps of adjustment, and actually I'm very happy. Come visit!

Lots of love,
Urvash

November 15, 1993
Provincetown, MA

Dear Mummy and Daddy,

I last spoke with you around my birthday. It feels momentous to turn 35. . . . The pace at which I've lived amazes me when I think of it. . . . This past month I traveled to New York to speak to a fairly high level gathering of corporate executives at Time-Warner about gay issues.

I've just come back from the annual NGLTF Creating Change Conference, held this year in Durham, NC. I started the conference six years ago while on the task force staff and it remains the best, most exciting gay political gathering in the country. It was great for me because it stimulated a lot of ideas in connection with the book. . . .

There are plans afoot between the US and Indian gay groups to produce the first Indian gay and lesbian conference in Bombay in late '94. I've been contacted about speaking and am very excited. So, who knows, this coming year may find me visiting you [in India] twice!

I miss you and send you all my love.
Urvash

February 11, 1994
Provincetown, MA

Dear Mummy and Daddy,

It's a sunny Saturday morning. Two feet of snow fell yesterday! This is the snowiest winter since the late 1970s, they say! It reminds me (a bit too much) of Potsdam snow! I was out at eight shoveling the walk and the driveway and now am at the dining room table writing letters in preparation (as a warm-up) to working on the book [*Virtual Equality*].

The writing is still painfully difficult—and the angst of it continues to surprise me. I did think it'd be easier because I have such strong opinions about what I'm writing about. But the actual act of saying it clearly, elegantly, simply is hard. I censor myself, think how dumb, so and so will hate this notion, can I say this? A million decisions at every sentence. But I'm doing it. . . . My editor—Charles—is very excited at what I sent him. He has lots of helpful ideas for revising. Kate also says I am writing well and she's very proud of me! Those are the only people who've read the raw draft so far. . . .

Other than this, I do very little. I'm working again with the paper I used to volunteer for in Boston years ago (*Gay Community News*) trying to revive it. . . . And we go to DC at the end of Feb—me to do some interviews and Kate to perform.

Love
Urvash

March 25, 1994
Provincetown, MA

Dear Mummy and Daddy,

I have lots of work ahead [on the book]. But I'm suddenly stalled. What an interesting journey. It's a constant battle for me—I am so used to the immediate response, the collaborative process of political organizing. This solitary existence is hard for me to create from, and yet I need complete focus in order to write at all.

Love
Urvash

FIGURE 2.1. "Power Lesbian," cover of *OutWeek* magazine, March 4, 1990. Courtesy of *OutWeek* magazine.

A NATIONAL LESBIAN AGENDA

Keynote Address at the National Lesbian Conference
in Atlanta, Georgia, April 27, 1991

We are here at the National Lesbian Conference because of the passion, love, excitement, and desire we feel for women.

We are here because spectacular forces of evil and prejudice threaten our very existence as lesbians.

It is this evil present in Judge Campbell's decision denying Karen Thompson guardianship of Sharon Kowalski.

It is this evil that murdered Rebecca Wight, and wounded her lover, Claudia Brenner, as they were camping in the mountains of Pennsylvania.

It is this evil found in the cowardly silence of all politicians who will not stand up to defend lesbians and our commitment to changing these realities.

Let us never forget the social context we gather in.

To be lesbian today means to face loss of our jobs, loss of housing, denial of public accommodation, loss of custody, loss of visitation simply because of our sexual orientation.

To be lesbian today means to face violence as a queer and violence as a woman.

To be lesbian today means to have no safety for the families we have created, to face the loss of our children and loved ones, to have no status for our committed relationships.

To be lesbian means to be invisible, as Kate Clinton says, like the stealth bomber, low-flying, undetectable. It is to be a stealth lesbian, hidden from a world whose sight is monochromatic and patriarchal—hidden even when we are out and powerful, by a world that is obsessed with the relationships between men.

To be lesbian means to work in social change movements, in gay and lesbian organizations, in civil rights and feminist organizations that still ghettoize the multiple issues of discrimination that we face and that still tokenize us and put our concerns and voices on the back burner.

To be lesbian is to have, until very recently, absolutely no images in mainstream culture of out, proud, strong, independent women.

To be lesbian today is to live in a society that identifies and defines us only through our relation (or lack thereof) to men—lesbians are masculine, man-haters, the sexual fantasies of straight men.

To be lesbian today is to face multiple systems of oppression—to face homophobia, sexism, racism, ageism, ableism, economic injustice—to face a variety of systems of oppression *all at once*, with the type of oppression changing depending on who we are, but the fact of oppression remaining constant.

We gather here at this conference in Atlanta in 1991, not 1951, not 1971, not 1981, but today. And the context of this time is ominous. The world in which we strive to live as openly lesbian has taken off its ugly white hood to show its sexist, anti-gay, racist, and capitalist face as never before.

When a Ku Klux Klansman can run for the US Senate and get forty-four percent of the vote, the hood is off.

When the president of the United States is elected on the heels of an orchestrated racist campaign, the hood is off.

When the campaign for Jesse Helms in North Carolina when he vetoes the Civil Rights Act of 1990, when he introduces a Crime Bill that will strip our civil liberties, when he speaks in strong support of the anti-choice, anti-woman, anti-abortion movement, when he opposes equal rights for women, when he lets our brothers and sisters with HIV die from negligence, and when he engineers a war to win reelection—the hood of evil is off.

A second piece of the context in which we gather is more hopeful: we meet at this lesbian conference at a historic moment in the lesbian and gay movement's history. Today tens of thousands of lesbians are actively engaged in the movement for lesbian liberation. At the workshops and caucuses I have attended, it is clear that the two thousand of us at the conference are deeply and intimately involved in our movement for freedom.

Today, we are truly a mixed movement through the involvement of lesbians. And through our involvement we are changing the face, the politics, and the content of our gay and lesbian organizations.

There is a revolution underway in the gay and lesbian liberation movement. The fact that organizations are developing multicultural plans and dealing with racism on their staffs, boards, and in their programs is a direct result of lesbian feminist organizing and politics. The fact that the gay and lesbian movement has begun to be multi-issue, that it is pro-choice, that it dares to speak out on the broad social issues of the day (like the war) is a direct result of lesbian leadership. The fact that the feminist health agenda of the 1970s—the agenda of disability rights, insurance reform, health care access for all, welfare reform, etc.—the fact that these issues are now on the central burner of the gay and lesbian movement is in part a function of the painful experience of the AIDS crisis and in part a result of lesbian feminist analysis and organizing.

The parallel contexts of great danger and great change frame our meeting together tonight as lesbians.

And as we have seen in this week together, the work we must do—our agenda for action—is large and quite specific!

There are two big pieces to our national lesbian agenda: one is movement building and two is public policy. Put another way, I believe that our lesbian agenda for the 1990s is about organizing and power; it is about "making," as Audre Lorde said, "power out of hatred and destruction."

These are not easy agenda items to move.

The experience of this conference suggests to me that we do not, in fact, have a national lesbian movement. We have a vast cultural movement, we have a huge amount of talent, we have a lot of grassroots leadership, we have lesbians active in a million projects—but the focus of lesbian communities in our cities and towns remains the same as it was in the 1950s—it remains the bars, augmented by women's cultural events, the festival network, and local feminist and lesbian bookstores.

We have no national movement, no national newspaper, no national annual gathering place for lesbian activists to meet and talk politics. We have one annual state conference I am aware of—in Texas—and for all the talk of a national lesbian organization let me remind everyone that we have a national lesbian organization that struggles for its daily existence—the National Center for Lesbian Rights. How many of us here support this ten-year-old pillar of lesbian advocacy?

The centerpiece of our national lesbian agenda must be the re-creation of a lively, open, organized, and unafraid lesbian movement. It existed once.

The challenges to this re-creation of a lesbian movement are manifest throughout this, our National Lesbian Conference (NLC). The NLC is a mirror to the current state of our movement. And the mirror shows us several harsh truths.

Truth: That we are not one lesbian community but a series of very splintered communities who have in fact not been working together at home or at this conference.

Truth: In this conference we have demonstrated that we do not trust each other at all; that we refuse to claim the cloak of leadership even when we have it—perhaps because we rightly fear the backlash or ostracism that all lesbians who dare say the word *leadership* fear; we have shown that we do not understand that diversity politics is not a knee-jerk reaction or paying lip service but about action and internalizing the message; it is not about making sure that we have one of each, but learning and accepting that we have each in one—in other words, that we respect and carry the commitment to act in ourselves.

Truth: In this conference 2,000 have gathered. I have met so many seasoned, powerful, interesting lesbians, and it pains me that any of us might leave this place feeling dejected and hurt, angry, and excluded. Let us not do that. Remember, we will never feel included entirely, because the big social context is what excludes us completely.

Truth: That developing alternative decision-making processes is wonderful and radical, but that all processes must be accountable and take responsibility for their actions.

Truth: That we can get so intense and focused on criticizing each other and focused on ourselves that we forget that we are in this together, that we are in this to change the fucked-up world outside.

We must begin in our own house, and put it in order. We must begin by taking a deep collective breath and looking around at the fierce, powerful women that we are. Let us look around at the skills we bring, and let us let go of perfectionism and purity politics based in fear. Let us enact instead a courageous and honest politics based in lesbian pride. It is time for lesbians like me and you to bring our energies back home into our own movement and into our own communities. It is time for us to mobilize at the grassroots level *first*.

Every state must have a lesbian conference to encourage involvement by lesbians.

Every city and town should have activist lesbian networking breakfasts or potlucks to reconnect us to each other.

Let us certainly do our organizing on our particular and separate piece of the social-change pie—but let us not forget that we are allies as lesbians. We are not the enemy.

Let us encourage and promote lesbianism! Let us link up across age to talk political vision. Let us not be afraid of doing the wrong thing—let us just do something!

On a political level, in the two years of planning for this conference, I have sat through many discussions on what is the lesbian political agenda. Lesbians have tried to define lesbian-specific issues. Well, that is not my vision of my lesbian movement's political agenda.

My vision is to claim quite simply the fact that the lesbian agenda is (as it has always been) radical social change.

It is the reconstruction of family; it is the reimagining and claiming of power. It is the reorganization of the economic system; it is the reinforcement of civil rights for all peoples. It is the enactment of laws and the creation of a society that affirms choice. It is the end to the oppression of women, the end to racism, the end to sexism, ableism, homophobia. It is the protection of our environment.

I have no problem claiming all these issues as the lesbian agenda for social change—because that is the truth. Lesbians have a radical social vision—we are the bearers of a truly new world order, not the stench of the same old-world odor.

This large agenda does not overwhelm me; it tells me how far I must go until we all win. It tells me who my allies really are.

How do we enact our agenda? We enact it by continuing to do what we are doing in each of our communities. We enact it by involving more of our sisters, the thousands of lesbians who do not interact with us or with our movement for social change.

We enact our lesbian agenda by building a movement for *power*. What are we afraid of—why are we afraid of power? We surely will not make things more fucked up than they already are.

I am not suggesting that all of us drop the work that we are doing to focus on this new exclusive lesbian thing called a *lesbian agenda*—I am suggesting that we continue to do what we are doing, but that we do it as *out* lesbians. That we claim our work as lesbian work, that we be out about who and why we are how we are.

I proudly claim our unique, multi-issue perspective. I am proud of my lesbian community's politics of inclusion. I am engaged in my people's liberation. Let us just do it.

FIGURE 3.1. from the Valda Lewis Collection. Urvashi speaks at the Creating Change conference, 1995.

3

WE STAND FOR FREEDOM AS
WE HAVE YET TO KNOW IT

Speech at the 1993 March on Washington for
Lesbian, Gay, and Bi Equal Rights and Liberation

Urvashi spoke to a crowd of more than 700,000 at the April 25, 1993, March on Washington for Lesbian, Gay, and Bi Equal Rights and Liberation—the third LGBTQ national march on the capital (the first march was held in 1979, the second in 1987).

Hello lesbian and gay Americans. I am proud to stand before you as a lesbian today.

With hearts full of love and with an abiding faith in justice, we have come to Washington to speak to America.

We have come to speak the truth of our lives and silence the liars.

We have come to challenge the cowardly Congress to end its paralysis and exercise moral leadership.

We have come to defend our honor and win our equality.

But most of all, we have come in peace and with courage to say, "America, this day marks the return from exile of the gay and lesbian people."

We are banished no more.

We wander the wilderness of despair no more.

We are afraid no more.

For on this day, with love in our hearts, we have come out, to reach out across America to build a bridge of understanding, a bridge of progress, a bridge as solid as steel, a bridge to a land where no one suffers prejudice because of their sexual orientation, their race, their gender, their religion, or their human difference.

I've been asked by the march organizers to speak about the Far Right—the Far Right which threatens the construction of this bridge. The extremist Right, which has targeted every one of you and me for extinction, the supremacist Right which seeks to redefine the very meaning of democracy.

Language itself fails in this task, my friends, for to call our opponents "the Right" states a profound untruth.

They are wrong. They are wrong.

They are wrong morally, they are wrong spiritually, and they are wrong politically.

The Christian supremacists are wrong spiritually when they demonize us. They are wrong when they reduce the complexity and beauty of our spirit into a freak show. They are wrong spiritually, because, if we are the untouchables of America, then we are, as Mahatma Gandhi said, children of God. And as God's children we know that the gods of our understanding, the gods of goodness and love and righteousness, march right here with us today.

The supremacists who lead the anti-gay crusade are wrong morally. They are wrong because justice is moral, and prejudice is evil. Because truth is moral, and the lie of the closet is the real sin. Because their claim of morality is a simple subterfuge, a strategy that hides their real aim, which is much more secular. Christian supremacist leaders like Bill Bennett and Pat Robertson, Lou Sheldon and Pat Buchanan, supremacists like Phyllis Schlafly and Ralph Reed, Bill Kristol and R. J. Rushdoony—these supremacist leaders don't care about morality; they care about power. They care about social control. And their goal, my friends, is the reconstruction of American democracy into American theocracy.

They say they have declared a cultural war on us. It's a war, all right. It's a war about values. On one side are the values that everyone here stands for, traditional American values of democracy and pluralism. On the other side are those who want to turn the Christian church into the government, those whose value is monotheism.

We believe in democracy—in many voices coexisting in peace, and people of all faiths living together in harmony under a common civil framework known as the United States Constitution.

Our opponents believe in monotheism—one way (theirs), one god (theirs), one law (the Old Testament), one nation supreme (the Christian, white one).

Democracy battles theism in Oregon, in Colorado, in Florida, in Maine, in Arizona, in Michigan, in Ohio, in Idaho, in Washington, in Montana, in every state where you, my brothers and sisters, are leading the fight to oppose the Right and to defend the United States Constitution.

We won the anti-gay measure in Oregon, but thirty-three counties and municipalities face local versions of that ordinance in Oregon today. The fight has just begun. We lost a big fight in Colorado, but thanks to the hard work of all the people of Colorado, the Boycott Colorado movement is working, and it's strong, and we're going to win our freedom there eventually.

To defeat the Right politically, my friends, is our challenge when we leave this march. How can we do it?

We've got to march from Washington into action at home.

I challenge every one of you—straight or gay—who can hear my voice to join the national gay and lesbian movement. I challenge you to join the NGLTF to fight the Right. We've got to match the power of the Christian supremacists, member for member, vote for vote, dollar for dollar.

I challenge each of you to not just buy a T-shirt but get involved in your movement. Get involved. Volunteer. Volunteer. Every local organization in this country needs you. Every clinic, every hotline, every youth program needs you, needs your time and your love.

And I also challenge our straight liberal allies—liberals and libertarians, independents and conservatives, Republican or radical—I challenge and invite you to open your eyes and embrace us without fear.

The gay rights movement is not a party.

It is not a lifestyle.

It is not a hairstyle.

It is not a fad or a fringe or a sickness.

It is not about sin or salvation.

The gay rights movement is an integral part of the American promise of freedom.

We, you and I, each of us, we are the descendants of a proud tradition of people asserting our dignity.

It is fitting that the Holocaust Museum was dedicated the same weekend as this march, for not only were gay people persecuted by the Nazi state, but gay people are indebted to the struggle of the Jewish people against bigotry and intolerance.

It is fitting that the NAACP marches with us, that feminist leaders march with us, because we are indebted to those movements.

When all of us who believe in freedom and diversity see this gathering, we see beauty and power.

When our enemies see this gathering, they see the millennium.

We Stand for Freedom · 49

Well, perhaps the religious Right is right about something.

We call for the end of the world as we know it.

We call for the end of racism and bigotry as we know it.

For the end of violence and discrimination and homophobia as we know it.

For the end of sexism as we know it.

We stand for freedom as we have yet to know it.

And we will not be denied.

4

A SHARED POLITICS OF SOCIAL JUSTICE: AN INTERVIEW WITH URVASHI VAID

This 1998 interview was published in Talking about a Revolution. *David Barsamian is the host of the syndicated radio program,* Alternative Radio.

DAVID BARSAMIAN: In the wake of social activism in the late sixties and early seventies, a number of social movements developed. One of them was the gay and lesbian movement. What are its goals?

URVASHI VAID: The goals of the gay and lesbian movement are full equality and human rights for people who are gay, lesbian, bisexual, and transgender. That means on a legal and legislative level, equal rights in every aspect of public and private employment, housing—the whole panoply of civil rights that everybody in this country should be able to enjoy. On a more social and cultural level, the gay and lesbian movement fights for respect, for understanding of the fundamental humanity and the legitimacy of our relationships, for the recognition that we have families as LGBTQ people that include children, parents, and extended families, in many of the same ways that heterosexual people have families. These other, extralegal issues are very important in the gay agenda.

DB: Why do you think some people feel genuinely threatened by gays and lesbians?

UV: There are many reasons people feel threatened. I think some of it is just lack of familiarity. The gay and lesbian communities in this country have just become visible in a short amount of time, the last few years. We're new to most Americans. Most people still do not understand that we are a part of every family because they don't know the gay siblings, aunts, uncles, nephews, or cousins in their own families. So, they see us as the Other, still, when we are very much a part of the fabric of this country—and in fact of every country.

Another source of uneasiness is misinformation. Some of that is fostered by the opposition movement that we face right now—the extreme, very conservative Right. Even the middle is sometimes opposed to gay and lesbian equality. They base their opposition on a fundamental misunderstanding about gay and lesbian people. We are human beings. We are not evil. We are not unnatural. We are ordinary people, some of whom are good, some of whom are bad. Some of us are talented writers and artists. Others are hardworking machinists. The spectrum is what we represent.

The misinformation that our opponents put out about us is very damaging. The anxious middle of the American electorate, the 30 to 40 percent of people who oppose discrimination but don't agree that gay people should have the right to have family or marriage, listens to this misinformation and gets swayed by it. We have to counter that misinformation by coming out in our families and our workplaces and everywhere in our lives, and by talking to heterosexual people about who we are and what our aspirations are. I think that does a lot to dispel the fear and anxiety that heterosexual people feel.

DB: The Christian Coalition is perhaps the most visible of the many politicized, sectarian groups now operating in the political theater. They certainly view gays and lesbians as unnatural, and they're making their views powerfully known within their own communities and within the national Republican Party.

UV: The most pernicious statement that is made by the Christian Coalition and its political mouthpieces like Pat Buchanan is that the acceptance of gay and lesbian people's existence will actually undermine western civilization. Buchanan goes on and on about this in his speeches: how no society that has tolerated homosexuality has survived. It's an illogical, ahistorical, bizarre statement, and yet it gets a lot of play. People really believe it. You could make that kind of statement about any number of historical institutions, for example: "No society has survived that tolerated slavery." (Not a statement that

Buchanan ever makes.) Slavery was a big part of ancient Rome and Greece. Perhaps that was their downfall.

As somebody who believes in democracy and participation, I think it's actually a good thing that all these people are being mobilized by groups like the Christian Coalition to get involved in issues that affect them. What's bad is the information they're getting about gay and lesbian people. The information the Christian Coalition gives its members is quite contradictory. It's essentially, "love the sinner, hate the sin." But gay and lesbian people are gay because sexuality is an integral part of our lives, just as sexuality is an integral part of heterosexual people's lives. You can't divorce the being from the orientation.

The energy that the Christian Right expends on demonizing gay people would be so much more productively spent on solving some of the serious problems in our society that have nothing to do with homosexuality. Gay people aren't the source of crime. We're not the cause of poverty. We're not the cause of illiteracy. We're not the source of the decay in the American family. It's the economic system that is the source of those kinds of problems.

We're convenient scapegoats. We're living in a time when scapegoating of gay people, of immigrants, of single mothers, of people of color, and of the poor is on the rise. And the reason scapegoating is on the rise is that it's a wonderful subterfuge. The Right attacks government instead of attacking big business. Big business is the reason people are losing their jobs, but the Right acts as if it's because of government bureaucracy.

DB: A segment of the political discourse not only incorporates this hostility toward homosexuality, but also has a very well-defined view of sexuality and the role of women: as homemakers, as mothers, as cultural protectors. It's not limited to the Christian Coalition. You also hear it from Louis Farrakhan and the Nation of Islam (NOI), for example.

UV: Central to today's struggles in the public sphere are different views of gender and the roles of women and men. The profound feminist contribution to the world has been to say that what it means to be a woman and what it means to be a man is manufactured. These meanings are artificial constructions. They change from period to period in history. What's appropriate for women in one time or place is inappropriate in others.

Opponents of that view say gender is biological. You're either a man or you're a woman. Everybody knows what it means to be a man. Everybody knows what it means to be a woman. So, we're having an argument throughout this society, in every culture, about the role of women and the role of men, what gender means, and how the acceptance of nontraditional families will affect the heterosexual nuclear family.

I think feminism is the antidote to conservatism. Feminism is not just about women. It's a fundamental way of approaching the issue of gender and equality and power in society. The women's liberation movement, and feminism as a political theory, have contributed so much of value over the last hundred years. They have changed the status of women in dramatic ways. Feminism and the women's liberation movement have also changed men's lives, opening possibilities for them to be nurturing, to reject the masculine stereotypes that have chained them. Feminism has changed the family in profound ways. For these reasons, conservatives have aggressively targeted feminism as evil.

DB: What you are saying brings up the issue of white male privilege—which hits a raw nerve. How do you talk to white men about it? How do you convince white men that they benefit, almost by definition, because of their gender and the color of their skin?

UV: I don't know that I talk very effectively to white men about this issue. I think there is a curtain that exists between me and many men that I meet, a curtain that is not of my own creation.

DB: Because you're a woman of color?

UV: Exactly. That's one of the most frustrating aspects of racism and sexism on a personal level—how we have these filters that we see each other through. I find that even when I'm saying something that has absolutely nothing to do with race or gender, it is heard by a white man in a very personalized way—as if it *did* have something to do with race and gender—because, when he looks at me, all he sees is Woman of Color. It doesn't work the other way around—when I look at white guys whom I know or work with, I don't see their whiteness or maleness as the first thing. So, for example, I may see the political ideology first. Am I talking to a conservative, a liberal, a radical, a moderate? That's what I often notice first. Or I see mannerisms, warmth, intangible human qualities. Is this somebody I can actually have a conversation with? Do I have to fear this person? Is he just a jerk?

The question you're asking, though, is a very important one. There has been a backlash among white men against the emergence of movements of people of color and against sexism. Progressive people have to speak more directly to this backlash and the anxiety that gives rise to it, although without badgering people or pointing fingers. The way I try to do it is to ask, "Are we committed to a shared politics of social justice, you with your identity and me with mine?" Often the answer, when you really have time to have a dialogue, is, "Yes, we are committed to a shared vision of social justice."

I don't think you have to be a person of color to be opposed to racism. I don't think you have to be a gay person to be opposed to homophobia. I don't think you have to be a woman to understand sexism and believe in equality of men and women. We have to move away from the notion that you can only speak to those issues if you are a member of those groups. I don't believe that. I'm not a nationalist.

I think one of the failures of our identity-based movements is that we let go of the project of developing common politics. We focused more on the identity and less on the politics. Now, I value identity. As I've said many times, I am who I am, a lesbian. I value that. I will always be, wherever I go, an out lesbian speaking about the world and the issues from my perspective as a lesbian. And yet, I very much believe I can link up and find common ground with a heterosexual mother who lives in the suburbs. I think I can link up and find common ground with a straight, white businessman who's working in a big corporation. I really believe that. Otherwise, I would be much more cynical, and I would be writing nasty books about how we can't get along.

I'm a progressive at heart. I believe that there is a progressive framework that I and many people subscribe to in our hearts, which we have to push for politically and implement in public policy. Many people believe that the prosperity we see in this society ought to benefit all the people in some way, for example in affordable education and health care. More people believe that than believe we should turn our backs on the poor and walk away from social problems.

DB: There are criticisms of identity politics—that it contributes to balkanization, to fragmentation, and to competition, and prevents building bridges. What are your views on that?

UV: I do not think that identity politics contributes to the balkanization of the movement. I think the lack of a broad movement contributes to our powerlessness.

There are many critiques of identity politics. They come from the Left and the Right and even from within identity-based movements themselves.

Within the gay and lesbian community, for example, there has been a big argument for many years. Are we a single-issue movement? Do we care about other issues? Are we a human rights movement in a broad sense? There is profound disagreement among us about this question. Gay progressives believe that we have to be multi-issue. The fight for gay and lesbian equality is a primary purpose of our work, but we also see how the changes that we need to make to gain our equality intersect with the issues of racism and sexism and economic injustice. But there are others who say, for pragmatic or ideological reasons, "There are no intersections. We're going after gay rights. We have to keep our focus on ourselves."

When I hear leftists say, "We have to move beyond identity," I hope they know that these kinds of debates are going on within identity-based movements. But sometimes when I hear leftists say that, they sound just like the right-wingers who argue that we have to move to some kind of "universal politics"—which really means that everyone is defined in terms of the old standard of white male patriarchy. We can't go back to that!

We have to come together in a new way, based on the understandings we've developed of ourselves as women of color, as people of color of whatever gender and nationality, as gay people, even as white men. I believe it's possible for us to come back together in new ways because we now have the self-confidence and maturity to do it. Thirty years ago, there was no gay and lesbian identity. Now there is. Thirty years ago, the idea of what it meant to be in a common movement meant something really different than it would if we were to do it today.

There's a feminist critic who has said that identity politics was a kind of necessary mistake. It's a formulation I appreciate. It was essential for us to deepen our understanding of our racial identities and various cultures. But for progressive people, it's a mistake to stop there.

DB: Does identity politics mean you contribute to your own marginalization? Isn't it a kind of victimology?

UV: I don't buy that! It's a convenient hook on which to pin the failure of the Left, which is due to many factors other than the emergence of movements of women and people of color. The New Left splintered for many reasons: ego wars between its (male) leaders; the systematic destruction of its leadership and its organizations by the government; its inability to translate its politics into electoral activism. It failed to politically institutionalize itself.

I actually identify my work in the tradition of the activists of that New Left, and I very much appreciate the work of the movements of the sixties and early seventies: the civil rights movement, the Black liberation movement, the antiwar movement, and the women's liberation movement. But what I saw was a splintered movement, a splintering that predates the emergence of identity-based movements. Leftists fail to see that the gay and lesbian liberation movement, for example, has been an incredibly active, in-the-streets movement. I could say the same for the women's movement, as it mobilized around reproductive rights, and against violence against women and sexual harassment. These primary sites of organizing and activism changed the minds and lives of millions of people. So, to dismiss these movements is the wrong approach—it prevents you from taking advantage of the energy and the talent that's in those movements.

There is an old guard of the New Left that is profoundly threatened by its loss of power. The women's movement's critiques of male-dominated institutions, and the Black liberation movement's critiques of white-dominated institutions are still relevant. Some of the folks who are running the remaining Left organizations are brilliant, dedicated people, and I respect their enormous contribution. But I want to challenge any assumption—like this one about the reasons behind the "splintering" of the Left—that they've got it right and everybody else has it wrong.

There are signs of hope. Some of the writing that I'm seeing in new books coming out and in publications like the *Nation* and the *Progressive* calls for us to come together. But we're not going to come together as the reincarnation of the Left of the sixties. We have to come together as a twenty-first-century movement that will look different from the New Left. It will also look different from our current identity-based movements. We don't have the platform right now. We don't have the relationships with each other today. But we're building them. I'm confident that we're going to see progressives create new institutions over the coming years. For the first time in many years, I feel like there's a desire on the part of all sorts of progressive people to come together and work together.

DB: I think there's a resurgence of patriarchy. Do you agree? Why is it happening now?

UV: I can't remember who said this, and I'm paraphrasing: "For every emergence of women there is an emergency of men." Sexism is real. It's institutionalized in the economic system, in our family structures, and in the way women and men still think of their roles in the family.

But when you say there's a resurgence of patriarchy, I'm not so sure I see it among young people. Of course, sexist attitudes still exist: you can see that in popular music and in the media. But young people are also challenging that.

There are some generational issues being played out. Many of the folks of my parents' generation, in their sixties and seventies, have fairly progressive views about gender and sexism. The problem comes with the boomers. Their generation is the one that fought the gender wars most personally, in their marriages and economic lives. Many of those men have a lot of personal resistance to women's equality, while the women feel a lot of pain.

Then you come to my generation. I'm thirty-eight. People in my generation have a different understanding of gender roles and sexism—perhaps because of the battles that took place before. It's not that patriarchy, the system of male domination, ever went away. But it is now being challenged globally. I was at the 1995 Fourth World Conference on Women in Beijing, organized by the United Nations. I encountered women from all over the world who are pushing against patriarchy and working toward societies that respect women and men in a whole different way than those based on male domination. They're challenging violence against women. They're challenging the unequal pay that women get for the same jobs. They're challenging restrictive laws and government control of reproduction. Clearly there's a profound challenge to patriarchy underway. That is causing tremendous uneasiness in this country and others. There is a resistance to that challenge, a backlash to that challenge.

But you know what? Women are not going to stop! There's a determination to improve our lives and the lives of the young girls coming after us. The fight against sexism isn't won. It changes from generation to generation. It gets rolled back. But I don't believe that conservatives like Phyllis Schlafly are going to be able to stop it. In fact, Phyllis Schlafly has benefited from feminism. She can be a strong leader with authority in her movement because of the accomplishments of the very feminism that she attacks.

I believe social change happens both incrementally and in flashes of illumination. For many years, I thought we would have a revolution that would overthrow existing structures and replace them with a society based on justice and equality. But I haven't believed that for a long time. I believe that social change is necessary, because we live in an economic and political system that is increasingly repressive, that hurts the majority of people in this country. Something's got to change.

And I'll put it out there: I believe that the way we will make that change is through a socially responsible capitalism. I don't believe we are going to overthrow capitalism. But I believe that we can make capitalism more responsive, accountable, and environmentally sound. We can make it fairer and non-discriminatory. We can take the benefits of this economic system and spread them out among everybody, rather than the five owners of everything. We can make the places where we work humane environments that meet our needs, whether for childcare or health care or Medicare or Social Security. We can raise the standard of living for all people without overthrowing capitalism. This is simply pragmatic.

Progressivism encompasses a spectrum of beliefs; it's not an ideology in which people are following one leader saying one thing. Our movement includes people who have wildly diverging opinions about many things. But, as progressives, if we could commit to a general frame of reference that we are about improving the quality of life for more people, that we're about helping working- and middle-class people and about taking care of poor people, we could really make some inroads in political power in this country. But, if we choose to be purists, if we choose to keep arguing for a consensus we will never reach, for agreement on every point, it's never going to happen. I think we are serious about our various beliefs—but are we serious that we can govern, that we can lead people?

I think we have great visions. We have great answers to the problems that face this country in every single area—in education and crime and poverty and welfare. We need a movement that unifies us to push for certain agreed-upon visions. We can't spend our time waiting for the Perfect Vision, the One and Only Answer, the Charismatic Leader. That's nirvana. It ain't gonna happen.

Instead, we've got to work with what we're facing right now. This is a time of enormous economic anxiety, which is being manipulated to scapegoat individuals or groups for problems that they have absolutely nothing to do with creating. Immigrants aren't responsible for the lack of jobs in this country; the movement of multinational capital to other places is. Gay people are not responsible for the decline of family. The changing roles of women and men, the dislocation caused by economic forces that force people to move and split families—all that stuff is responsible. Let's talk about the real sources of those problems and put out our answers, our suggestions. Then, you know what? We'll suddenly find ourselves having a lot of people who will say, "Yes, I'm a progressive."

DB: How does social change happen?

UV: I have an incremental theory of social change. The epiphany moment is just as important, though. Social change can happen through illuminating personal experiences. If you experience discrimination, whether you're a man, a woman, a young person, whatever the source of discrimination is, you are absolutely going to be transformed through that experience. Anybody who has walked a picket line, who has been out on strike, is transformed by that experience. Somebody who organizes their neighborhood to deal with environmental pollution is transformed. Many times, in my experience, people are moved to have faith in the possibility of social change by moments like these.

When we as gay people come out to our families, it's that kind of moment of transformation. You have to go through a lot, internally, to get to the point where you can say, "I'm gay." Society doesn't provide affirmation to gay people and we have to find it within ourselves. You have to come to a sense of self and self-esteem in a whole different way when you're a gay, lesbian, bisexual, or transgender person.

When I talked with my parents about being gay, it changed them. It changed our dynamics. It changed the whole understanding my family had about homosexuality. It suddenly got personal. It didn't suddenly make my parents or my family into gay activists from day one. I wouldn't say even today, after many years of my work in the movement, that they're on the front line—but they have become absolutely supportive of non-discrimination, of equality. They will not stand for anybody who says that their daughter is somehow less human than a heterosexual, or more immoral. They don't believe that. That's a really great change.

5

AWAKENED ACTIVISM:
AIDS AND TRANSFORMATION

This essay is an edited version of chapter 3 from Urvashi's book Virtual Equality: The
Mainstreaming of Gay and Lesbian Liberation *(1995).*

AIDS will do more to direct America back to the cost of violating traditional values and to make
America aware of the danger of certain behavior than anything we've seen. For us, it's a great
rallying cry. —NEWT GINGRICH, 1995

January 1994

Walta lies on his side, anxiety and fear in his eyes. The air in the room is still.
He had a transfusion two days ago. Michael says he was walking around the
apartment, but today he has no energy. Last night, he had diarrhea. I don't
think he knows we are in the room.

"Walter?" Michael asks, saying his name as if it had an *r*.

Walta, curled in a fetal position on his bed, does not move.

"Walter?"

There is no response.

"Walter, are you all right? Do you need anything? Walter? Urvashi's here.
Walter?"

"Yes."

"Are you all right?"

Walta starts suddenly, as if someone has shaken him. He tries to raise
himself and can't. He stares at me blankly, then turns to Michael for reassur-
ance. His right eye is glassy and moves in a different direction from his left
eye. *Has he gone blind in it?* I wonder. I don't ask Michael. There is a shadow,

like a dark bruise, on his left cheek. He is very thin. "Cheekbones for days," he would have said, as he did about my friend Betsy the first time they met. "Betsy's beautiful. Cheekbones for days."

Michael tells him, "I'm going to hook up some IV, Walter, because I'm worried about the fluid you lost last night. Let me find your IV thing." He kneels beside the bed and fumbles under the covers. Walta does not move or respond. I stand by, doing nothing.

"Where is that thing? Ah. Here it is." Michael clips the IV bag to the catheter attached to Walta. He times the drip with a wristwatch. "One, two, three, four, five . . ." he counts out loud and adjusts the flow. "There." Walta lies on his side; his eyes are wide and open, looking past us.

Michael picks up the conversation exactly where he and I left off, without missing a thought. We are talking about what we've discussed so often in the fifteen years we have been friends: the endless drama associated with keeping afloat the progressive nonprofit newspaper *Gay Community News* (GCN). *Gay Community News* is our common political work, our collaborative creation, our means of resistance, the family network through which we know most of our friends. It is how we will live forever. The operations of gay and lesbian nonprofit organizations are like soap operas: love, passion, excitement, vendettas, jealousy, sex, betrayal.

Walta Borawski, Michael Bronski, and I met in Boston through GCN in that time before AIDS. I was twenty-one. They seemed so much older, although they were only in their early thirties. They became two of my mentors in gay and lesbian liberation and, in a way, I grew up with them. They had been together for nearly twenty years, but theirs was unlike any marriage I had seen: open and totally committed, independent and yet stable enough to manage dinner together most nights, full of love and barbed humor at each other's peculiarities.

Together, they were encyclopedic in their knowledge of gay and lesbian history and culture. Michael is frighteningly smart and totally skeptical. He's the most original gay critic in the country, an old-fashioned intellectual, with a post-Stonewall race, gender, and class consciousness. Walta was a poet who could knowledgeably dish out the life and career of nearly every female torch singer who has recorded an album. Michael has cooked me more meals than I can count—talking the whole time he cooks—while Walta sat at the table and smoked, or played his latest favorite record for us, or told us some Streisand trivia.

We became friends through endless arguments, all trying to define what *progressive gay and lesbian politics* meant. The GCN crowd was an offbeat, nationwide network of writers, artists, cartoonists, activists, and readers. We organized, analyzed, wrote, traded gossip, fell in and out of love with each other, had feuds, made up, and even lived together in collectives and group houses. The Fort Hill Faggots for Freedom was a collective of gay men who lived in a group of houses in Roxbury in the mid-1970s; in the early 1980s, I lived in an updated, lesbian-feminist version. We shared our lives, food, houses, books, music, films, plays, and political organizations and built friendships around never-ending conversations. We attended hundreds of political meetings; wrote leaflets, articles, and books; produced conferences and readings; planned demonstrations, rallies, and pickets; and organized fundraisers, benefits, potlucks, neighborhoods, and even unions.

At GCN, we argued constantly with each other about sex and politics. We fought about whether pedophilia and NAMBLA (the North American Man Boy Love Association) belonged in the gay and lesbian movement. We fought about pornography and feminism, about sexual differences and similarities between lesbians and gay men, about bisexuality, about gender, about S&M, about power and sex, about both the Right's and Left's dislike of sexual pleasure. We alienated the traditional gay political activists at the national level with articles calling them *homocrats*; we alienated leftists with articles critical of Cuba; we angered lesbians with sexually explicit illustrations to stories; we angered gay men who were offended by seeing women's breasts depicted in a cartoon; we lost advertisers after reporting on violence outside gay and lesbian bars; we infuriated gay conservatives by arguing that our movement was one that fought homophobia, racism, sexism, and economic injustice; and we reached and educated tens of thousands of gay, lesbian, and straight readers.

It was GCNers—like John Mitzel and Charley Shively—who organized pickets against Anita Bryant in 1977. GCNers again led the organizing against police entrapment of gay men in the late 1970s. In February 1979, GCNers Amy Hoffman, Eric Rofes, and Richard Burns went to the first planning meeting in Philadelphia of the first National Lesbian and Gay March on Washington, and Eric served on the march's steering committee. When I got involved with GCN in 1979, I worked on pickets against two homophobic films, *Cruising* and *Windows*. In 1980, we organized two gay and lesbian buses from Boston to Washington to have an openly gay presence at the national demonstration against US intervention in El Salvador. In 1982, we literally raised GCN from the ashes when arson completely destroyed its offices. We started the Prison Project to advocate for lesbian and gay people behind bars. We began to cover racism and sexism within the movement; that led us to cover class in a more serious way. By 1983, we had become one of the principal gay sources of information about AIDS.

When did it all change? When did our lives go from the optimism of people developing a whole new politics to the numbness of a people experiencing survival as a disaster?

Was it the year that Walta started to fade? Was it when Richard, Amy, Kevin Cathcart, Catherine Hanssens, and I had dinner together in 1981, the week that the *New York Times* reported the cases of an odd cancer in five gay men? Was it when Michael Bronski wrote about the *gay clone* as a political phenomenon? Maybe it was in 1987, after the second March on Washington, when Jesse Helms got nearly unanimous support in the Senate for his ban on the use of federal funds for gay-specific AIDS education. It could have been in 1982, when we all argued against the closing of gay bathhouses. Was it in 1984, the first time I returned to Boston since moving to Washington, and Michael and Walta threw a party to welcome me back? Maybe it all changed in 1985, when Dr. Jim Gleason, one of Michael's lovers, was diagnosed. Or in 1986, when the Supreme Court ruled that gay and lesbian sexuality could be criminalized by the states. Maybe it was in 1988, when Bob Andrews died. Or in 1987, when Steve Ansolabehere died. Or in 1992, when Mike Riegle died. Or any week in between, when hundreds of people we knew and loved were diagnosed with AIDS, fell ill, got better, went into the hospital, came out of the hospital, came over for dinner, went to the movies with us, went back to the hospital, came out again, went on an international cruise, and then, always too suddenly, died.

The AIDS epidemic so transformed the gay and lesbian political movement that, as with our personal lives, we can mark two distinct eras: Before AIDS and After AIDS. At the outset, AIDS presented a pair of political dilemmas to gay and lesbian activists. How were we going to get a response from an administration that did not care about us? And how were we going to motivate and mobilize a community that was largely in the closet and invisible?

In the 1980s, gay and lesbian advocates made four strategic choices whose results affect us to this day: degaying, desexualizing, decoupling AIDS-specific reform from systemic reform, and direct action. At the time, those decisions seemed the best responses we could come up with, but they were short-term, quick-fix strategies that yielded dramatic but short-lived gains. As a consequence, we failed to tackle the underlying problems that still exacerbate the epidemic: the problems of homophobia, sexual denial and repression, racism, sexism, and the dictates of a profit-driven health care system.

In the early years of the epidemic, gay rights advocates faced monumental problems. How were we going to make gay and bisexual lives visible to straight legislative bodies that had never even known we existed? How were we going to motivate political leaders to spend money on the unpopular segments of society affected by AIDS? In the context of a sex-phobic society, filled with secrets and shameful lies about human sexual behavior, how could we explain a sexually transmitted epidemic in terms that everyone could understand? How could we ensure that the maximum number of people—gay-identified and straight-identified—would protect themselves and not treat this as someone else's problem?

Degaying AIDS promised an answer. Coined by the activists Ben Schatz and Eric Rofes, *degaying* meant decoupling the stigma of homosexuality from the stigma of AIDS in order to win the access and attention we needed. In short, homophobia required gay people, nationwide, to create an AIDS-specific movement. We chose to focus on AIDS rather than on homophobia and racism, even though homophobia and racism were the causes of the governmental and societal paralysis in the first place.

We degayed AIDS when we put forward nongay public health officials as our spokespersons and when we pressed forward on AIDS-specific issues while avoiding gay and lesbian rights issues. Because we believed gay people did not carry the same moral authority or influence as public health officials, we asked the latter to speak for us.

In a panel at the Fifth International AIDS Conference, held in Montreal in June 1989, Ben Schatz challenged the movement for stating that "AIDS is not a gay problem; it's a human problem"—which implied that being gay and being human were not the same. With our frequent pleas to the government to spend funds for AIDS because straights can get ill too, we promoted the homophobic subtext that AIDS would not be as important if only gay or bisexual people were susceptible. We drew attention to worldwide statistics that show that heterosexual sex transmits HIV as easily as homosexual sex. But by emphasizing the risks to heterosexuals and playing down the staggering decimation of the gay community, AIDS activists established the fledgling AIDS movement as separate from the gay and lesbian civil rights movement. In a sense, it is: the AIDS-specific movement is focused narrowly on services and securing a response to the epidemic.

Yet, from the beginning, efforts to deal with AIDS were stymied by homophobia. AIDS-prevention efforts were frustrated by the closet: in order to get gay people to come forward to deal with their HIV infections, we had to overcome their fear of discrimination. We had to convince gay people not to worry about losing their jobs or having their sexual orientation disclosed to coworkers and families. In addition, homophobia prevented health officials from funding gay-specific AIDS-education programs.

Further, the politicization of AIDS by the right wing held back any national response to AIDS for many years. The first comprehensive piece of AIDS legislation, the Ryan White Care Bill, was enacted in 1990, nearly ten years into the epidemic. The Right early on equated AIDS with homosexuality, so AIDS policy became a referendum on gay and lesbian rights. If only we had seen these policy fights in the same way, we might have devised one unified movement rather than the bifurcated one we did create.

Let me be clear: the degaying of AIDS was not a lie. The things we said were true. It *is* true that AIDS is sexually transmitted and certain acts (like receptive intercourse) are more likely to result in transmission than others (most kinds of oral sex). Worldwide, AIDS *does* affect large numbers of heterosexuals. Moreover, an AIDS-specific movement *was* needed to provide services for hundreds of thousands of HIV-infected people. The tragedy of our separating AIDS from its gay roots is not that we misled America—in fact, we saved a lot of lives by urging heterosexuals to practice safer sex and by explaining to them how they are at risk.

Rather, the tragedy of degaying has been internal, both in terms of more gay lives lost and in the size, scope, and politics of the gay and lesbian movement itself. Questioning the divorce of AIDS-service organizations from the gay and lesbian political movement, Eric Rofes discussed degaying in *Outlook* magazine in 1989. He cited the repeated refusal of AIDS organizations that grew out of the gay community—like AIDS Project Los Angeles, the Names Project AIDS Memorial Quilt, and the San Francisco AIDS Foundation—to use the words *gay* and *lesbian*. He remembered a 1986 AIDS Walkathon in San Francisco, and a 1988 National AIDS Candlelight Vigil in Washington sponsored by the AIDS Memorial Quilt, at which no gay-identified person spoke. Rofes pointed out that this repeated dissociation of AIDS from the very community that was struggling to deal with it prompted the late AIDS activist Michael Callen to write angrily, in the March 1989 issue of the *People with AIDS* (PWA) *Coalition Newsline*: "AIDS is a gay disease! There. I said it. And I believe it. If I hear one more time that AIDS is not a gay disease, I shall vomit. AIDS is a gay disease because a lot of gay men get AIDS.... More important, most of what has been noble about America's response to AIDS has been the direct result of the lesbian and gay community."

The splintering of the AIDS movement from its gay roots has depoliticized it as a movement; it is like all the other disease-centered national charities (cancer, cerebral palsy, multiple sclerosis, etc.). Closeted gay men and women began to donate to gay (but not gay-identified) community institutions. As AIDS activism and fundraising developed a social cachet—through the involvement of straight celebrities and wealthy individuals—more gay people felt comfortable getting involved. Throughout the 1980s, people wrote checks to AIDS organizations who had never supported organizations working on the homophobia that inhibited the federal response to AIDS. This lack of support, before 1992, drastically held back the gay political movement. It felt surreal, in the late eighties, to be involved in AIDS issues yet to be unable to talk about its connection to anti-gay violence. Or to point out that the lack of attention to AIDS was the same as the lack of attention to all other gay problems.

Another way to understand the depoliticization is to note that, although the AIDS-service movement reaches thousands of people who are touched by AIDS, it has never systematically organized them into a political bloc for AIDS-policy fights. For example, the AIDS Action Council (AAC) does not have access to the mailing lists of every single AIDS organization in the country. So even on the direct mail level, the AAC is unable to compete on AIDS-policy issues with the religious conservatives who amass millions of names, which they marshal to obtain support and to start letter-writing campaigns.

Although AIDS did accelerate gay and lesbian political participation, the results were mixed for the mainstreaming of the gay and lesbian movement. On the one hand, AIDS integrated us into the broader political culture by forcing us to focus on national politics, public policy development, lobbying, and electoral politics. Driven by the urgency of anger and loss, gay and lesbian organizations asserted themselves in the legislative or political sphere; we brought gay perspectives and realities into areas that had not heard from us before. Legislative bodies, government officials, and corporate and business leaders all started to interact with openly gay advocates. Through this steady process of interaction, AIDS issues were partly mainstreamed.

On the other hand, because we had defined our political purpose as AIDS work rather than as gay or lesbian work, our newfound access did not automatically help our movement for gay and lesbian equality. This paradoxical truth was one that gay and lesbian advocates faced as we began to come out of the political closet. We rapidly improved our AIDS-related lobbying but gained little ground on gay and lesbian issues. Gay political organizations remained marginalized in Washington throughout the 1980s, even though gay- or lesbian-led AIDS organizations grew in clout and visibility. So, in the time I worked at NGLTF, AIDS lobbyists were able to get meetings with high-level Bush officials while lobbyists pursuing gay or lesbian issues were denied access.

Visibility

The AIDS epidemic made our lives and our political movement more visible than ever. Younger gay and lesbian activists are sometimes disdainful of the priority that middle-aged and older queer activists place on queer visibility. Our cultural integration seems so pervasive that it feels secure. But invisibility and silence about homosexuality are our two oldest enemies. As recently as ten years ago, major newspapers refused to use the word *gay*, preferring *homosexual*. As recently as 1991, obituaries in major papers did not mention the surviving lover of a gay person who died.

Before AIDS, the gay and lesbian media were the principal location of any conversation about gay and lesbian issues. Our communities, our disagreements, our sexual mores, and our institutions were thoroughly debated in the pages of lesbian and gay publications. Even after the advent of AIDS, the gay and lesbian media remained the principal source of information. In a very real sense, the gay and lesbian press saved many lives. It published much of the early political analysis of the AIDS epidemic. It was gay and lesbian media that covered the first PWA conference, held in Denver in 1982, and published the Denver Principles, which became the rallying cry for an entire movement. It was lesbian and gay media that promoted the idea of safer sex, carried ads for benefits, exposed the government's lack of response, and covered the traumatic early political fights within the gay and lesbian communities (over bathhouses, testing, promiscuity, poppers, and much more). It was in the gay and lesbian press that fights about the value of AIDS Coalition to Unleash Power's (ACT UP) tactics were conducted. It was our press that carried details of medical treatment and scientific information, teaching thousands of people with HIV how to respond to the crisis long before the medical establishment caught on. Finally, it was the gay and lesbian media nationwide that promoted the growth of AIDS education, outreach, and political organizing.

The mainstream press did not cover AIDS seriously until the late 1980s, when two events triggered the coverage: public shock at Rock Hudson's diagnosis with AIDS, in 1985; and the publication of Randy Shilts's history of AIDS, *And the Band Played On*, in 1987. I would argue that such visibility required desexualizing our community, which ultimately did not dissipate homophobia but only glossed over its presence. Notably, straight culture has elevated lesbians (seen as asexual women and thus safe) over gay men (seen as sexual problems and dangerous) in terms of cultural appeal. Despite our cultural visibility, the equation for most Americans is not Silence = Death, but Gay = AIDS.

In a sense, AIDS outed our entire community. Perversely put, we won visibility for gay and lesbian lives because we died in record numbers. The sheer number of these deaths, and the far larger and sobering number of gay or bisexual men and women still living with HIV and AIDS-related illnesses, made us a population impossible to ignore. Families had to come to terms with lovers and friends left behind—even if some chose to ignore them. Co-workers had to confront the unacknowledged homosexuality of people they had worked alongside. Problems like the closet, employment discrimination, loss of health care benefits, the denial of care by medical and service providers, were not news to gay and lesbian people, but through the visibility that AIDS gave to our lives, they became more noticeable to others.

But our cultural visibility was not easily obtained. For years, the government ran away from AIDS, the media resisted coverage, and conservative religious leaders were silent or hostile. Visibility was won through calculated and sustained mass-media campaigns waged by gay activists to seize the attention of the nation. These campaigns were coordinated by public relations and advertising professionals fighting homophobic referenda; by lawyers and lobbyists pressing for reform; by gay and lesbian media advocates; and eventually by ACT UP and the direct-action movement.

AIDS media activists began work to influence straight media coverage from the first reports of the disease, in 1981. The mission was twofold: to secure accurate coverage of the burgeoning epidemic and to counter inflammatory or homophobic coverage. We saw media coverage as a means to advance our public policy agenda, a way to win more AIDS funding and nondiscrimination measures.

Through it all, the movement became adept at building coalitions with straight medical and public health associations and with a range of non-gay allies. Although media campaigns worked to win important electoral victories, we lost ground in a sense. For one, the gay movement was forced to spend millions to defend itself rather than to advance queer equality. In the 1990s, the Right has used this strategy quite effectively to frustrate gay and lesbian progress at the state and local level. Second, we were forced into a battle that had some ambiguous consequences. From the outset of AIDS, the

Right has portrayed the gay community as selfishly concerned with its civil rights at the expense of the public good. Gay activists like Jeff Levi and Tom Stoddard eloquently argued that the public good required attention to civil rights, but the question continued to be framed as a debate. With its initiatives, the Right was able to repeat this charge and others against gay people.

In many ways, the visibility we have won through AIDS has been double-edged, contradicting myths about gay people as much as confirming them. Among the truths are that gay, lesbian, and bisexual people are a part of every extended family; that we have been genuinely heroic in our response to this tragedy; that our response to AIDS developed new models of community engagement, volunteerism, and activism; and that gay and lesbian people come in every shape, size, color, and type.

But public information polls reveal that AIDS has not significantly changed heterosexuals' opinions of us. Visibility has also reinforced old attitudes about homosexuality and about homosexuals: homosexuality as illness, gay men and lesbians as uncontrollable sex fiends, gay sexual acts as inherently unhealthy and deadly, and being gay as an immoral condition. AIDS-phobia has persisted, ebbing and flowing but always present. A national telephone survey done in 1991 revealed that a quarter of those surveyed felt disgusted by or angry at people with AIDS; more than a third agreed that people with AIDS should be quarantined and their names published; and more than a fifth that people with AIDS deserved their illness.

Desexualization

AIDS exposed our sexual cultures to an uncomprehending straight majority. Public debates recurred in policy fights about abstinence, sex education, condom use, the production of AIDS educational materials that use sexually explicit images and texts, and promiscuity. Congress enacted a sexual standard into law when it passed an amendment, initiated by Jesse Helms in 1987, outlawing federal funds for AIDS education that "promotes or encourages homosexual behavior." This effectively cut off federal monies to the population most affected in the United States. Known as the Helms Amendment, the measure is attached to every bill that may affect gay or lesbian people.

There was no early consensus in the movement on how to handle AIDS and gay male sex, and there still is not. Initially, there was tremendous denial about AIDS among gay men, who trusted the government very little; given the long history of police harassment, they had good reason. With the emergence of AIDS, it seemed too odd and too predictable that government officials now told us to close bathhouses and urged gay men to have less sex, fewer partners, and more monogamy, and to abstain from or circumscribe the way they had certain types of sex. AIDS struck at the heart of the sexual freedom that many gay men believed constituted gay liberation. It became harder to explain to an increasingly conservative country, which believed gay men were dying because they had too much sex, why gay sexual freedom was important.

The mainstream gay and AIDS movements devised a complex response: distancing themselves from the sexual liberation ethic of the seventies, while at the same time developing new ways to talk about sexual practices and transmission (media ads, safer sex workshops, videos, posters, and countless other campaigns). We quickly revised our community's sexual history to point out and play up those in committed relationships and cited the dramatic decline in rates of new infection among gay men as a sign of gay men's sexual responsibility. Because of our fear of homophobia, we responded to the cultural visibility that AIDS gave to gay male sexual life with a politically motivated effort to de-emphasize the importance of sexuality in the lives of gay men.

Decoupling AIDS from Systemic Reform

A basic reality of gay lives is that we take care of our own. AIDS service organizations at once grew out of and depoliticized the pre-AIDS gay and feminist health movements. AIDS activists did not so much invent a gay health movement as reinvent it. During the 1970s, the early gay and lesbian health movement established community-based health clinics, including the Howard Brown Memorial Clinic in Chicago, the Whitman-Walker Clinic in Washington, the Fenway Community Health Center in Boston, and the Lyon-Martin Lesbian Health Center in San Francisco. It organized the National Lesbian and Gay Health Association and held an annual conference.

The pre-AIDS gay and lesbian health movement adapted the feminist health movement's critiques to challenge mainstream medicine's pathologizing and discrimination-ridden view of homosexuals. Mental health activists counseled gay people to accept themselves and to understand the homophobia of our culture, instead of counseling them on how to become straight. Lesbian self-help health collectives taught women to use speculums and do breast self-exams. They demystified women's gynecological needs and questioned the heterosexist bias of mainstream medicine. Gay and lesbian associations of medical professionals, starting first as support groups, eventually became strong advocacy groups, like the Gay and Lesbian Medical Association (founded in 1981 as the American Association of Physicians for Human Rights).

As a consequence of the epidemic, the feminist health agenda became the health agenda of the gay and lesbian Lambda Legal Defense and Education Fund began to explore issues they had never before concentrated on: health insurance reform, welfare reform, eligibility for Social Security Disability income, Medicaid eligibility, access to affordable and quality health care, sex education, and nondiscrimination in health care delivery.

But the absorption of this health agenda did not answer the more radical feminist criticism. The feminist movement analyzed the health care system as a politicized arena in which homophobia, sexism, racism, and economic disparity were institutionalized. The feminist mission was the construction of a more just, accessible, and fair health care system, guided by and empowering the people it served.

The AIDS-service organizations, in contrast, positioned themselves squarely within the health care system and sought to accommodate us to it. And the gay movement relied on and tried to strengthen the hand of public health officials: we went for the AIDS fix and left systemic problems largely unaddressed. Whereas the old gay and feminist health movement was grounded in criticism of the economics of health care, the AIDS service movement reproduced the dominant class, race, and gender biases within the organizations, legislation, and delivery systems it created. In fundamental ways it shied away from seeing itself as part of a broad anti-poverty, health care reform movement. Largely ignoring how a profit-centered health system does disservice to gay men and lesbians, AIDS service organizations molded themselves into traditional health care bureaucracies—vying for the same funds, creating the same structures, and adopting many of the same attitudes toward patients that radicals in our movement challenge.

Interestingly, the one part of the AIDS movement that did adopt the radical empowerment stance of the feminist health movement was the PWA Coalition. The embrace of feminist principles by the PWA Coalition had a lot to do with the feminism of one of its founders, the extraordinary songwriter and singer Michael Callen. Callen lived with AIDS for over fourteen years, before succumbing in 1994, and was at the forefront of several innovations in AIDS activism. Callen advocated a greater voice for people with AIDS in all aspects of the health crisis, from representation on boards of organizations to involvement in decisions about medical research, drug testing, and public policy. But Callen's prophetic voice was not heeded as often as it should have been, and in this decade the crisis is dealt with on a more traditional model, in which people with AIDS are the "clients" of a paternalistic health care and social service system that takes care of them until they die.

Whereas the explicit goal of the early gay and lesbian health clinics and venereal disease clinics was community organizing and political reform in addition to services, the goal of AIDS service organizations has largely been medical and social service delivery. Most devote only a small fraction of their resources to public policy advocacy, to political education, or to community organizing. Sadly, the inattention has limited our ability to mobilize constituent pressure on AIDS policy fights. Without a strong political mission, the AIDS movement turned into just another liberal social service movement— although it was still a step forward for gay people, because we had never had social service organizations to take care of our needs.

The New Face of the Lesbian and Gay Movement

AIDS dramatically changed the composition of the gay and lesbian movement. Millions of gay and lesbian people became politicized as they saw the government fail to act while scores of friends and loved ones suffered. Men who had never been political, never considered coming out of the closet, never attended a gay or lesbian fundraising event, began to do so in large numbers. Lesbians who had shunned the mixed gay movement, choosing to work on women's rights, grew alarmed at the exploitation of AIDS by the Right and decided to confront the homophobia of the medical, political, and legal systems. Straight friends, family members, and colleagues of people with AIDS were moved, through their personal experience, to support a movement they had previously ignored. This awakening took place not only in the consciousness of middle- to upper-class men and women of all colors and types, but also among poor and working-class people. Because AIDS affected so many kinds of people, a broad segment of America began to turn to gay and lesbian organizations for representation and assistance. In the 1960s and 1970s, the gay rights movement was the province of a small group of "politicos." By the late 1980s, gay organizations were being asked to serve white, Black, Latino, and Asian gay people.

The movement was poorly equipped to deal with this influx of new energy and different kinds of people, which helps explain both the movement's growth and the increased tensions within it. For example, as people of color turned to gay and lesbian organizations for culturally specific and culturally sensitive AIDS services, they encountered a lack of comprehension, outright resistance, and sometimes racial prejudice. In response, gay people of color established AIDS service groups that were racially oriented.

There is little question that AIDS organizations for people of color have expanded the reach of AIDS education and prevention. But they have not transformed the racial or class politics of mainstream AIDS organizations. In this sense, the failure of the mainstream gay and white-dominated AIDS movements to take up systemic reform must also be seen as a failure to address racism and sexism. Cutbacks in social services will hurt those people with AIDS and HIV who are dependent on such services. Yet AIDS organizations have not been at the forefront of opposing these cutbacks. We seem to have bought the myth that we will be all right as long as AIDS-specific expenditures, like the Ryan White Care Act of 1990 or funding for AIDS research, are not cut.

Perhaps the most notable way in which AIDS changed the composition of the movement was the awakened activism of middle- and upper-class gay white men. Until the epidemic struck, many of these men had never experienced prejudice directly or even through their friends. AIDS exposed their sense of security as false. As Rodger McFarlane, an early executive director of Gay Men's Health Crisis (GMHC), observed, "For a white man with a graduate degree and a good job who can pass, [discrimination was] not an issue. Never was. Until [AIDS] really got down to it and you realized they want you to die. If you want to be the way you are and not play their way, you're dead meat. You are literally left to die."

Of the six founders of GMHC, several had never been active in the gay and lesbian community or been out of the closet before AIDS. These men came together because their lovers and friends were getting sick and they feared that no one was acting to save them. The men brought donors, contacts, and experience in mainstream business, medicine, and politics into the gay movement. With these skills, contacts, and resources, GMHC, originally an entirely volunteer organization, has become the largest and most politically influential AIDS service organization in the world, with a staff of more than two hundred and an annual budget of over $20 million.

The new energy from the gay and lesbian middle class helped build a social service apparatus throughout the country. Community centers, youth projects, anti-violence projects, substance-abuse programs, housing projects, and legal services projects grew larger or were established.

We need to value the contribution that upper-middle-class and professional gay men and women made to the gay movement in the 1980s. The engagement of this stratum in gay politics has been a key factor in the cultural revolution we witness to this day. But no one can deny that these gay men and women brought their own values and ideals into the existing gay and lesbian movement. The newly activated gay people made the post-AIDS movement more conservative in at least three ways: by the reformulation of the liberation-oriented goals into reform; by the substitution of institution building for movement building; and by their outright rejection of grassroots political organizing as the best means to build gay and lesbian power. In place of liberation, the AIDS movement substituted nondiscrimination; instead of building a movement, it built agencies and bureaucracies; instead of placing its political faith in training and organizing gay and lesbian people and our allies into an electoral coalition, it placed its faith in friends in high places....

The Direct-Action Strategy and Its Decline

On March 10, 1987, the playwright and AIDS activist Larry Kramer gave a speech at the New York City Lesbian and Gay Community Services Center. He passionately criticized the gay movement's lack of political advocacy and media presence on AIDS and asked the crowd of two hundred and fifty men and women, "Do we want to start a new organization devoted solely to political action?" Days later, at a follow-up meeting at the center inspired by Kramer's address, and attended by more than three hundred, ACT UP was born. ACT UP New York began drawing more than eight hundred people to its weekly meetings at the center. And ACT UP chapters quickly appeared throughout the country. By early 1988, strong chapters existed in Chicago, San Francisco, Boston, and Los Angeles. By the end of 1989, ACT UP boasted more than a hundred chapters worldwide, including scores of chapters in small midwestern, southwestern, and southern cities in the United States.

ACT UP gave to gay people affected by AIDS a vehicle through which to organize. Motivated by their own HIV status or by a sense of outrage at the government's inadequate response to AIDS, thousands of people flocked to ACT UP groups. Fueled in part by anger, many were also driven by a pragmatic critique of why AIDS was not getting the response it deserved. Kramer correctly pointed out that politicians listened to the media and that, except in isolated incidents, the media had not yet been reached by AIDS activism. The deepening epidemic and Kramer's urgent call for action tapped into energy that the movement had not before reached on a national level: the desire among gay and lesbian people to engage in direct action on behalf of their own lives.

From the beginning, ACT UP attracted a wide mix of people in New York—from closeted gay professional men who were HIV-positive, to veteran lesbian-feminist organizers, to gay activists frustrated by traditional political strategies, to straight celebrities, to young gay and straight activists whose first-ever political involvement was often an ACT UP meeting and demonstration. Indeed, ACT UP grew in part because it provided an easy, local, and direct way to participate in gay politics—something that no national gay or lesbian project had given large numbers of people up to that point, or since.

Direct action works because everyone involved shapes the way it takes place. There is no third party mediating the experience; the idea most often originates with the people who carry it out. Pickets, sit-ins, small demonstrations, rallies, speak-outs, leafleting, carrying a protest sign into a meeting, risking arrest by committing civil disobedience, writing chants, using a bullhorn, spray-painting, wheat-pasting, preparing placards for a march through the city streets—all these forms of protest are very immediate, very personal. The exhilaration of direct action is profound. And the sense of moral purpose—of being united with the other people one acts with—can be passionate and affecting. As ACT UP member David Barr recalls, "It was really exciting to watch people go through this process of finding ACT UP, getting politicized, figuring out what that means, how they can do some work, and how they grew from that."

ACT UP gave people a sense of belonging and a creative outlet for despair. It became community, family, and faith all rolled into one. Gay men found in AIDS activism the courage to confront their mortality, the vehicle to express their anger, and the hope that, through their action, research and treatment would be accelerated. Lesbians, many of whom had worked in and even led various non-LGBT-oriented social justice movements, were long familiar with systemic inequities. They came home into their own movement through AIDS activism. Hundreds of straight, bisexual, and allied folk got involved with AIDS activism and direct action to express their anger at the government, which appeared to condone the death of people with AIDS.

At least four historical developments contributed to the national emergence of ACT UP and accelerated the reach of its direct-action strategy: the intransigent policies of the Reagan and Bush administrations; the impact of the 1987 March on Washington for Lesbian and Gay Rights; the national media coverage captured by ACT UP; and the inability of traditional gay and lesbian groups to involve the large number of people who wanted to take action on AIDS and gay rights at the local level.

Both the Reagan and Bush administrations behaved reprehensibly in response to AIDS. For several years, Reagan ignored the problem completely. His Secretary of Health and Human Services, Margaret Heckler, met with gay lobbyists in 1983 and promised to make AIDS a priority. But that promise was frustrated by the internal politics of the administration; the Moral Majority and religious Right wanted the government to have nothing to do with gay men. By 1986, when Surgeon General C. Everett Koop began to press for a greater response to AIDS, he encountered opposition from Secretary of Education William Bennett. Over Bennett's objection, Koop published and distributed the first government mailing on AIDS, which he sent to every household in early 1987. For his moral courage, Koop earned the lasting gratitude of gay and lesbian people. By 1987, the year Reagan finally uttered the word AIDS, gay and lesbian anger at the administration was at a boiling point. *San Francisco Chronicle* reporter Randy Shilts's book, *And the Band Played On*, on AIDS and politics, made the government's irresponsibility vivid to his colleagues in the media and to the public at large. All this set a highly politicized stage for ACT UP's emergence.

The impact of the Second National March on Washington for Lesbian and Gay Rights, in 1987, on gay and lesbian activism cannot be overstated. Planned for over a year and a half, the march was an enormous success, exceeding the wildest expectations of any of its organizers. The timing was right, and the word was out at the grassroots level. The march drew more than 650,000 people, and for the first time gave massive visibility to the epidemic's effect on the gay community. As part of the march, the AIDS Memorial Quilt was displayed on the Capitol grounds, providing an emotional and moral anchor for the protests held throughout the weekend. At the march, the colorful and exciting presence of ACT UP attracted the attention of thousands of gay and lesbian people—and drew widespread media notice. On October 12, the day after the march, a widely covered, national civil disobedience action at the US Supreme Court by five thousand protesters made direct action a top national news story.

The march weekend ignited gay and lesbian activism. Marchers went home and formed scores of local political, direct-action, cultural, social, and professional groups. The NGLTF national office had a fourfold increase in the number of calls it received from gay and lesbian activists seeking technical assistance, organizing materials, and advice. Each year after the march, the movement seemed to grow, a trend that has, in fact, continued into the mid-1990s. ACT UP both benefited from and contributed directly to this heightened awareness and activism.

Through the media coverage it secured, ACT UP contributed to a greater awareness of AIDS issues within the gay and lesbian community, and in society at large. Media interest in ACT UP was immediate—from its first demonstration, on March 24, 1987, at Wall Street, targeting the Food and Drug Administration's (FDA) bureaucratic logjam on experimental drug development. The coverage ACT UP won remains unprecedented. Never before has an organization of gay and lesbian people been as widely covered by the straight press. The media success was both carefully orchestrated and organic. On the one hand, many early ACT UP organizers were savvy media veterans. Some, like Ann Northrop, worked in the news media; others, like Michelangelo Signorile, were skilled at public relations.

ACT UP New York inspired some of the finest visual artists in the country—including the graffiti artist Keith Haring; the Gran Fury Collective, which developed ACT UP's signature Silence = Death image; and the documentary filmmaker collective Testing the Limits—and made their political art available to others across the country. The artists' arresting graphic images were printed on posters, T-shirts, and leaflets; and their films were broadcast on cable TV and in national news media and distributed worldwide. These images made an enormous impression on viewers. The lime-green poster of Reagan with the pink word "AIDSgate"emblazoned on it, which we carried during the 1988 Republican Convention protests in New Orleans; the American flag labeled "Bush AIDS Flag," with skulls instead of stars; the red-and-black posters citing the AIDS death toll so far and asking, "Where Was George?"—all became graphic reminders of AIDS. ACT UP media committees everywhere planned actions with an eye toward media coverage: What was the visual, who would do the press conference, where would they stage the backdrop, what media outlet would be the best to cover this event?

Along with these calculated attempts to gain coverage was the inherent drama, tension, and theatricality of ACT UP demonstrations in particular and of direct-action protests in general, which made them telegenic and newsworthy. I still remember the orchestrated, chaotic beauty of the 1988 FDA action, at which a thousand protestors surrounded the FDA's bleak building in Maryland; the 1989 demonstration at the US Civil Rights Commission's hearings on AIDS, at which many in the audience donned clown masks and held up watches to protest the ineptitude and wastefulness of this body; and the shock of ACT UP's 1989 Stop the Church demonstration against the Catholic Church, which interrupted a church service at St. Patrick's Cathedral in Manhattan. The life and death drama of furious people with AIDS and HIV screaming at officials and bureaucrats riveted the nation's attention for several years.

Ultimately, such actions also angered many people. ACT UP was controversial from the start. Many people loathed its confrontational tactics. Some in the community feared that ACT UP would alienate the general public. Others feared that it would jeopardize hard-won political access. Still others feared that direct actions against political friends would estrange them. Yet others deplored the use of direct action in most circumstances, arguing that traditional political activism was the best way to win AIDS policies. The self-righteousness that was the hallmark of ACT UP galled many of its erstwhile supporters. ACT UP chapters seemed to thrive on these controversies and exploited them. Among the most polarizing actions in the history of ACT UP was a spring-summer 1988 "freedom ride" by four members of ACT UP New York through the South, ending at the Democratic Convention in Atlanta, which both alienated and inspired southern gay and lesbian activists from North Carolina to Louisiana; a pitched, year-long battle in 1988 and 1989 over the appointment by New York City Mayor David Dinkins of Woodrow Myers, who supported identifying people with HIV and AIDS and quarantining them, as New York City Health Commissioner; the 1989 protest by ACT UP San Francisco that disrupted the opera and another that stopped traffic on the Golden Gate Bridge; the 1989 Stop the Church demonstration; a demonstration against George H. W. Bush's Health and Human Services Secretary Louis Sullivan at the International AIDS Conference in San Francisco in June 1991, at which activists prevented him from being heard; and a 1992 demonstration by ACT UP members at a meeting of gay and AIDS lobbyists with the Centers for Disease Control about its policies concerning women with AIDS.

Direct action and traditional politics have always clashed in the gay and lesbian movement. Although some veterans of the post-Stonewall generation embraced ACT UP as a return to the radical politics they felt the gay movement had wrongly abandoned, most gay political veterans looked down on direct action in general. Conversely, many ACT UP members were contemptuous of and hostile to the mainstream gay and lesbian rights movement. "People are dying," they argued. "This is no time for business as usual."

The resistance of traditional political activists to direct action was deep. Some seasoned lobbyists felt that direct action was ultimately beside the point: they believed substantive knowledge of the issues and specific policy advocacy would finally win the day. Others, like congressional Representative Barney Frank of Massachusetts, argued that, while there was a time and place for direct action, it tended to alienate more people than it reached. Still other traditionalists took a pragmatic, even opportunistic, view: they supported the street activists as long as they "legitimized" conventional lobbyists. So, for example, immediately after the ACT UP protest at the FDA, a high-level meeting took place among gay and AIDS lobbyists, and the FDA bureaucrats. The lobbyists put forth the same message that the AIDS protesters had carried, but consciously positioned themselves as a "more reasonable" alternative to the mob outside. Such a technique, while effective for policy writing in the short term, provoked tremendous ill-will and lasting distrust between traditional political organizers and street activists.

ACT UP itself believed its direct-action tactics were the most effective. The unglamorous, behind-the-scenes lobbying process, it argued, was not only too slow to save lives; it was also undemocratic, because it did not allow for the participation of all who were interested. As ACT UP gained more media attention, and as it was credited with many political successes—some of which it was directly responsible for and others to which it contributed, alongside traditional lobbyists—its prestige grew, but at the expense of traditional activists whose work took place behind the scenes.

In a real sense, each strategy played off the other to increase its political strength, with gay mainstream groups, seen as reasonable, enhanced in the eyes of state power structures, and direct-action adherents idealized by grassroots queers.

Direct-action believers had several different kinds of critiques of the mainstream movement. Some, like Larry Kramer, were simply furious at gay and AIDS organizations, labeling them the enemy because they failed to take actions he felt they should or to act aggressively enough on AIDS. They distrusted mainstream gay groups. Thus, ACT UP and Queer Nation refused to work at the 1992 Republican Convention within a gay and lesbian coalition that included the Human Rights Campaign Fund, the NGLTF, and the Log Cabin Republicans. Others, like the feminist movement veteran and ACT UP activist Maxine Wolfe, believed that direct action was more inclusive, democratic, and honest than closed-door lobbying. Finally, a handful of ACT UP members functioned as provocateurs, stirring up conflicts within the movement and thriving on fomenting division.

I experienced the hostility of both sides of the direct-action/traditional politics divide. Because I came up from a grassroots wing of the feminist and gay movement, I championed direct action—alongside traditional political activism. In 1990, as executive director of the NGLTF, I protested President George Bush at his first (and only speech) on AIDS and incurred the wrath of conservatives on the NGLTF board and in the community at large. In contrast, in February 1992, I hastily and mistakenly agreed to be involved in a direct-action protest that called for protestors to handcuff themselves to the gay and AIDS lobbyists attending a small meeting with the Centers for Disease Control. The handcuffing was perceived, rightly, by the lobbyists as a hostile and troubling act. When I objected that people were uncomfortable being handcuffed and wanted to be released, the group refused to unlock them. I then withdrew from the action, because it violated my sense of what was right. This withdrawal was wrong on my part, because I had made a commitment to serve as a legal observer for the protesters, but necessary because I disagreed with the action. People on either side were angry at me: numerous ACT UP members branded me a traitor, while the AIDS lobbyists, many of whom I had worked with for several years, eyed me with anger and dismay.

For years, our anger was aimed at the federal government, federal agencies, Congress, drug companies, the media, and homophobic politicians. But as we became polarized among ourselves, the protests, anger, and direct action turned toward proponents of traditional political activism. Refocusing the anger we felt at AIDS on one another, or on AIDS organizations with whose policies we disagreed (as ACT UP did in New York when it picketed the Hispanic AIDS Forum), undermined the solidarity we needed to function as a movement.

Meanwhile, the Bush administration stepped up its rhetorical attack on ACT UP, calling it terrorist and militant. The attacks by straight homophobes like Bush were picked up and repeated by gay and lesbian conservatives—and liberals—many of whom had never believed in the value of direct action in the first place. The pages of the gay and lesbian press in the early 1990s are filled with criticism of ACT UP as a group that had outlived its purpose. As direct action ran into greater resistance, some who had participated in or endorsed it backed away.

In addition, the novelty and efficacy of direct action began to wear off. It became difficult for AIDS activists to obtain media coverage for their protests. Searching for new angles on a familiar story, the media began to report on dissent about direct action within the gay community. In the process of reporting the argument, the media, gay and straight, deepened the splits between opponents and proponents. By 1992, despite the visibility of ACT UP activists who challenged presidential candidates on the campaign trail, the consensus among gay people was that direct action was no longer an effective strategy.

Interestingly, those who disagreed most with that notion were feminists and lesbians. As ACT UP's popularity declined among men, new feminist direct-action groups rose up: the Women's Action Coalition (WAC), the Women's Health Action Mobilization (WHAM), and the Lesbian Avengers. Within ACT UP, lesbians asserted themselves, pushing for direct action to change the definition of AIDS for women and pressing for equal access to clinical trials. The new groups reflected alienation between progressive lesbians and the mainstream gay movement and, to some extent, represented a new type of lesbian activist. Thus, the activist Ruth Schwartz wrote, "Many ACT UP women represented a new dyke generation, more queer than feminist. Next to their early-twenties bravado, punk haircuts, and sticker-plastered jackets, lesbian AIDS service providers often looked like the establishment."

Lesbians are, as a whole, more politically progressive than gay men. Our skepticism about government, family, and patriarchy draws many of us to grassroots political action and to the democratic participation and individual control that direct action fosters. Yet there are several key exceptions to this general rule, based to some extent on generational, racial, and class differences. For example, with the exception of some of its founders, those active in Lesbian Avengers chapters were mostly young women, often experiencing their first organized lesbian or gay political campaigns. Middle- to upper-middle-class gay professional women were more likely to be active in traditional political organizations, like the National Organization for Women (NOW) and the Human Rights Campaign Fund (HRCF). Sadly, the racial separatism of the AIDS activist movement was reproduced in the new wave of lesbian direct-action groups. Lesbians of color are largely absent from these circles of activism and are more likely to be involved in non-gay anti-racist or economic justice projects. In the end, direct action did not help us resolve the old splits of political ideology, race, gender, and class. Instead, direct action reinforced them.

As the tide of cultural conservatism launched by the New Right in the 1970s hit its stride in the 1990s, the popularity of direct action diminished: media scrutiny exposed contradictions within the direct-action movement; direct action failed to transform mainstream gay institutions and to build the lasting, grassroots political presence we needed; and, sadly, many people involved in direct-action groups grew sicker, walked away in disgust or exhaustion, or died.

In addition, the mainstream gay rights movement came into its own during the 1990s, seeming to fulfill its promise of political access, cultural visibility, and social legitimation. After a decade of painful transformation induced by AIDS, mainstreaming gayness seemed to many to be the strategy offering the clearest short-term gains and the best hope for long-term equality.

PART 2. EXPANDING ITS SCOPE

6

INCLUSION, EXCLUSION, AND OCCLUSION: THE QUEER IDEA OF ASIAN-PACIFIC AMERICANNESS

This was a keynote speech at the East Coast Asian Students Union Conference, Brown University, on February 20, 1999, published in Amerasia Journal *in 2000.*

At the risk of debunking a premise many of you may consider central to the work ahead, I want to speak first today about the queerness of the very idea of Asian-Pacific Americanness. I want to propose to you that there is a difference between organizing an identity-based movement and a progressive and human rights-based one, and that at this moment in our history as political activists, the Asian Pacific American (APA) movement ought to choose the latter.

My talk makes a four-part argument. I begin with a personal piece that locates me in the soup that is race, gender, identity, sexuality, and class. It is my own self-assessment of where I stand today on these intersecting realities in my body. Second, I argue that we need to examine the paradigm of ethnic organizing that we are implicitly adopting when we take on the notion of an Asian-Pacific identity. Instead of a race- or ethnic-based model, I wonder if an economic model of understanding the experience of Asians in America would provide more fruitful grounds for organizing. Certainly, I believe that racism is a serious reality and obstacle for Asian Pacific Americans and for the political movements we are building in the United States. But the racism we as Asian Americans encounter differs from the racism encountered by Latinos or African Americans in this country, and we would be well served to note those differences, even as our immigrant communities have comfortably ignored issues of class and economic justice among our own. Third, I believe history teaches us that creating identity-based politics does not lead to liberatory outcomes. But this conclusion begs the question of what the goal is of the new APA politics we discuss here. What are we trying to achieve by attempting to create an APA movement? Do APAs even agree? Will we ever agree? Will the goals that we agree on be better served through another, non-identity-based political movement? Finally, I want to propose that, both to address the political challenges that Asian Americans face and to include sexuality, the APA movement must be willing to question and re-envision the heterosexual Asian family: no progressive Asian movement can emerge without such a re-envisioning. And I am not at all confident that we are at a place where such re-envisioning and redefinition are possible; I suspect that many of you will disagree with this last premise, and that is okay!

I argue overall that identity-based organizing is indeed vital and urgent—no matter if we are first generation or fifth. And making visible and included the different sexualities within Asian American communities is very important to those of us who are queer. But, ultimately, inclusion and visibility are the easy parts. The harder questions that confront a progressive APA movement are: What is the movement's commitment to economic justice, and is the movement willing to transform fundamental institutions in Asian societies in order to foster a genuine inclusion of feminist, gay, lesbian, bisexual, and transgender Asian sexualities to bring about meaningful societal change?

As Dana Takagi has noted in her essay, "Maiden Voyage," the adding-on or adding-in of sexuality into the melange of Asian identities in America is, on its own, not enough. If sexuality is submerged into the preexisting, hierarchical, ethnic-based narrative, we are not redefining very much and not, in fact, opening up very much space for queer Asians like me. Nor are we making real social change.

Personal Identity Formation

As a child, I was one of about fifty Indians in a small rural upstate New York college town in the late 1960s. I remember the first questions my childhood peers asked me: Did we live in a teepee in India? Were there roads in India? Did we have hospitals and telephones? Were Indian women born with a dot on their foreheads? The ignorance of these questions and the jarring uniqueness of our family's daily life in that little town instilled in me an early awareness of my difference—and an early desire to run away from it, to blend in and not be noticed. Sadly, this running away from my Indian self to assimilate was something I continued well beyond college, and it was a process that accelerated when I started to come out as a lesbian.

My assimilation was more defined by a bifurcated existence than it was by my wholesale acceptance of all things American. Like many immigrants, I felt detached from mainstream American values and rejected many of them. But I felt a similar skepticism toward the Indian values my parents tried to get me to adopt. Quite deliberately, I lived in two worlds—American outside the home and Indian with family and friends. This split grew dramatically when I went to college.

At home, our struggles and tensions centered on how to maintain a connection to a homeland ten thousand miles away. In college, my struggles revolved around my growing political awareness of sexism and racism and my recognition of my own sexual orientation. Because I had no Indian community outside of family and felt little political kinship with other Indian students beyond ethnicity, the place where I discovered and defined my identity was inside grassroots political organizations. It was political work on issues like apartheid; poverty in Poughkeepsie, New York (where my college was located); and rape and violence against women, that taught me lifelong lessons about race and gender.

After I came out as a lesbian, my worlds became even further splintered—I had a queer life, a mainstream American life, and an identity within my Indian family and community. I came out to my parents early because the activist path I had chosen left me very little space to hide. When I began the process of coming out, I was unaware how long-term it would be. Over time, my family and I have moved apart, come closer, and finally arrived at what I would characterize as acceptance. But for many years, being openly gay led me away from Indian family and community because I felt there was no way I could be out and present in both those places.

I had developed a racial and gender identity through feminist and multiracial political work. But while I could apply feminist analysis to question what it meant to be an Indian woman, with all the sexist nonsense I was expected to maintain, race was another matter. Part of the problem for Indians—and especially for a light-skinned one like me—lies with our own (racist) difficulty in identifying as people of color. This is not the experience of Indians in the United Kingdom or Canada, who have a strongly developed sense of racial and cultural difference. Many Indians in the United States use class and skin color privilege to pretend that we are Caucasian. Curiously, as Ronald Takaki notes, one of the first legal issues presented by Indians to the American legal system was the question of what race we were.

In my own history, I identified first as a woman of color, then as Black, and much later as an Indian or South Asian. In part, I believe this happened because at the time I came of age, few politically active and progressive Indians were writing about race, much less acknowledging that there were queer people of color—the notable exception has long been South Asian feminist activists and writers in the subcontinent and in the diaspora. Thus, my newly emerging sense of racial identity did not bring me "home" to other Indians, but rather brought me into a wider, multiracial political circle. As an activist working in largely white women's and gay organizations, my support came from other people of color and from progressive, multi-issue activists—of all colors and often Black.

But my tardy identification also derived from the absurd nature of the term *South Asian*—what, after all, did being a South Asian mean? The Indian subcontinent did not shape my identity; my family of origin and Indian roots did. So, it was not until the emergence in the 1990s of an out, loud, and proud South Asian queer movement, with the formation of groups like Trikone; the publication of the anthology, *A Lotus of Another Color*; and the launching, by queer South Asians in Toronto, of Desh Pardesh that I went through a third identity shift. Until the 1990s, I had never had an ongoing personal connection to a network of other political, gay and lesbian South Asians; never had a group of friends and colleagues with whom to discuss the experience of our multiple identities and the different worlds we negotiate. Through this contact, I realized the depth of my estrangement from my Indian self. And I consciously adopted the hyphenated identity as an effort to rebuild a connection back to my roots. I began to name myself *Indian American*, to acknowledge the simultaneity of cultural assimilation and cultural difference that warred inside me, to begin to face how I was not assimilated and why I was. I began to make peace with some of the traditions I had run from.

Over the nearly two decades that I have been out in my family and in the world, I have been able to integrate many aspects of my family of origin with my queer family. My parents have always been honest and loving, but we have disagreed mightily over my choices of work, of being an out and open lesbian, of the feminist politics I hold. As a lesbian in a committed relationship with my partner of eleven years, I still encounter their homophobia and discomfort with my personal life. They are not comfortable integrating me as a lesbian in the way that they integrate and treat my sisters and their straight partners. After all this, I would still say that my parents do not accept who I am or that they feel comfortable with my role in the world as a gay activist. As a consequence, I have had to stand far outside the parameters of the Asian family and, I admit, that makes it easier for me to question and challenge some of the basic assumptions and exclusiveness of those structures.

I have also encountered the serious limitations of this hyphenated existence: neither *Indian American* nor *South Asian Lesbian* nor *Indian Lesbian Feminist* quite captures the blend I feel I am. A hyphen cannot embody synthesis—a synthesis of identities that some may term *assimilation*, but which is also quite radical and transformational as well. What lies beyond merely adding another hyphen to the multiple identities we each carry? What is our investment in the maintenance of racial and gender categories? I have learned so much in the process of developing a racial and sexual identity. Does rejecting identity as a basis for organizing mean that I would have to abandon this self-awareness? Would I somehow lose myself to gain the world?

Inside, I am a hybrid of several cultures and multiple identities—Indian, immigrant, queer, feminist, progressive, Asian, American. Outside, I face the challenge of articulating this hybridity as a politics that could make a cohesive movement for racial justice, economic democracy, the abolition of gender roles, and the liberation of human sexuality and family. We need to create this new common social change movement which allows us both the mooring and the freedom to work on the racial, gender, immigrant, economic, queer, and other human issues we face. My search for a new synthesis of identity with politics is rooted in the faith that we can find or will found this common social change movement.

The Limits of Ethnic-Identity-Based Organizing

The idea of an APA political movement is rooted in the model of ethnic-based organizing that has characterized the civil rights struggle in the United States. Ethnic- or race-based organizing has been an effective strategy in American politics to assert political power, to secure public policy solutions that meet the needs of the particular constituencies that are organizing, and, perhaps most importantly, to develop a stronger sense of self and self-worth in a context that whitens all difference. For these reasons, organizing as APAs is politically important to our immigrant communities.

We live in a moment in which racism, disguised as "race-neutral" policies, is dominant. The goal of this resurgent racial bias is to reimpose white supremacy in the workplace, in the awarding of government contracts, and in the allocation of public resources. Conservatives want you and me to believe that by erasing race, by getting rid of affirmative action, people of color will be "freer"—but this claim obscures the truth about institutionalized and embedded racial prejudice and how linked racism is to class. Few of us are "free" to move up the ladder of success, business, and educational hierarchy on our merits alone—opportunity and freedom are conditioned by economic privilege. Few are "free" to go to college without financial assistance; few of us are "free" to break out of the class lines assigned us by our race and our class of birth.

We live in a moment in which conservatives wage a sophisticated attack on Black majority voting districts through redistricting laws and complain about voting fraud when they lose. We live in a moment of incredible immigrant bashing—where punitive measures are passed to punish both legal and undocumented immigrants, by the same economic and political system that benefits enormously from the labor of these workers. We live in a moment when the attack on single, poor women of color is disguised as "welfare reform"— reform that will hurt millions of women and children most. This is a moment in which working parents suffer needlessly because the nation cannot find the willpower to fund affordable daycare or can't find the dollars to provide free, high-quality education through college.

We live in a moment in which the white Right cleverly plays to machismo and patriarchal attitudes among communities of color, in which traditional masculinity is invoked, and Ralph Reed and other white right-wingers (like the Promise Keepers) talk about racial reconciliation, while at the same time endorsing racist criminal justice policies which incarcerate huge numbers of Black men and poor men of color; 13 percent of all Black men are disenfranchised. Out of the other side of their mouths they demonize and criminalize youth of color—through calls for curfews, bans of youth from malls and certain communities, bans on the free expression and lyrics and culture that youth are creating. We live in a time in which class divisions splinter people of color from each other—operating as a vicious circle, in which Asians distrust Blacks, who distrust Latinos, who distrust Asians. These are big challenges for us as people of color and an APA movement focused on them can provide us a space to discuss and learn and strategize how we will respond.

Within this broader context of racial prejudice, many grave issues confront the Asian American communities in this country: one only has to read the newspapers to identify them. Immigrants are being demonized and attacked widely: the cuts in services to legal immigrants as well as the targeting of undocumented immigrants seriously affect our communities. Thousands of people have lost access to Social Security benefits, health care, education, and basic human survival needs—while funds for immigrant-specific social services are inadequate. Hundreds of refugees and immigrants are incarcerated when they come here and are deported with no right to appeal. Immigrants and undocumented workers are exploited inside US sweatshops run by members of our own communities or exploited as domestic workers by other Asians, as well as non-Asians. Global multinationals that have set up operations in Asian countries bank their prosperity on the exploitation of labor in those countries.

Violence toward Asian communities is very high: there was more than a 100 percent increase in reports of violence in New Jersey between 1996 and 1997, and over 481 incidents were documented by the National Asian Pacific American Legal Consortium.

There is huge generational conflict and tension within our communities and families between first-generation and fourth-generation immigrants. The pressure of your parents' generation on your shoulders is a pressure I feel and know intimately. How are young Asian people handling this pressure? What resources and places do we have to talk about these issues and to support each other in dealing with our families? In both these contexts, it makes logical sense to organize as a racial or ethnically linked movement and around racism. There is much urgent work we need to do and to be part of in a broader racial justice movement. And yet, I am skeptical of this strategy as a panacea or even the best model for APA organizing.

For one, I believe that economics as much as race conditions the experience of racism of APAS in America. Our APA movement thus far has had little to say about economic justice. Second, the irony of the framework of APA is that *American* defines and unites us far more than *Asian* or *Pacific*. And third, the model of race-based or ethnic-based or even identity-based organizing is very valuable in terms of definition, individual empowerment, and community organizing. But it is of limited value as a transformational device.

My parents came to America for economic opportunity, like many Asian and South Asian and Pacific people, who arrived either by choice or as laborers brought in to build American railways and infrastructure at the turn of the century. Asians in this country have by and large completely bought into capitalism. This is despite the fact that capitalism is now strip-mining the economies of many of our countries of origin. It has not provided relief to the millions in the world who are poor and living at subsistence levels, and it has created enormous disparities in freedom, opportunity, and power between the rich, middle class, working class, and poor.

We are model minorities in our acquiescence to the system. So, in this country, the same immigrants who are suffering from the racist immigration policies of the Republican Right staunchly oppose health care reform or a social safety net. Indians in the United States—at least of my parents' generation—are quite conservative and more often than not Republican (although being Democrat these days offers little solace to those of us who are progressive).

Many people I know believe that if you work hard, you can get ahead; that people who are poor and on welfare are shiftless; and that economic security and property are the ultimate goals of life (all framed in the guise of providing for your family, but at its core no different from the insatiable greed that motivates all capitalists). Ironically, the condition of Asian and Pacific people in America is more linked to economic forces and the ups and downs of capitalism than it is to racism. American labor is already resentful of immigrant labor. The boom in high-tech jobs that has created great opportunities for Asian engineers and computer programmers hinges on the success of speculative and volatile markets that have inflated the value of internet and computer stocks, creating a wealth that cannot last and will benefit only a very few. I do not see a progressive APA movement dealing with these and other economic contradictions and tensions.

A second reason I am skeptical of the term *Asian Pacific American* is that it means so little. We are more tied together by our shared experiences or marginalization in white America than we are by our Asian Americanness, or our links nationally, historically, linguistically, or culturally. Most of us do not know a thing about each other's countries of origin or histories. For second- and third-generation Asians in America, it's enough of a challenge to learn about our own ethnic and cultural heritage. To forge a sense of common solidarity with each other has thus been difficult. I do not believe that the large numbers of Indians in America feel a sense of kinship with Japanese-, Chinese-, or Filipino-Americans. Instead, they feel kinship along the tradition-bound lines we have always followed: family, caste, state or origin, language—the conventional links. Given this truth, are we in fact trying to force on to our wildly diverse immigrant cultures a commonality that will never be shared? Is the commonality more about expediency in American politics—the need to be counted, to be able to marshal votes, etc.—than it is about reality? Will we ever be able to deliver a voting bloc as Asians given our radical diversity?

This brings me to a final point for us to consider as we think about the APA identity formulation: Does identity politics work? The answer is, it depends on your goal in using it. For what does it work and for what does it fail? I think it works to create self-esteem, empowerment, and visibility in the American political system, community building, and organizing. But it fails as a vehicle to revamp the social service system in this country. Ideology-based movements are more valuable than identity-based ones.

A massive context of discrimination and institutionalized racism, homophobia, and sexism explains why we have single-issue movements dedicated to the eradication of these forms of prejudice. It also illuminates the dilemma that confronts each civil rights movement. They all reach the point of partial fulfillment, where the system accommodates somewhat to admit us; but the underlying prejudice and structural barriers to full equality remain in place. That is the truth we face now in the LGBT movement: what I've called our "virtual equality," or the creation of zones of freedom inside a fundamentally intransigent social system of family, marriage, state, and economy. In terms of public policy, we end up working piecemeal on small solutions that benefit particular communities in the short run, rather than working in a more concerted way to make systemic change that could benefit all of us in the long run.

We find ourselves at a crossroads as a gay and lesbian movement. Down one road lies the direction we have been pursuing—of working solely or exclusively within the lesbian, gay, bi, transgender context, on so-called "gay rights" issues. Down the other road lies the project not just of trying to fit in, but of trying to change the world and institutions we encounter.

If we walk down this second road, we quickly realize that our fight to end discrimination on the basis of sexual orientation intersects with women's efforts to overturn our second-class status, with the struggle for racial justice and equality, and with the quest for a fairer economy and a cleaner environment. What we attempt in walking down the second road is the project of building a kind of political and social change movement beyond the civil rights movements we have built thus far. We must build a movement that is all about economic change and through that we will create massive social change.

Let me stress, neither choice—single-issue politics nor multi-issue politics—is right or wrong: they are, however, quite different. Let me also stress that I am not arguing that we must abandon all the single-issue or identity-based work we are doing—just that we have got to supplement it with new organizing that we are not doing. I want a movement that is not just focused on identity but that is engaged in defining what the kind of society we want as we move into the twenty-first century will look like.

Is this possible? I don't know. Is this necessary? Yes. Why? It is necessary to create this common movement because we face a totalizing right-wing opposition that is not capable of being defeated by anything but a systematic counter mobilization.

Right-wing ideas about public policy and the ordering of cultural life are not merely cyclical swings in the historic pendulum of policy ideas. They represent a serious effort to restore the very values and hierarchies that social justice movements have struggled to transform, and to construct something that has not before existed in America—a theocratic state. In place of gender equality, the Right advocates male supremacy. In place of remedies aimed at addressing centuries of racial discrimination against African Americans, the Right proposes policies that ignore the impact race plays on economic opportunity. In place of a social welfare role for the state, the Right proposes either the elimination or privatization of all government service programs. These ideas are antithetical to the policies and values of social justice movements.

Because of the way we are structured—issue by issue, or identity by identity —social justice movements cannot boast the kind of ideological or political unity that is found on the conservative Right. Because we have invested less time and skill in organizing, social justice movements seem to have less clout to deliver on our goals. We can and we must rebuild a constituency for social justice. We can and we must make a new structure out of the way we now operate to succeed nationally and locally. We can and we must have the courage of our values to take the risk of joint action and new cooperation. We can and we must take the leap of faith in order to build the trust that common purpose requires.

Queering APA Organizing

Your conference is to be commended for acknowledging that heterosexuality is not the only sexuality in Asian and Pacific communities. This is a truth denied in most Asian contexts. All too often, one still hears the canard that homosexuality is a Western thing or a corruption of truly Asian values. The histories of Asian sexualities in each of our countries of origin remain to be discovered and uncovered by scholars of your generation in the years ahead. The truth is that, of course, there is a rich tradition of same-sex love and experience in every culture and continent of the world. Whether it understands itself as *gay* or *lesbian* or *transgender* or *bisexual* is debatable, but the existence of same-sex behavior and same-sex love the world over ought not to be obscure to anyone.

Queers in America face tremendous barriers to fully living our lives: discrimination, violence, and prejudice are pervasive and are the norm. So, yes, a progressive movement of Asians and Pacific people in America ought to take up the challenge of being allies to the LGBT movement, and ending prejudice based on sexual orientation is a progressive stand that the APA movement should take. We all benefit from strong civil rights laws, from the idea of a nation that is inclusive of many kinds of people. And, as you see embodied in me, queer Asians like me need the alliance of mainstream APA groups speaking out on sexual orientation issues.

But more fundamentally, there is another challenge that I think queerness poses to Asian communities and it is similar to the challenge that feminism poses—and it is a challenge I am not so sure our people, even progressives, are willing to take up. The challenge is to the notions of family that we are raised with and to their unyielding patriarchal, heterosexist, and authoritarian terms.

What does it mean that we are all raised in families where compulsory marriage and compulsory heterosexuality is the unquestioned norm? Or that to stand against that is to be ostracized by family and community and, in some instances, to be killed by one's own father or brother for disobedience and violating the family honor? Why do we tolerate and accept the blatant double standard in Asian families for girls and boys? Why do young Asians in America feel they must go along with this and that they have no recourse short of radical rebellion and acting out? What does it mean that there is no youth movement that is explicitly about the liberation of young people from this oppressive and destructive form of patriarchal family? We need to create ways to organize around the so-called "private family issues"—to publicize what has been privatized.

What does it mean that we have not created a movement that dethrones the patriarchs of our families—our fathers, no matter how beloved, and our mothers who made their bargain with a system that they are now hell-bent on enforcing on their daughters and sons? How can a gay or lesbian person ever be "accepted" in this heterosexual conception of family? No wonder the idea of sexual agency that feminism brings up is so threatening.

Questions like these may be heresy to bring up in a gathering like this. I risk incurring the wrath of those who will twist what I am questioning and take it as disrespect instead of frank interrogation and disagreement. But this to me is the undone work of internalizing the meaning of movements for women's liberation and sexual freedom into the APA movement. There can be no more than token integration of these issues unless we are willing to examine the gender biases of the families and communities we come from.

Here is what I believe we need to work on.

1 Increase the level of political participation and awareness in our communities. We could be an electoral bloc to be reckoned with on issues like race, immigration policies, education policy, and so on.

2 Develop ways to have cross-generational dialogue that is outside the structure of Asian families.

3 Continue to build support systems for each other.

4 See our work as tied with the freedom of other people of color.

5 Envision and articulate through our organizations the kind of progressive social policy agenda we believe in, the kinds of vision for social justice we want. Envisioning is the first step to seeing ourselves as part of a larger social justice movement—to moving into politics, beyond identities.

Gandhi wrote that morality consists of doing what we ought to do. He argued that mere observance of custom was not morality. Instead, moral actions are those guided by justice and respect for the divine will. They involve no coercion and are not motivated by self-interest. If I help my neighbor because he is suffering, I commit a moral act. If I help my neighbor because I want credit for helping him through his suffering, my action may still be a good deed but, in Gandhi's argument, is not moral. Merely by pursuing our own liberation and freedom we are not engaged in a moral course. If we place our liberation movement in the service of building a more just society, then we will be a movement that is unstoppable because our course will be spiritually and politically just.

7

RACE, POWER, SEX, CITIZENSHIP, AND THE LGBT MOVEMENT

These invited remarks were given at the keynote panel of the Conference on Race, Sex, Power: New Movements in Black and Latino/a Sexualities, April 11, 2008, University of Illinois, Chicago.

The times in which we live attest to the continued salience of what the Marxist-Leninist study group that one of my friends once belonged to called "the primary contradictions." From my perspective, the hierarchies of dominance and submission that those primary contradictions—of class, race, sex, gender, and sexuality—represent continue to operate in the same ways as they ever did. Inequality has not been eliminated; it has only been born again in new forms in the new economy, in the various global governance regimes, and even within the social movements to which many of us belong.

My perspective on racial and social justice comes from a queer place. I am one of the dinosaurs—the much derided "1970s radical lesbian feminist." The one who still applies concepts like patriarchy to explain the glass ceiling to women's power; the one who values participatory forms of decision making over business school models; the one who still maintains that women's liberation will also mean a transformation of men's lives away from deadening, competitive, and violence-based forms of masculinity.

Call me naive, color me "old school," critique aspects of my politics as essentialist—I will admit to all these flaws. What I will not concede is the claim that we are living in a post-gender, post-racial, post-gay world where somehow the old primary contradictions no longer operate, where racism, misogyny, and homophobia are somehow less relevant. I do not believe that we are in an era of Politics 2.0, where the age-old battle lines between right wing and left wing have been replaced by a third way. I do not believe that the bitter power struggle progressive movements have been waging with authoritarian movements can be wished away by speeches seeking a new national consensus or by centrist policy accommodations.

What I do believe is that power yields nothing without a demand and without some kind of countervailing power to win that demand. I believe that organizing to redistribute power and access more democratically is how we will bring about change. I believe that sex is as central to human beings as food, and as potent a motivator in our lives. And I believe that the biggest job of intellectuals—be they in activist or in academic realms—is to disturb power and challenge tradition.

As many of you have noted, racism today is perpetuated by the interaction of race and class, more than by any other factor. Class interacts with race to create disparities or exclusion. But, like the Lord, class too works in mysterious ways. Class not only causes and exacerbates structural racism; it also makes it less visible while not really dislodging its operation. This fact is clear especially if we look at the role the "talented tenth" plays in relation to the larger power structure, and within each community of color.

The current form of racism requires that in order to succeed, people of color must erase—or at least mute—their racial identity in favor of a class-based solidarity with the upper middle class and the rich. The erasure of racial identity is the price of admission to the inner circles of power. You have to talk differently (no accent), walk differently (no swagger if you are a man), act differently (don't make white people at the table uncomfortable), and even start to think differently about what you see as the solutions to the continued subjugation of large numbers of your own people. If you do all this, you succeed. That is why people like Colin Powell and Condoleezza Rice have made it. That is why a Black presidential candidate from Harvard does better than would a Black presidential candidate from South Carolina. That is why immigration policies favor the specialized skills of "exceptionally talented people" (or whatever the H-1B visa language currently states) over the day laborers who pick the apples from the orchards. That is why Asians are held up as model minorities and why we must challenge the way we are used in America's racial dynamics—challenge what Vijay Prashad has called the *Karma of Brown Folk*, in his wonderful book of that title.

In our time, the emergence of rich people of color is taken to mean that race is no longer a barrier. Green is said to trump Black and brown. We are told that racism is a relic from another era—deep racial disparities in education, health care access and delivery, criminalization, housing, and wealth notwithstanding. We dismiss Jeremiah Wright as just a 1960s radical speaking an outdated politics. We are told that structural racism and white supremacy are irrelevant in the virtual world where having a "second life" online is more real than the real life off-line.

The work that many of you have done exposes the falsity of these arguments, but I would like to offer one reason I think they are made.

From the upper-middle-class white person's perspective, the race question remains, "What can brown do for me?" People of color's success (in business, in nonprofits, in politics, or in the academy) is still linked to how comfortable they make white people feel about their own racial identity. (The 2006 film adaptation of Jhumpa Lahiri's novel, *The Namesake*, illustrated this vividly when it showed how a young Indian boy—Gogol—assimilated and was accepted into the Upper East Side family in New York as long as he kept his background at an appropriate level of exotica but not when it disturbed his girlfriend's white upper-middle-class comfort zone.) This is a key dilemma for successful people of color.

This is why I think Barack Obama's presidential campaign has been championed by people whose politics have been arguably racist or at best racially ignorant in the past. How else do you explain that some of the most conservative people around—those who have opposed any focus on racial diversity, affirmative action remedies, or other race-specific remedies—supported Obama?

What do we make of this? I suppose their support could be proof of their claim that the world is merit-based and does not see race when it comes to talent and skill. But I would submit that it is equally arguable that for many white people—liberals and conservatives alike—President Obama's success assuages white guilt and is seen as being about their own and America's redemption from its long historical legacy of racism.

Middle America seems to be saying, "See, it's over, we can see the talented man, the inspiring leader, the generational paradigm shifter, the new visionary who can unite this country again; we don't just see a Black man." But to me, these voices want to move beyond race without having solved the barriers and obstacles that hundreds of years of racism have created. It's easy to proclaim a post-racial world and much harder to change the structures that still reproduce racial inequality.

Do people of color also want to move beyond race, or are we too busy being stuck inside it to get out? To my mind, going post-racial requires a self-immolation that kills people of color (and I would argue that a comparable self-immolation occurs in all other "post" framings—post-gay, post-feminist, etc.). Naming and challenging racism disturbs America and for that reason alone it has *not* become an effective strategy for getting the mainstream to address structural racism. But the post-racial paradigm appeases the powerful without yielding much in exchange other than their comfort. Poor people of all colors are often more honest about race—there is not a lot of denial possible when you feel you are in a struggle for survival and that you are threatened economically by somebody else.

Middle-class and upper-middle-class people of color have to speak to the racism we encounter, find new ways to connect to both poor and rich white people, and new ways to live with the racist dynamics in our neighborhoods, social lives, classrooms, boardrooms, churches, and indeed in every institution in our society. President Obama's genius was to try to find this new language, to reframe this dynamic and not allow erasure. But for most of us, our own confrontation with race and power is rarely done with that kind of eloquence or clarity.

How to challenge the department committee from passing over the woman of color candidate's credentials while allowing those of someone else who is less qualified? How to question the lack of authority accorded to women? How to confront the dynamic of comfort and discomfort around race within our social circles? How to hail that goddamn cab in New York? How *not* to have my nephew shave their beard so they will not be stopped and detained at the airport because they look like a young Arab man?

As a starting point, we need to look much more critically at how green has colonized brown and Black and white, at how it has made us its vassals. Green does indeed trump Black or brown. But not in the way that conservatives promise. You are still colored and subject to those codes of inferiority, violence, and exclusion even if you are the most respectable, rich, and brilliant person in the world.

And what is the current form of sexism? The vileness of the current landscape for women—the extreme hostility and subjugation that especially straight women encounter—is vividly evident to anyone interested enough to think about women's status. When women's power is still primarily channeled through men, when they are still seen primarily as "holes" or "cunts" who are there to please men rather than as agents of their own sexual pleasure, when women's genitalia are still mutilated in the name of tradition, when they are raped and abused in massive numbers in every culture and country, and there is no penalty that men as a class bear for that violation—we have not at all achieved women's liberation or men's transformation.

The Hillary Clinton presidential campaign makes visible many sad facts, chief among them that there is no longer a movement in the United States that is mobilized to defend and represent women. Hillary's image reveals the dilemma of strong women everywhere: How do you lead without being picked apart for everything and anything you do? If you say something strongly, you are too strident; if you fight back, you are defensive; if you cry, you are weak and playing the gender card; if you stand without a man, you are a man-hater; if you stand by your man even when he does you wrong, you are hated by women who wish they had the courage to leave their own men and hate you because you didn't—and hate themselves because they haven't. Your hair, clothes, weight, age, smile, gestures, and even your big laugh, are criticized.

The obstacles to women's progress remain—whatever the level of organizing in the women's movements around the world. The obstacles stem first from the resistance of traditional cultural institutions to change: religion, media, family structures, and governments have been less than friendly to women's liberation. And second, they stem from the resistance of women themselves to change—to changing the way they raise their children, to the way they engage with their men, and to the way they feel about themselves and each other. There is little more to female solidarity today than there was in the 1950s.

An even sadder truth is that the women around the world are at a stalemate over how to transform male privilege and power: we have not been able to dislodge it except in the tiniest of ways. Indeed, male power and prerogative are being advocated and asserted more vigorously than ever in many parts of the world (from the Promise Keepers in the United States to Islamic fundamentalists to Hindu fundamentalists to Orthodox Jews). We need courageous avenues for resistance.

I think we need a movement willing to challenge the morality of tradition as the primary guiding force in our lives. And we need a movement of women and men willing to stop making endless excuses for men's behavior. In my view, the hatred of women that is expressed in violence, in misogynist disregard for women, in the reassertion of tradition in the face of women's liberation—is rooted in fundamental problems in the parenting and nurturing of boys and men by their fathers and in the social channeling and control of men to be soldiers for the state.

We need a movement of people that prioritizes issues of gender—of women's roles and men's roles, of what is acceptable and what is not in what we say and how we behave toward each other. It needs to question the oppressive foundations of machismo *and* female victimhood; it needs to address economic and structural barriers to the equality of women.

I have always been grateful that I got to be a lesbian. *Lesbian* is a status that sits outside the traditional traps of male-female dynamics. I do not have to see men with anything but empathy and equanimity—because they have no power over my happiness. I get to actually like and admire women and men for who they are and not for their gender. This makes it easier to live in a sexist world.

But being a lesbian feminist of color inside the gay, lesbian, bisexual, and transgender movement for the past thirty years has been an interesting challenge. Somebody asked me if I thought things around race, sex, and class had changed a lot in the LGBT movement in the time I had been involved. I had to answer *yes* and *no*. Yes, there are more of us today than before, more queers of color, more straight friends and comrades working alongside us from every kind of background, and more support for and awareness of intersectional politics. But there is still very little of what we might call intersectional practice. The institutional LGBT movement is still overwhelmingly white and male in its leadership. The boards of our institutions and how they prioritize what they see as the community still reflect the biases people like me and my predecessors Barbara Smith and other leaders of color were critiquing in the 1980s.

The dynamics of green affect the lavender bubble too. Philanthropy American style is a byproduct of inequality. It is about love of our fellow man—literally. And such a tiny amount goes to support LGBTQ causes that it's remarkable that we have the thriving movement all over the world that we do. But inside the movement the same mechanisms I described in racial landscapes operate. I've always felt that my success as a woman of color in the world of gayness was a function of my ability to pass among many classes—a product of my own migration with my family of origin from lower middle class to middle class to upper middle class to ruling class.

Money in America brings with it the power to set agendas. Why are certain issues on the top of the list for the LGBT movement and others are not—why marriage as opposed to HIV/AIDS among Black gay men? Why domestic partnership instead of universal health care? Why second parent adoption instead of parental rights for poor women whose reproductive lives are criminalized if they do not conform to the state's orders of how they should conduct their pregnancies?

Who decides the agenda of a LGBT movement? In truth, it is decided quite undemocratically. It is determined by the urgency of crisis and the ordinary bravery of someone resisting prejudice. We have had our agenda set at times by individuals petitioning the courts for redress for bias—the marriage case in Hawaii in 1992 put that issue on the map. But would that issue have become the media force it did if it had not also been picked up and amplified by the voices of a handful of conservative gay writers, or if it had not been seized upon by the anti-gay right wing as a wonderful tool for them to exploit as a wedge?

The question of what gets put on a movement's agenda is a combination of political opportunity and opportunism, a mix of intention coming from a coherent, thought-out strategy and happenstance coming from the biases of the people in the movement who have influence over its agenda. Race, class, power, and sex all play a role in what gets put on a movement's agenda and what gets left out.

Two final points on the LGBT movement. There is a vast difference between the goal of sexual freedom and the goal of sexual citizenship. Perhaps it should not be one or the other, but a quick recap of queer history would suggest that the latter has replaced the former almost entirely, with interesting consequences. Where gay liberation sought to transform the nuclear family and invent new forms to protect a wider circle of kinship relationships, gay rights seeks access to the traditional forms of family for LGBT people. Where gay liberation argued that straight society would be transformed for the better by openly accepting and welcoming queerness, gay rights contends that our integration will change very little. I have argued that both are true and that citizenship is a precondition to freedom.

But what is citizenship anyway? As Shane Phelan writes in *Sexual Strangers: Gays, Lesbians, and the Dilemmas of Citizenship*, "The question of citizenship does not concern only what rights, offices, and duties are to accrue to citizens but also how the polity decides who is eligible for them; that is, it concerns the structures of acknowledgment that define the class of persons eligible for those rights, office and duties."

The mainstream struggle for LGBT rights in the United States is squarely at the place of acknowledgment—that is the basic rights agenda, still unfulfilled, that is the agenda of every LGBT organization you can imagine. But the deeper struggle for LGBT liberation is focused on full moral and cultural acceptance around the world. It seeks the fundamental redefinition of what is good and what is evil when it asserts that gayness is a moral good, that sexuality is good, and that sexual freedom—defined as the cultural transformation and opening up of ideas of sex and gender—must also be an integral outcome of our struggle for full human rights.

8

WHAT CAN BROWN DO FOR YOU?
RACE, SEXUALITY, AND THE FUTURE
OF LGBTQ POLITICS

This is a condensed, edited version of a talk that was given as the 2010 Kessler Lecture at the Center for Lesbian and Gay Studies, CUNY Graduate Center, on November 18, 2010, published in Irresistible Revolution: Confronting Race, Class and the Assumptions of LGBT Politics *and in* Queer Then and Now: The David Kessler Lectures 2002–2020. *A section from a previous, unpublished version has been included.*

As the 2010 US midterm elections came and went, I found myself thinking of the memorable opening paragraph from Charles Dickens's *A Tale of Two Cities*:

> It was the best of times, it was the worst of times, it was the age of wisdom, it was the age of foolishness, it was the epoch of belief, it was the epoch of incredulity, it was the season of Light, it was the season of Darkness, it was the spring of hope, it was the winter of despair, we had everything before us, we had nothing before us, we were all going direct to Heaven, we were all going direct the other way.

This passage describes the perplexing dualism of the present moment—an age of remarkable technological change and human possibility, in which more wealth exists than ever before yet objectives like ending hunger and poverty seem unreachable. We live in an "epoch of belief"—millions upon millions of people fervently embrace their faith traditions, filled with absolute certainty that they are on the righteous path. At the same time, we live in an "epoch of incredulity," in which millions of others are so disillusioned and alienated by corruption or fear that they are apathetic.

It seemed we had everything before us in 2008 when President Obama won. I remember feeling that way in 1992 with Bill Clinton as well, or even in 1968, only to watch that hope turn sour in 2010, as it did in 1994, or in 1968 when Bobby Kennedy was killed. The merry-go-round of political promises keeps us bobbing up and down with excitement at each revolution, but our enjoyment and engagement in the process leaves us sad at the end of the ride, awake to the fact that we have only gone around in a circle.

A similar dualism—of growth and inertia, progress and stagnation, optimism and frustration—exists today in the LGBT movement. The scale and size of the mainstream movement remains significant. According to the Movement Advancement Project (MAP), a national think tank on the LGBT movement, there were, as of 2010, over five hundred LGBT organizations focused on issues in eight broad categories: community centers, arts and culture, social/recreational, service provision, research, advocacy, issue-based, and legal organizations. These organizations had combined expenses of $500 million, with half of the expenditures going to advocacy, legal or other issues, and research. Moreover, the thirty-nine largest LGBT organizations annually surveyed by MAP employed nearly nine hundred paid staff and had over seven hundred board members. The mainstream movement is a large infrastructure indeed.

Yet, the LGBT political agenda at the national level, especially before the US Congress, is stalled. The largest LGBT advocacy organization, the Human Rights Campaign (HRC), managed to secure full passage and implementation of only one LGBT rights bill in Congress over the past twenty years: the Shepard/Byrd Hate Crime Act, passed in October of 2009. The second largest political organization, the National Gay and Lesbian Task Force (NGLTF), seems great at managing coalitions, producing trainings and conferences, conducting research, and policy analysis, but unable to move those into muscular leadership for results. The mainstream gay rights legal movement, which still has the most successful strategies in the LGBT movement, remains an island unto itself—making its own decisions in small conclaves, rarely consulting in a meaningful way with grassroots activists, limiting participation in key strategic meetings to those who agree with the strategies underway, and rarely coordinating its efforts with political advocates so that a powerful media, educational, and organizing push could be made alongside each major new direction in litigation.

The anti-gay military policy was repealed but barriers to transgender participation in the armed forces remain in place, and the military's epidemic levels of violence and sexual harassment of women (and also of significant numbers of men) remain unchallenged by the LGBT mainstream movement. The Employment Non-Discrimination Act is not moving, leading some to assert that it will advance if gender identity is removed. It will not, in my view, because that obstacle is simply a pretext for a deeper lack of political support in Congress for LGBT equality. Immigration equality is also stalled and, with the election of an anti-immigrant Tea Party minority, the chances for comprehensive immigration reform are minimal. The appointments of talented, openly LGBT leaders to key positions in a friendly administration continue to be stymied by hostile and vigorous opposition.

The gains made during the Obama years have come about for the same reasons as they did during the much more hostile Reagan, Bush I, and Bush II years: through the efforts of a small group of people lobbying behind the scenes within the executive branch of government, making quiet and significant changes in agency-led actions and regulations at places like the US State Department, the Department of Health and Human Services, and the Department of Labor.

Even this is not a complete picture. Because of the inability of the existing larger infrastructures to represent the diverse constituencies and issues that LGBT people face, the movement has spawned a number of even more specialized, single issue–focused organizations at the national level over the past ten years, each addressing a particular subject or constituency (freedom to marry, health, immigration, military, transgender, family policy, youth, community centers), and even two Republican organizations—because the first was deemed too liberal by the second.

Indeed, it could be argued that there are at least two movements fighting for LGBT equality and freedom today: one explicitly anti-racist and the other doggedly single-issue. One that is progressive and one that is center-right. One that consists of locally based grassroots advocacy, organizing, and service-oriented groups (Queers for Economic Justice, the Audre Lorde Project, the Sylvia Rivera Law Project, FIERCE, Southerners on New Ground, the Community Center movement, the HIV/AIDS organizations, the youth groups, and key public community foundations like Astraea) supported at the national level by the NGLTF; and the other, which consists of larger, more national organizations (HRC, ACLU, Lambda Legal, Gay and Lesbian Alliance Against Defamation, National Center for Lesbian Rights, the Gay and Lesbian

Victory Fund), supported by mainstream corporate and private philanthropic institutions. These movements share a common history and they often share institutional origins. They overlap, they coexist, they cooperate, and they compete. But they are not coterminous: their end points differ dramatically. And their power to determine the course of queer politics varies as well.

It is my contention, however, that neither the grassroots (race-inclusive) nor mainstream (liberal) parts of the LGBT movements have yet meaningfully tackled structural racism and racial privilege. Neither has made more than a superficial dent in the way racial separation exists in our communities. Neither has convinced the majority of LGBT people who are active in the movement that race is and must be our issue.

Indeed, advocates of racial justice in the LGBT movement still find ourselves having to make the case again and again, year after year, about why race matters to the achievement of LGBT equality. The LGBT movement should work on racial justice, I've argued repeatedly: because it is a matter of justice and we are about a fairer society; because we need to reciprocate—so when we ask communities of color to support us around sexuality, we need to show up on issues of race; because there are LGBT people of color in our communities and racism affects us, so our movement must deal with it; because dealing with race is in the mainstream gay community's self-interest, and brown will help us win at the ballot box.

Not only am I tired of having to make this speech; it saddens me that, while most of the audiences to whom I have spoken have no problem hearing the argument framed in those terms, they resist implementing the idea that the LGBT movement must make racial justice a core commitment. The existence of LGBT people of color is simply not deemed important enough to warrant what many white gay and lesbian people see as a diversion from the LGBT agenda to address race. As a result, race in our movement is seen largely as something that affects a subset of LGBT people. When race is addressed at all, it is done primarily under the rubric of diversity or outreach, occasionally as a matter of equity, but rarely as a substantive matter, integral to the goals of LGBT rights and central to its success or failure.

The key structural reason why neither branch of the LGBTQ movement has operationalized its stated intersectional politics is quite simple: the default definition for what gay means has been set by, and remains dominated by, the ideas and experiences of those in our communities who are white, and this has not really changed in more than fifty years. Issues, identities, problems that are not "purely" gay—read as: affecting white gay men and women—are always defined as not the concern of "our" LGBT movement. They are dismissed as "non-gay" issues, as divisive, as the issues that some other movement is more suited to champion. We have our hands full, we are told. We need to single-mindedly focus on one thing.

This is an argument that both LGBT liberationists and gay equality–focused activists have made and bought wholesale for decades—without malice, without prejudice—just because there has been an unquestioned assumption that this narrow focus works, that we are getting results because we are making a "gay rights" argument, that this is smart and successful political strategy.

Limits of Single-Issue Politics

This narrow focus, I would argue, is causing us to stall in our progress toward formal equality and to abandon or ignore large parts of our own communities, making us a weaker movement. The gay-rights focus may have been needed at one point in our history, but it is a vestigial burden we need to shed. It narrows our imagination and vision; it does not serve large numbers of our own people; and it feeds the perception that we are generally privileged and powerful, and not in need of civil equality.

Single-issue politics, rooted in the interest group approach, was adopted by most US social movements after the 1950s. It has provided coherence, helped us build infrastructure and visibility, and certainly helped us achieve progress, but in the LGBT movement it has done so at the expense of people of color, transgender people, the working class, youth, and those who are less empowered in our communities. And its success has reached a limit. Single-issue politics leads to single-issue results. So, we created HIV-specific remedies in the 1980s that did not help other people with life-threatening illnesses facing the same mismanaged health care system. And we work on school bullying as if gay kids are the primary targets, when it is a much larger and more pervasive problem of in-groups and out-groups, gender performance by insecure young people, or prejudice stoked by structures of religion-based ostracism of the Other. A holistic policy response is needed, not a single-issue solution.

From a broad liberationist agenda—in which LGBT groups marched to end US intervention in El Salvador, in which lesbians led the US peace movement and the anti-nuclear movement, in which lesbians and gay men spoke out passionately in support of Black civil rights and against racist drug and sentencing laws, in which we demanded that government save our lives and that we get our fair share from it—we have become an ever narrower, individual rights movement, where the freedom to assert our individual right to marry is argued by some to be the most radical thing we could ever seek. Issues of reproductive freedom, sexuality and birth control, challenges to the patriarchal nuclear family, support for working families, ending violence against women, prison reform, poverty, redistribution—all once critical parts of our LGBT liberation movement's agenda—have disappeared in the national movement discourse.

As these issues have receded in our movement, we have lost our past alliance with the feminist movement, with the peace movement, with anti-poverty movements, with the environmental movement, and with the labor movement. We never had much of an alliance with the civil rights movement. Because we cannot win on our own, weak alliances are obstacles to our movement's ability to enact pro-LGBT policies at every level of government.

The past three decades have witnessed a series of critical public policy fights on race that have given LGBT leaders at the local, state, and national levels many chances to speak up and organize alongside the interests of people we claim as our allies. Examples include the welfare-reform fights of the Clinton era and ongoing efforts to cut back benefits and services for poor people; the effort to overturn and roll back affirmative action; an escalation of anti-immigrant lawmaking and nativist sentiment; the over-incarceration of Black and Latino people in our prisons and jails; the branding of Islamic and Arab-appearing people as "terrorists" and their targeting by immigration, police, and media entities; the decline of public education in urban and minority schools; the high drop-out rate among Black males in high school and college; the very high rates of violence against people of color, including continuing and pervasive police brutality; the widening gap in health care access, and disparities in health by race (such as in maternal health). These are all issues that have been discussed at one time or another in ballot initiatives, lawmaking, campaigns, and the public sphere.

Yet there have been only a handful of instances where LGBT organizations stepped forward to raise their voices and expend their political capital in support of these major civil rights issues facing communities of color. One example was when the Task Force went door-to-door in gay districts in California to urge opposition to the immigration and affirmative action ballot initiatives (we lost); another example was when groups like the Arcus Foundation opposed the anti-affirmative action measure in Michigan in 2006 (we lost); and a third example is the ongoing work that local people of color LGBT groups like the Audre Lorde Project have done to join campaigns against police violence and over-incarceration of people of color.

It is in this broad context of the national LGBT movement's ineffectiveness, and the larger increase in racial and economic disparities overall, that we need to look more closely at the movement's difficulties with claiming racial justice as a central and core issue.

Parts of our movement are working for racial justice, to be sure. These efforts are primarily being initiated by the queer people of color groups I have mentioned already and by non-gay progressive groups like Applied Research Center (ARC), Center for Community Change, and the Highlander Center. Groundbreaking work is being done by grassroots progressive groups in arenas like the criminal justice and prison systems, welfare organizing, homelessness, housing, youth development and leadership, immigrant rights, detention of immigrants, and schools. Creative work is also underway to strengthen investment in LGBTQ people of color organizations (Funders for Lesbian and Gay Issues' Campaign for Racial Equity) and to build people of color leadership (The Pipeline Project). There is potential also for linkages across national boundaries that might illuminate ways that the US movement's framing of identity is more limited than that of activists elsewhere, say, in Nepal or Africa.

But these efforts need more support to be effective.

Barriers to Incorporating LGBT Issues in Racial Justice Groups

In a landmark survey of eighty racial justice organizations for its 2010 *Better Together* report, the Applied Research Center (ARC) identified three barriers to the organizations' work on LGBT issues. The biggest barrier was a perception pervasive in racial justice organizations that most LGBT people are white and that our movement is not interested in race. The low visibility of LGBT leaders of color and the limited funding directed at racial equity fuels this perception. ARC called for a greater investment in people of color organizations working on both sexuality and race, an increased investment in the development of people of color leaders, and an increased investment in media and other outlets that can engage people in communities of color.

A second barrier identified by ARC was a lack of understanding about how to apply a sexuality lens to racial justice issues. We need to make clearer how LGBT people are affected in particular ways by issues that are currently seen primarily through a racial lens, such as police violence, homelessness, immigration, prison and incarceration, schools, and harassment.

A third barrier ARC identified was the fear of community resistance, both actual and perceived. Interviewees cited fear of religious organizations' reaction to working on LGBT issues, fear of causing internal divisions in racial communities, and lack of demand for work on LGBT rights from communities of color. All these challenges point to additional work for LGBT movement leaders to do. But it is equally important, I feel, to consider what might account for the resistance of the mainstream movement to a deeper incorporation of racial justice into its agenda.

Mechanisms of Avoidance of Race in the Mainstream LGBT Movement

In an excellent essay, author and anti-racist activist Tim Wise proposed three mechanisms that liberals and progressives appear to rely on to avoid addressing racial justice: colorblindness, colormuteness, and white privilege. Wise also identified something he called *class reductionism*: the notion that it is economics more than racism that needs to be addressed. Let me talk about each of these as they seem to be operating in the LGBT movement.

Colorblindness. Neo-conservatives like to quote Rev. Martin Luther King Jr.'s line from his famous "I Have a Dream Speech": "I have a dream that my four little children will one day live in a nation where they will be judged not by the color of their skin but by the content of their character." However, to claim that color does not matter in this moment is to ignore how racially biased outcomes arise out of the structure of our social, economic, and daily lives, not just as a result of intentional and malicious racial prejudice.

There is a perverse way that the election of a Black man to the role of president has made the expression of racism even more permissible. Assertions rooted in age-old bias are now simply and hotly defended as not racist, as being merely comments on President Obama as a leader. The very people who do and say the most white-supremacist things hotly deny the charge of racism. Race-based prejudice is all over the Tea Party and the Republican Party's skillful exploitation of lies like "Obama is a Muslim"; "Obama is un-American"; "Obama was not born in the US"; "Obama takes care of his own (read: Black people)"; "Obama does not get or care about ordinary (read: white) Americans." These kinds of comments are treated by the media as if they only arise from fringe elements, instead of showing them for what they are: the most effective tool deployed by right-wing tacticians to undermine the President's support among independents. President Obama was elected despite the country's racism, not because the country had transcended it.

Ironically, race and racism have become the hate that dares not speak its name, while sexuality and homophobia have become the love shouted from every media outlet, championed by corporations (who surreptitiously continue to donate to antigay causes and candidates), the subject of music and video by every superstar, and the new cause célèbre among liberals.

The pretense of colorblindness allows for these and other forms of conscious and unconscious racism to be asserted. In LGBT organizations, it operates to maintain racial exclusivity in our spaces. A clear example is in the racial composition of the leadership of our national movement's key organizations. When I started organizing in the movement, LGBT organizations' staffs were small and generally not diverse. But there was a lot of conversation about the urgent need for racial representation in all parts of our movement. Most feminist and LGBT groups had specific targets they set for the number of people of color they wanted on their boards. The Marches on Washington in 1979, 1987, and 1993 set high targets for racial representation. These were soundly derided as quotas and thus as bad in the 1990s, by which time a reactionary gay wing of the movement had crawled out of its closet.

As a result of this critique, I suspect that few of our national organizations have any formal targets or prioritization of representation. The data speak for themselves. Of the thirty-nine national LGBT movement organizations surveyed by the Movement Advancement Project 2010, only two had CEOs who were people of color, and one of these ran an African American LGBT group. Of the sixty-six LGBT community centers surveyed by MAP, fewer than 5 percent had people of color at the CEO level. Outside the LGBT movement, there are strong and brilliant LGBT leaders of color who are running multimillion-dollar organizations. There are powerful and successful professionals, lawyers, business people, academics, political figures, artists—all of whom LGBT groups could tap to be board members. Yet, every LGBT organization will tell you it is having a hard time doing its outreach. What should we make of this weak diversity at the board and CEO level?

I think the reason has everything to do with a lack of specific commitment to racial inclusion, a lack of focus on issues that matter to people of color, and the low comfort level of the board members, donors, influencers, and decision-makers in our movement with a racially diverse group of peers. It is my experience that many leaders in our communities are not comfortable with the voice, leadership, and political orientation of LGBT leaders of color, and are even less comfortable when those individuals come from anything but the middle or upper middle class. I can see this in my own experience. We are not given opportunities to be seen as leaders capable of representing an entire movement. When I was first appointed to the leadership of NGLTF, the old guard board members sought to have me sign an employment contract that would have precluded me from taking any public position, giving a speech, or committing the organization to a direction without their prior written consent. I refused and they backed down. This was an example of their discomfort with my race, gender, and class politics.

Leadership is promoted through networks: through social capital or relationships, as well as through the influence of economic capital. LGBT people of color do not have this kind of social capital because we live in race-segregated social worlds. This is why I think it is very difficult for a person of color to be selected as a nonprofit CEO. It generally requires a campaign to convince a board that the candidate can raise money from and command the respect of the largely white donor and member base of our organizations. I would not have become the head of NGLTF in 1989 without such a campaign. I banked on the social capital and leverage of a vast network of grassroots allies and colleagues in the movement who lobbied the task force's board on my behalf through phone calls and letters.

Colormuteness. This mechanism for race avoidance, as described by Tim Wise, refers to a tendency of white liberals to neither see nor give voice to race and racism as central issues in their communities and institutions. The LGBT movement's muteness with regard to race is shocking not only because a significant number of our community members are queer people of color, but also because of the pervasive and overwhelming evidence of race-based disparities, which show the United States to be a deeply divided society. Race, gender, and class operate to produce starkly different options even for people who are similarly situated.

Structural racism operates even where individual racism is less vivid. As the media and education–oriented think tank the Opportunity Agenda noted in its annual *State of Opportunity Report* in 2010, there are widespread racial disparities in every arena: health care access, infant mortality, educational access and completion, criminal justice prosecution and sentencing, home ownership, college completion, wages, and many other measures of equal opportunity. And economic disparities are widening, with the middle class of all colors shrinking and being hurt most by the policies of the past thirty years (post-Reagan).

Muteness about the interrelationship of race and the LGBT agenda is the norm, even when the connections are clear. So, for example, during the Clinton years, the NGLTF Policy Institute and grassroots people of color groups like the Audre Lorde Project were among the few groups to engage with the welfare reform fight, arguing that these so-called reforms would have a destructive impact on poor women and children, and pointing out the blatant heterosexism of the policies. In the present marriage battle, few, if any, connections are made to the way that a focus on marriage equality has dramatically narrowed a larger and more diverse family policy agenda that once was an LGBT movement staple, an agenda that would also benefit a large number of people of color who do not live in so-called traditional families.

Critiques have been advanced by queer theory and critical race scholars like Roderick Ferguson, David Eng, Jasbir Puar, and Dean Spade; by progressive grassroots organizations like AgainstEquality.org; and by legal scholars like Nancy Polikoff—all of whom have urged the movement not to rely solely on marriage equality as the index for family protection in the LGBT community and not to tie the receipt of benefits to marital status. They have urged it to build a family protection agenda that includes a larger number of diverse families (such as, for example, the more than 4.5 million families that are grandparent-led in the United States). Despite these critiques, the LGBT movement's family recognition agenda has narrowed drastically since the 1990s.

Underlying this narrowed agenda is a desire on the part of the mainstream middle-class LGBT movement to be integrated into existing societal institutions. However, getting admitted into the mainstream not only risks being absorbed without deeply changing the status quo—but the very act of admission requires that the outsider disaffiliate from those others defined by the existing power structure as illegitimate. As queer theory scholars have argued, for sexual outlaws and gender nonconformists to make themselves intelligible or coherent to the status quo requires a necessary submission to regulation. Roderick Ferguson notes that "the assertion of gay identity ceases to suggest an alienation from [heterosexual normativity] but rather an intersection with [it]," a process he calls *homonormativity*. Jasbir Puar goes even further, drawing a parallel between a form of sexual exceptionalism associated with the emergence of a national homosexuality, which she calls *homonationalism*, and "the exceptionalism of American empire . . . a commitment to the global dominant ascendancy of whiteness that is implicated in the propagation of the US as empire as well as the alliance between this propagation and this brand of homosexuality."

In other words, there is a connection between the narrowing of the LGBT agenda from its anti-militarist, anti-racist, and feminist origins in the late 1960s to its present patriotic, patriarchy-accepting nationalism and its acceptance by the mainstream. Normativity and acceptance of imperialism is the price the LGBT movement pays for its integration into the state—at the very instant that the American state is increasingly racially biased toward immigrants, at war with poor and low-income people, and in the hands of the corporations.

Finally, colormuteness can also be seen in the lack of attention by the mainstream LGBT movement to what many surveys of people of color in the movement consider to be important policy issues to work on. In a 2007–2008 survey by the Human Rights Campaign that obtained responses from 727 LGBT people of color and from nine focus groups, the issues that the respondents ranked as most important to them were, in order: affordable health care, jobs and the economy, equality for people of all races and ethnicities, prevention and treatment of HIV, and equality for LGBT people. The Arcus Foundation has also funded extensive national research on African American attitudes toward LGBT issues and white LGBT attitudes toward African Americans. These data reveal that issues of common and overlapping concern include jobs, health care access, and education. The Zuna Institute's survey of Black lesbians also found a high percentage of concern about jobs and financial security, health care, and education—all before civil rights issues like marriage and partner protection.

Yet the issues of generating jobs and financial security, of health care reform, of reducing violence or HIV are not the top four issues of any of the major national LGBT organizations. Instead, we have developed a system of issue-specific LGBT groups that also exist—on immigration, on the military, on family, on health, on HIV. Although the issue-focused groups are more receptive to a racial and class lens, they are still not leaders in making the linkages. The point here is that a key reason for our colormuteness is not that we don't know what issues to work on, nor that problems facing LGBT people are so radically different from the problems facing communities of color that our movement cannot address them coherently. No, indeed. The real issue is an absence of leadership on the part of the white LGBT movement to champion race.

White Privilege. This is the third mechanism that Tim Wise notes for how liberal groups avoid working on race and racism: white privilege, or the favoring of perspectives of white people over those of people of color. Frustration with the unexamined and unquestioned—if well-intentioned—white privilege within our LGBT movement is what prompted me to attempt this talk. The privileging of white LGBT experience shows up again and again in ways small and large, visible and hidden. From the wrong analysis of the defeat, in 2008, of Proposition 8 (resulting in a banning of same-sex marriage in

California) which blamed it on African American voters instead of on white Protestants, for example, who were a larger share of the electorate; to the naming of the 2009 Matthew Shepard/James Byrd Jr. Hate Crimes Prevention Act, to which James Byrd Jr. was added late and only after pressure from civil rights allies; to the absence of women of color from the leadership of the fight to allow LGBT people to serve in the military despite the fact that they are discharged in huge numbers, one can see a racial privileging of certain experience over others.

Another example of how white privilege works in our movement is the extent to which donors—individuals and institutional—help determine and control the movement's agenda. The generosity of these individuals has helped to build a multifaceted movement, and it is to be applauded. Yet the donors to our movement bear significant responsibility for the lack of focus on racial justice by our research, organizing, legal, and advocacy organization.

There are very few champions of funding for LGBT people of color. Fewer than half of all autonomous people of color organizations received foundation funding in 2007 and the majority had budgets under $100,000. As a result, across the country, donors do not offer incentives to LGBT organizations to engage in work on racial justice. For example, the NGLTF was often told by its donors that they were not interested in funding work on race (like affirmative action or immigration reform). National LGBT organizations that took a stand against the death penalty after the Matthew Shepard murder trial lost donors and board members over their position.

The organizations engaging in work on racial and economic justice in our movement are all grassroots-based and have been led by innovative groups like Sylvia Rivera Law Project, the Audre Lorde Project, Project Fierce, Housing Works, and Queers for Economic Justice, to name a few. Their challenge in getting a majority white infrastructure to face white privilege is tough, because they depend for their funding on a constituency whose privilege they are questioning. The new engagement of non-LGBT funders, like Ford Foundation, the Open Society Initiative, and others, should prove useful to the grassroots racial justice movement.

Examples from my own experience in the mainstream LGBT movement as the only woman of color in leadership positions for decades may also be instructive regarding the way the white racial frame dominates the mainstream LGBT movement. When I was appointed head of the NGLTF in 1989, a prominent donor called the task force offices and said to a development director there that he could not believe the task force board had hired "that radical woman" who was "practically a nigger." More than once, white gay activists have questioned my claim of being a person of color; as one colleague noted, I was "practically white." Brown is an intermediate state that occupies a complex place in the American racial consciousness—but after 9/11 and the decade of anti-immigrant bashing that ensued, brown and Black are both more stigmatized than I could ever have imagined they would be twenty years ago.

Over the years, I have experienced viscerally the awkwardness and discomfort of some male donors with me because I am a woman, an awkwardness that increases when I do anything that reminds them that I am also not white. My girlfriend loves me to wear Indian outfits like kurta pajamas or saris to LGBT formal dress events, but my experience in them is uncomfortable—not just because I am more used to wearing jeans, but also because I already feel so highly conspicuous in the largely white and largely male gatherings I attend regularly and wearing Indian clothes makes me feel even more so. My discomfort has been confirmed on more than one occasion, when well-meaning colleagues have joked that I am "going native" or "putting out the Kente cloth" on occasions when I have worn Indian clothes.

Throughout my time in the movement, I have raised issues of racism, sexism, economic equality, and privilege with very mixed response. Sometimes I have succeeded in creating innovative new programs to impact racial disparities in our communities, but at other times, I have had my suggestions ignored and my ideas marginalized. Some doors were open to me because I was a woman of color and the movement wanted "representation," but others were not open far enough, or simply never pointed out. Yet I have succeeded—in large measure because of the class privilege that my education gives me and the social capital that I have cultivated that comes from being successful, and being backed by people with money and resources.

But I never deluded myself into believing that my success proved anything more than the exception to the general experience of most of my colleagues. Because so many major donors are most comfortable giving to people like themselves, women and people of color have a hard time raising funds in our community of donors. Making people in the middle, upper-middle, and wealthy class in the LGBT movement comfortable is critical to one's success as a leader. The funder community will need to take a good look at itself and will need significant education if we are to reorient the LGBT movement toward new issues and leadership.

Class Reductionism. This is the argument that class, more than race, is the most important thing to focus on. It is certainly true that class and race are linked, and that economic-justice remedies—such as insuring that people make living wages or that communities of color have access to a great and affordable local health clinic—might actually result in some positive impact regarding racial disparities in wages or health. But it is also the case that Black and brown folks who are not poor or working-class—indeed, those who are upper-middle-class and affluent—are still subjected to discrimination regularly, across several spheres, from the housing market to health care delivery, the workplace, and education.

This is an interesting point for LGBT people to consider with respect to our movement because, in truth, we don't deal with class much at all—ours is not so much reductionism with regard to class as it is class denial. The LGBT movement has not developed a policy agenda that comes out of the needs of working-class or poor LGBT people. Indeed, there is a significant part of the LGBT community (a full 30 percent, if we are to believe national 2010 exit polls) that votes for an economic agenda that dramatically favors wealthy people and is extremely antagonistic to the needs of middle-class and poor people.

Until very recently, few data sets have developed the LGBT picture. In its groundbreaking analysis released in 2019 titled *Poverty in the GLB Community*, the Williams Institute reviewed three existing data sets to draw conclusions about the actual economic situation of GLB people. They found that poverty in the GLB community is "at least as common" as poverty in the broader world and, like that broader world, has a racial dimension as well. LGBT youth comprise from 4 to 10 percent of the juvenile justice system population in New York State; same sex couples raising children are more diverse by race than heterosexual couples. When it comes to adoption, gay and lesbian couples are raising 4 percent of all adopted children in the United States. Indeed, researchers noted that GLB couples are adopting at a higher rate than single heterosexuals (3 percent). Yet the Evan Donaldson Institute did a survey of 307 adoption agencies nationwide in 1999 and 2000 and found that more than a third would reject a gay or lesbian applicant.

There are many unaddressed class issues among people of color, within and beyond the LGBT community. These class issues produce tension between African Americans and Asians, between Latino immigrants and African Americans, and within the Black community itself, where there is a long-standing tension around the Black bourgeoisie and its "politics of respectability"—as Melissa Harris-Lacewell labeled it at the Applied Research Center's "Facing Race" Conference in 2010. To what extent is secondary marginalization of LGBT people within communities of color itself a byproduct of class? How does the class allegiance of people like me, who have skipped several class levels in my lifetime, change our politics, as we move on up? These and many other questions are yet under-discussed and would be worth raising inside the relatively narrow circles of the people of color elites of the LGBT movement.

My point here is that we cannot see race as a problem entirely of the white parts of the LGBT movement. We need to consider the extent to which those of us who are people of color contribute to the failure to address racial justice and how class facilitates or inhibits that effort.

Action Steps to Set a New Course

In a 1997 speech to the National Black Gay and Lesbian Conference, the poet June Jordan said, "[P]olitical unity based upon sexuality will never achieve lasting profound victories related to the enlargement of freedom and the broadening of equality of entitlement unless . . . [it] become[s] a political unity based upon principles of freedom and principles of equality."

Ultimately, this is what an LGBT politics for the future must articulate with regard to race: our shared "principles of freedom and principles of equality." I believe there are three principles we need to be guided by in the future course of the LGBT movement.

Principle 1: No Queer Left Behind

LGBT liberation stands for a change in the lived experience of *all* LGBT people. We must explicitly commit not to leave anyone behind when partial equality is won for some of us. This principle would not only commit donors and institutions to fulfilling equality for those most vulnerable in our communities, but would also commit the resources that are needed to implement equality once we have won.

Equal rights guarantees in law are always contingent upon their enforcement. Outcomes gained by other social movements show us that the achievement of formal equality—although essential and urgently necessary—produces mixed results because of the differences in people's economic and social status. This is because equality is not evenly distributed: its realization is affected by one's economic status, race, geographic location, religion, and many other factors. Thus, women's equality has resulted in it being very difficult for poor women to get abortions, while wealthy women can access them anytime.

I would urge the movement to adopt the principle that our movement is not over until the weakest among us has seen the benefits of freedom.

Principle 2: Racial Justice Is an LGBT Issue

We need to commit to this truth by putting it in the mission statements of our organizations and in the policy agenda of our legal and advocacy movement. This means LGBT organizations, once and for all, must broaden the definition of who is included in the LGBT community, and what constitutes a gay issue.

Job security is among the top issues of concern raised by LGBT people in poll after poll. Economic anxiety is the legacy the baby boomer generation has left its successors, and our communities are no different in their concerns. Within this context, nondiscrimination is an important but inadequate goal to address the concerns of all classes and races of LGBT people. So, LGBT organizations at the state, local, and national level must support campaigns to extend unemployment benefits, expand workforce development for low-wage workers, support training and jobs for ex-offenders, work to pass living wage laws, and develop microfinance strategies to help US-based low-income entrepreneurs. These are all are examples of policies that could increase economic security for working LGBT people and express the commitment of the movement to achieve social justice, not just equal rights.

Choice and reproductive health, access to health care, and ending health disparities are critical issues for LGBT women and men of all colors, as is adequate resourcing of the ongoing HIV/AIDS epidemic. These issues must be restored to prominence on the LGBT agenda. Similarly, reducing the over-criminalization of certain communities, sentencing reform, support for better treatment of prisoners, and working to end to rape inside prison are all issues that affect many LGBT people and disproportionately affect LGBT people of color. Defending a robust role for the state in securing economic prosperity for all is a meaningful LGBT issue. The tax-cut mania of the moment has never been more than a thinly disguised attempt to shrink the size and social-democratic role of the state.

A critical part of adding race to our agenda requires of LGBT politics a confrontation with this era's anti-government sentiment: we are ironically a community that needs much more government investment to address many of our biggest challenges. Yet we are also a community rightly skeptical of state power, having experienced its abuses. How do we reconcile this complex historical relationship with the state? What new ideas can we introduce to the polarized debates that emerge from our experience of being regulated, managed, and negated by state power? How would we structure the kinds of services that state funding enables, such as elder care, youth services, school curricula that teach tolerance, alternatives to incarceration, affordable housing, mental health services, drug and alcohol programs, HIV prevention, treatment and care, and support for people facing life-threatening illnesses? How can we engage with government in ways that do not expand its police power to target parts of our communities?

Principle 3: Enhance the Leadership Voice of People of Color

The third principle to which we must commit is to increase the representation and to enhance the leadership voice for LGBT people of color at decision-making tables. LGBT institutions and leadership must reflect the racial and gender composition of our communities. LGBT movement organizations should set voluntary goals and targets for the representation of people of color on boards and staff senior teams and conduct annual reviews to insure the organization is making progress toward its targets. LGBT board members and major donors need to have space to have frank conversations with each other about the reasons why they have had difficulty supporting and nurturing leaders of color. There is a critical need to invest in and resource grassroots organizations and LGBT people of color-oriented programs that network, nurture, and strengthen leaders who come from under-represented communities. We need programs that reach out to corporate, philanthropic, and academic sites to recruit out and diverse LGBT leaders who might be willing to lead a board or a staff.

Principles are the guidelines that can help set our future course. But action must also be taken. For the LGBT movement to work in a meaningful way on race, we need to reconfigure the definition of which allies we work with, what we work for, and how we work for LGBT freedom. We need significant consolidation and restructuring in our national movement organizations. And we need to take up some new campaigns that put into practice our long-held theories that sexuality, race, economic status, disability status, gender, and gender identity and expression are all interconnected. So, at the US Social Forum, the Queer Caucus, led by FIERCE, the Audre Lorde Project, and SONG—all organizations that are members of the ROOTS Coalition, a national coalition of collectives engaged in multi-issue organizing across progressive movements—led hundreds of LGBT attendees in a participatory process to determine if they would be willing to join forces in non-gay campaigns working to achieve specific policy change in education, criminal justice, or health care policies. Such grassroot innovations hold the key to breaking through the impasse of present racial justice politics.

Let me propose three additional examples of experiments to incorporate race into existing forms of LGBT organizing.

Experiments in Organizing

First, I'd like to see our movement consciously and significantly support Latino, Black, and Asian candidates of color who are pro-LGBT at the national level and mobilize the rather significant LGBT vote in some of the midsized and smaller cities not known for such a vote at the state and local level, especially in the South and the Midwest.

A second experiment I would propose is to commit to a race-based ballot measure and mobilize a significant and serious effort as a sign of our commitment to align our political interests with that of racial justice organizations. Such a measure could be an affirmative action initiative, an immigrant rights initiative, a criminal justice initiative, or a schools initiative—all critical issues with huge impact.

A final set of interventions could involve making the case for LGBT equality to a wider set of audiences in a particular community, to meaningfully shift public opinion. Let's take our stories and lives, our families, and relationships out of the context of the reactive anti-gay campaigns that our opponents thrust upon us, and instead plan and pursue a pro-LGBT educational campaign to build more allies and support in particular communities.

Conclusion

The poet June Jordan wrote:

> What is the moral meaning of who we are?
> What do we take personally?
> How do perceived issues propel or diffuse our political commitments?
> I think these questions can only be answered again and again, and with difficulty.

They are the questions we face in this moment of partial fulfillment of LGBT formal equality. The moral meaning of who we are will be determined by our actions, by what we stand for, and by whom we stand with.

LGBT identities are changing and LGBT politics must as well. The LGBT politics of the future—LGBT politics 3.0—must be a more inclusive, democratically determined, decentralized, and multi-issue politics.

To succeed, it must be a politics that speaks to critical issues like racial and economic equity, gender inequality and justice, the role and value of government in our society, the role and value of the market and economic sector when it is harnessed for socially responsible and sustainable ends, global justice, and the need to end racial and tribal hatreds and nationalist mindsets arising from a purity-based politics of ethnic superiority. It must be an LGBT politics willing to provide leadership to a wider progressive movement that is desperate for new voices and new energy.

We need an LGBT politics of the future that seeks respect instead of pity, affinity instead of tolerance, connection instead of isolation, and full citizenship on queer terms. A politics that does not need crutches like the biological argument—"we were born this way, so don't hate us"—to assert our moral integrity and win our civil equality; a politics whose goal is to deliver equality and social justice and access to the "good life," where we are free to be as diverse, nonconforming, and inside or outside of heterosexual structures as we each desire.

9

ASSUME THE POSITION:
CLASS AND THE LGBT MOVEMENT

This essay is based on an invited keynote address at a 2011 conference at Vassar College, on the occasion of the college's 150th anniversary. It was published in Irresistible Revolution: Confronting Race, Class and the Assumptions of LGBT Politics *(Magnus Books, 2012).*

My favorite Patti Smith song has long been "Privilege/Set Me Free" from the *Easter* album, in which Patti intercuts the Lord's Prayer with an existential cry to God to set her free from her seeking, her desire, her youth, her angst. (I once put that record on my friend Robert's stereo in Vassar's Main dormitory, pointed the speakers out his window, set the record player to repeat play, cranked up the volume, and went outside on the lawn. Poor Robert heard that Vice President Natalie Marshall herself pounded on his door to get him to turn the record off—but of course no one was there.) The song has served as an anthem, rallying me again and again to rebound when I feel defeated by privileges that I cannot access, or trapped in my own heady melodramas within the privileges I occupy.

The irony of my discovery of the song on this hallowed campus is obvious. The common element in our diverse experiences of Vassar as queers is that we benefited from attending one of the most elite institutions in this country, an institution built upon economic privilege and dedicated to its continuance, an institution inaccessible to most people, that operates in both overt and informal ways to keep people frozen in their social and economic class positions. The fact that we found in this place a world of amazing ideas, people, and knowledge, and a questioning and even at times radical spirit of inclusion or expression, does not change the structural reality of Vassar's impact on our lives: by virtue of our attendance here, we each assumed, and have been assumed into, an upper-middle-class position.

I was not "to the manor born," yet over the years since I graduated from Vassar, I found and in many ways placed myself in positions to work within and sometimes even to run the manor. Vassar changed my socioeconomic class status forever, from immigrant working-class to upwardly mobile and securely middle-class. Attending Northeastern Law School changed it again, to the professionally employable, credentialed managerial class. Working at the Ford Foundation changed it yet again, to the really comfortable upper-middle-class, with the first pension plan I ever had. And working for a billionaire to help build his Arcus Foundation changed it yet again, from comfortably upper-middle-class to a platinum card–carrying member of the class that staffs, supports, and serves the ruling elite.

My friend Henry van Ameringen, the gay philanthropist, once observed to me drily, "For a socialist you certainly are surrounded by a lot of money." I answered that, as a socialist, my job was to redistribute the wealth, so I needed to be surrounded by lots of money. But the underlying and cynical truth of his observation is that when you ascend to a certain economic class position, by virtue of education, labor, or inheritance, you also assume a certain position in the social order. You become one of the elite few, going along and getting along in the system, and demonstrating a certain level of subservience to those others whom the system benefits.

Many tangible forms of power accompany the opportunity that goes along with economic status, education, and social privilege. These include, most practically, the power to live comfortably and securely, the material opportunity to fulfill wants, to provide for loved ones, to access health care and social services with ease, and to be heard in ways that people without money are not heard. You are promised, even if it proves to be a form of false consciousness, to be able to achieve the "good life." Specifically, being part of (even a servant to) the ruling class brings with it forms of power:

· The power to see and be seen;
· The power to transform one's identity and experience in material ways.

Class positions embody and generate a way of seeing and being seen—and like all observation and experience, this way of seeing is raced and gendered. Socioeconomic class affects whom or what you notice and with whom you affiliate. It shapes what you see and what you remain oblivious to; it determines whom you must please and whom you can disregard. Class-based seeing is aspirational. It is fantasy-based. So, we see people richer than ourselves and identify with them more than we see and affiliate with our own class peer-group or with those poorer than us. Poor, working, and middle-class people have a lot of anxiety and shame at not being better off. Upper-middle-class people spend more than they can afford in order to be seen as belonging to the class they aspire to become.

Class also affects who notices you. I've always wondered, for example, why the horrific murder of the white college student Matthew Shepard struck such a strong chord not only with LGBT people but also with non-queer folks. The outcry against the attack was enormous and contributed to an increased political commitment to challenge violence. It set the stage for a decade of new work on LGBT rights. Yet the same year his murder took place, dozens of queer, lesbian, and trans people of all colors were also killed, and grassroots organizations launched several campaigns to seek justice for these murders. In my thirty years of work in the LGBT movement, I can remember no nationwide mobilization comparable to that around Matthew Shepard, around the murder of a poor, nonwhite, queer person.

Class is a way of wanting. It informs our desires and what we aspire to—not to mention whether we can meet those aspirations. Class-based wants for most people include the desire for various forms of material comfort and security: a job; a home that we own, or affordable rent; a stereo; the ability to take a vacation; the ability to afford transportation; the ability to provide a good life for our kids. Wanting is about our imaginations and fantasy life as well—and class colonizes our creativity. Those of us who lived through the emergence of HIV/AIDS in our communities in the 1980s remember the many battles we fought against the right wing to gain attention to this epidemic. But equally bitter battles were fought within the LGBT movement over what we wanted, over our political imaginings. Did we want treatment or prevention (or both)? Did we want to push the FDA or push for health care reform (or both)? Did we want to ensure that funding for HIV went to poor Black and Latino intravenous drug users or to white gay men (or both)? Did we want to fight for Medicaid reform overall or make the AIDS-specific fix that would take care of HIV-positive people (or both)? These were class-based fights, and while the way the lines got drawn and who sided with what position was not always determined by class positions, the battles themselves certainly revealed them.

Money and education allow transformation. They bring about the magic of migration, of transition, and even erasure. Money can transform one's race or gender in a way that appears to mitigate the usual race or gender-based exclusion—although it does not change the structural barriers and exclusions that those without that same access to money experience. So Puff Daddy is a fixture on East Hampton's social circuit, although a rarity (I suspect even he still finds himself excluded from certain enclaves in that world). Women like Meg Whitman or Sheryl Sandberg may rise to the top in business and run Fortune 500 companies, but their success does not change the structural fact that fewer than 20 percent of corporate board members are women or that women earn less than men for performing the same jobs. Wealth and educational privilege transform race and gender for the individual beneficiary, but not the class from which they come. Still, the transformational power of money drives us to earn more and to try to change our lot and provide a better life for our families than we had ourselves.

These three intangible yet material impacts of class status—seeing, wanting, and transforming—operate in stark ways in the LGBT movement. To explore the operation of class in our movement, I want to spend some time on the example of a major fundraiser held by conservative donors in 2011 that was cochaired by Republican Michael Bloomberg, Republican hedge fund manager Paul Singer, and the brilliant, long-time Democratic and philanthropic innovator Tim Gill (on whose foundation's board I currently sit). The *Advocate* reported that the cohosts also included Tea Party Founder David Koch and the hedge fund manager Daniel Loeb. The event reportedly raised $1.2 million to support four Republican members of the New York State Senate who voted for marriage equality and who had been targeted for defeat by the National Organization for Marriage.

Those of us with memory and history had to shake our heads. What a difference thirteen years makes! We recall that in October 1998, the Human Rights Campaign (HRC) infuriated LGBT activists by endorsing the conservative Republican incumbent Alphonse D'Amato for the US Senate from New York State over the Democratic candidate Chuck Schumer. Local activists denounced the HRC and vowed never to work with them again. Irate board members of the HRC resigned and decried "sleeping with the enemy." By contrast, the Paul Singer–led fundraiser raised nary a peep from most New Yorkers.

It is neither logical nor possible to argue against the strategy of bipartisan politics: Republican and conservative votes are needed to advance LGBT rights (and all civil rights) in state and national legislatures. Nor is the idea of being a friend to get a friend offensive. Additionally, since so many conservatives have LGBT members of their families, it makes sense some would support LGBT equality (Singer has a gay son; Koch is rumored to have a close gay relative). Nevertheless, the LGBT political elite's embrace of conservative reactionaries raises many troubling questions: about whom the movement sees as part of our community and whom it sees as dispensable; about the broader vision the movement wants to achieve; and about what exactly movement leaders are seeking in alliances with those who see aspects of our queerness as a problem. Writer and organizer Kenyon Farrow asked in a blog post, "What does it mean when so-called progressives celebrate a victory in large part won by GOP-supporting hedge fund managers, Tea Party funders and corporate conglomerates—the outspoken enemies of progressive causes?"

In my view, the LGBT movement's embrace of Paul Singer, David Koch, and hard-right business people reflects a class bias that we do not often acknowledge. It demonstrates whose agendas and values dominate elite LGBT political strategy. By accepting the support of folks like David Koch and Paul Singer, the LGBT political movement prioritized an alliance with conservative donors and politicians over an alliance with those who have supported the LGBT movement for decades. Thirty-six Democrats also voted for the New York state marriage equality bill—but no comparable fundraising effort was launched to defend them. Unions invested heavily and lobbied hard for marriage equality in New York—but the LGBT movement embraced Koch, who funded the defeat of collective bargaining rights in Wisconsin and who is identified with nationwide efforts to destroy union power. Koch, Singer, and others actively oppose President Obama, who despite his flaws is one of the most pro-LGBT presidents in American history. Singer reportedly plans to raise $30 million to defeat President Obama.

What values is the mainstream LGBT movement compromising through these kinds of acts of collaboration? Should the LGBT movement care only about gay rights? What about the environment or women's reproductive rights or immigrants' right to fair opportunities, or labor's right to organize, or people of color's right to not be treated as second-class? Gay conservatives, be they Democrat or Republican, have long argued that we are and should remain a single-issue movement. What they fail to see is that such narrowing of the LGBT agenda has a cost. At best, it alienates LGBT people from long-standing allies who have helped us advance in the workplace, the courts, and the legislatures. At worst, taking the position that anyone who supports gay rights is our friend aligns us with political partners who promote policies that will maintain inequality and misery for large numbers of LGBT people.

The common argument for making these alliances with conservatives is that their endorsement of LGBT rights will persuade more pro-corporate Republican and Democratic politicians to opportunistically support LGBT rights. We are told this is smart politics, savvy, even necessary in today's polarized political climate, and the reason why we are winning. I question these rationalizations. They obscure the outright danger of such alliances. LGBT movement support for Republican candidates has been irrelevant: it has had no impact on the homophobic platform and politics of the Republican Party itself. It places the LGBT movement in a coalition with people who have funded and fought vigorously to recriminalize, repathologize, and discriminate based on sexual orientation and gender identity.

Elite donors to our movement claim that they are acting in the best interest of the community. They assume that all LGBT people will benefit if LGBT rights are advanced. But this is not necessarily true. When the HRC endorsed passing the federal Employment Non-Discrimination Act without protections for gender identity, they put the economic interests of middle- and upper-middle-class queers above those of a much poorer population of transgender folks. Similarly, when gay donors ally with right-wing elements in the Republican Party on marriage, they concede enormous influence to yet another set of moneyed interests. In so doing they put their economic and social class interest above those of poor LGBT folks, immigrant LGBT folks, and others targeted by the policies of the right.

In moderating its broader social justice aspirations to make new alliances with right-wing elements, all the LGBT movement will accomplish is to mitigate the feelings of marginalization felt by some privileged gay men and women. In making such alliances with the right, the male-dominated, largely white, and comfortably wealthy advocates sitting at the tables of political decision-making promote our acceptance into existing systems of power. We reassure the wealthy and powerful that LGBT admission to the club will not challenge their worldview, that we are just like them, that we believe in what they believe, and that we are even willing to sacrifice parts of our own souls to belong.

What Class Is the LGBT Movement and What Classes Make Up the LGBT Experience?

If economic class informs a way of seeing, a way of wanting, and a way to transcend experiences of oppression, what is the actual socioeconomic status of LGBT people? What do the data tell us about ourselves?

The limited available data on the demographics of LGBT populations reveal two truths: first, that significant percentages of LGBT people are low-income and poor; and second, that most of the staffs, boards, and members of mainstream queer organizations are middle- to upper-middle-class. The class composition of LGBT communities is quite different from that of many of the people who staff, fund, and lead our movement's mainstream institutions.

The Williams Institute's groundbreaking report, *Poverty in the GLB Community*, released in 2009, and the NCTE/NGLTF *Survey of Transgender Persons*, released in 2011, document significant economic diversity within LGBT populations. The Williams Institute report concludes that poverty is at least as common in LGBT populations as in the general population: 22 percent of lesbians and 15 percent of gay men lived in poverty versus 19 percent of women and 13 percent of men in the general population. When census data on LGBT couples is parsed by race, the rates grow even starker, especially for African American LGBT same-sex couples, who have higher poverty rates than heterosexual African American couples.

The NCTE/NGLTF study collected data from more than 6,500 transgender and gender-nonconforming respondents. It revealed that trans people are nearly four times more likely to live in poverty than the general population. The respondents reported extremely high rates of discrimination in employment, housing, public accommodation, medical care, access to police and other emergency services, and family rejection. Trans people in general have twice the rate of unemployment as the national average and trans people of color experience four times the national rate of unemployment. Discrimination is rampant: 19 percent report being refused a home and 11 percent report being evicted. Queer youth are also extremely vulnerable financially, especially if they are on their own. All studies of homelessness demonstrate the over-representation of LGBT youth among those who are homeless. In 2010, the Center for American Progress estimated that more than 100,000 LGBT youth were homeless in the United States. Both the Williams Institute and the Movement Advancement Project's (MAP) report on LGBT families note that LGBT families experience more financial hardships than heterosexual families. MAP reports that one in five LGBT families are raising kids in poverty, as opposed to one in ten heterosexual families. The Williams Institute reports that children in LGBT families have poverty rates twice that of the general population, and that 20 percent of kids growing up in same-sex households are being raised in households that meet the poverty threshold (this compares to 9.4 percent of kids being raised by heterosexual households that meet the poverty threshold).

The pervasive myth that LGBT people are high-income earners is dispelled in several online surveys that asked people to self-disclose their wages. Despite the tendency of such samples to over-represent higher earners, the data show that millions of LGBT people are low-wage earners. For example, 27 percent of respondents to the NCTE/NGLTF transgender survey reported earning less than $20,000 per year. And in 2008, in an HRC/Hunter College poll of 768 randomly selected LGBT people, 33 percent reported incomes under $25,000 a year.

A very different archive of research was gathered by the Welfare Warriors Research Collaborative, under the auspices of Queers for Economic Justice (QEJ). The participatory action research study of poor LGBT people found that 69 percent reported being homeless at some point in their lives; 58 percent currently lived in a shelter; 80 percent used need-based public benefits (food stamps, public assistance, and housing assistance); and more than 70 percent used health benefits like Medicaid, HIV/AIDS Services Administration benefits, SSI, and Social Security Disability (SSD). Most participants reported very high levels of police harassment, violence, and harassment by government agencies.

A Movement of the Middle and Upper Middle Class

Social movement theorists have long documented the middle-class nature of most post-1960s social movements, such as the peace, environmental, and women's movements. Whereas previous social movements, such as unions, were grounded in material interest, the new social movements were often focused around claims for rights, assertions of identity, desires for community, and assertions of values. Frederick Rose notes, "By measures of occupation, education and income, membership in new social movement organizations is disproportionately upper middle class." This is certainly borne out in the LGBT movement.

MAP collects data annually on the thirty-nine largest LGBT organizations. The 2010 MAP Report listed the demographic composition of boards and staffs of the thirty-nine largest organizations. Racially, staff identified as 68 percent white, 12 percent African American, 12 percent Latino, 7 percent Asian Pacific Islanders, and 1 percent Native American. However, boards were less diverse. They were 58 percent male, 40 percent female, 6 percent transgender, and 2 percent gender queer or "other," and they were 75 percent white, 11 percent African American, 8 percent Latino, 5 percent Asian Pacific Islander, and 2 percent Native American.

Data about the economic situation of donors to the LGBT movement are limited, as most organizations hold that information in a proprietary way, but MAP estimates that fewer than 3.4 percent of all LGBT people actually donated to LGBT movement organizations in 2010. Most gay people are not members, not contributors, and not connected to the work of the organizations that strive to speak, lobby, and campaign on their behalf.

A Mainstream Movement Agenda That Is Silent on the Needs of Many LGBT People

The class position of the people who staff and volunteer for LGBT organizations impacts the agenda of these organizations. This is clear from the programmatic priorities of LGBT mainstream organizations. It is no coincidence that the leadership of LGBT grassroots organizations derives more widely from poor and working-class backgrounds. QEJ did a fascinating report called *Poverty, Public Assistance and Privatization: The Queer Case for a New Commitment to Economic Justice.* In it, an array of leaders in the grassroots racial and economic justice wing of the queer movement talk about their class backgrounds. They share their experience with being on public assistance, coming from poor and working-class families, and the importance of this experience to their work as queer activists. These working-class leaders are pursuing a very different political agenda from that of mainstream leaders. They sought the expansion of the mainstream rights agenda to include a defense of public assistance, government control versus privatization of basic social support services, support for public infrastructure and investment, and support for human needs such as housing, food, health, and education. The overall silence of mainstream LGBT policy, legal, and advocacy organizations on bread-and-butter economic justice and social welfare issues is noticeable—and remarkable, especially in the post-2008 global economy.

Perhaps in response, over the past two decades, a grassroots LGBT economic and racial justice movement has emerged that has a very different economic and policy agenda from that of the mainstream movement. It advocates for low-income people. It allies with the broader social justice community of advocates, but it remains dominated by the larger LGBT establishment. The divergence between grassroots and mainstream movement advocates becomes apparent upon consideration of just about any of the LGBT movement's approaches to policy in areas like health care, jobs, and taxes.

Under the guise of marriage equality, the mainstream LGBT movement pursues tax policies that benefit the wealthy. For sure, the marriage agenda has many emotional dimensions, but it also has many material benefits for people with assets. A marriage agenda is not the same as an equitable tax agenda, which would benefit poor people, single people, and unmarried people. It is not the same as a family-recognition agenda that expands definitions of family and separates access to benefits from marital status. Indeed, if a gay organization were to take a position on tax increases for the wealthy, the significant gay Republican part of our community would object, and irate wealthy donors would condemn the so-called socialism of the movement's leaders and claim that they are out of sync with a (fantasized) LGBT majority.

There is an increasing divergence between the mainstream LGBT movement and a smaller, more creative, more multi-issue, grassroots LGBT movement. Whereas grassroots LGBT organizations—like the Sylvia Rivera Law Project, Queers for Economic Justice, the Audre Lorde Project (ALP), and Critical Resistance—are working extensively on issues of criminal justice reform, police harassment, and the exploitation of those who are homeless, transgender, or working in underground economies (like prostitution), the mainstream LGBT movement is disengaged from these issues.

A Movement That Avoids Race

An abiding myth about class status in America is that it is tied to merit, rather than to factors like race, gender, and geography. When data on household net worth are analyzed, the sharp income disparities among whites, Blacks, Latinos, and other poor people without assets become starkly evident. Class mobility is shrinking: the rich get richer—their kids do too—while the poor just stay poor. Socioeconomic class is tied to assets, which are tied to race. The Economic Policy Institute's report, *The State of Working America*, reveals that while the median net worth of white households in 2009 was $97,900, the median net worth of Black households was $2,200. In 2009, one in four households had a negative net worth (up from 18.6 percent in 2007); for Black households, that total was 40 percent. Despite such evidence, the queer mainstream has not placed race on its agenda. It does not see the issues for which it lobbies through the lens of the different communities that make up this movement.

Access Politics

A striking aspect of mainstream, gay-equality politics is the extent to which mass-based and public forms of political and cultural engagement are being replaced by elite-based, largely private or hidden forms of lobbying and litigation.

The structure of American politics requires politicians to raise money, and disproportionate time and attention is paid by these political leaders to people who are organized to give. Class-based access—and providing access to LGBT people with money—is the currency that makes the Human Rights Campaign the largest LGBT organization in the national movement and the most dominant mainstream LGBT movement entity in Washington. In 2010, the HRC raised more than $38 million and spent $35 million on educational activities and lobbying. It raised $9.4 million from major donors (who give between $1,200 and $5,000 a year). An additional 15 percent came from special events, and nearly 40 percent came from smaller, individual donations. With a network of dozens of city-based dinners around the country, a mailing list of several hundred thousand people, and a staff of more than three hundred, the HRC is a giant—a successful organization built and supported by middle- to upper-middle-class people. Critiques of the effectiveness of the HRC are as ubiquitous as its presence, but none can doubt the huge space that it occupies, or its class orientation.

Should we take pride in the fact that we are now in the back rooms where deals are being cut and politicians are being lobbied? I've been in these rooms. I do not feel pride at the devolution of our democratic, diverse movement into a moneyed elite pressing for rights (largely for itself). Who has access to tables of decision-making and power? In my experience, access is available to those who can bring money to the table. (Delivering individual bodies—or an entire constituency—can also give one access, but few queer LGBT organizations are yet able to present such large constituencies.)

Throughout the 1980s and 1990s, and long before the new anti-globalization movement, LGBT national agendas were articulated through public and open-ended, accessible processes of consultation: town meetings (which involved endless processing), meetings to determine what the demands of national marches should be (this happened for the 1979, 1987, and 1993 marches), statewide conferences, local political club meetings on endorsements, and ACT UP meetings at which everyone could (and often did) speak. These formats were unruly and imperfect.

Ironically, since the late 1990s, although the technologies exist to allow greater consultation and engagement than ever before, a narrower group of decision-makers is setting and controlling the LGBT agenda. So, the 2000 Millennium March was simply declared by the HRC (and was little more than a big street fair for that organization); and the 2009 National Equality March was called and declared by a handful of people, although it was mobilized using the new technologies and brought together more than a hundred thousand people. Decisions to bring major lawsuits that will have serious implications for the future of LGBT rights for all (such as the case being handled by David Boies and Ted Olson) are made by a handful of people—generally upper-middle-class, generally wealthy, and overwhelmingly white, gay male people. Decisions to engage in fundraising alliances with right-wing Republicans are similarly made without much consultation: "It is my money," say the donors. "I'll do what I want."

The politics of access has triumphed over democratic participation in agenda-setting in the LGBT movement. What this means is that people with money and political access have replaced grassroots activists as the key arbiters of which issue is foregrounded and which placed on the backburner, which arguments are made and which downplayed, who makes the case and who is left out of the room and the picture, and what is compromised and what is deemed non-negotiable.

An LGBT Movement for Social and Economic Justice

Columbia University professor Alexander Stille noted the contradiction in the United States between increased equal rights and increased economic inequality: "It's a puzzle: one dispossessed group after another—blacks, women, Hispanics and gays—has been gradually accepted in the United States, granted equal rights and brought into the mainstream. At the same time, in economic terms, the United States has gone from being a comparatively egalitarian society to one of the most unequal democracies in the world." Progress on rights has coincided with the destruction of economic security for the middle class and the consolidation of wealth and power by the most wealthy and powerful.

US social movements have generally pursued claims for equality of opportunity divorced from equality of condition (sometimes called "equality of result"). The existing power structure of neoliberal capitalism readily accommodates demands for equal rights, equal protection, and equal opportunity. But demands for racial equity, economic support for poor and working people, and social justice—all of which require some form of redistribution of power, taxes, assets—are largely ignored or actively undermined. Stille notes a key reason for such resistance: the rich have organized effectively to protect and advance their economic privileges. "One of the groups to become mobilized in response to the protest movements of the 1960s and early 1970s was the rich," Stille writes. "Think tanks dedicated to defending the free-enterprise system—such as the Cato Institute and the Heritage Foundation—were born in this period." So, even as racial barriers in higher education, professional employment, and cultural recognition fall, even though a Black president is elected, the actual economic status of Black America is worse today than it has been in several decades.

It is the same with LGBT equality. LGBT rights are advancing within the context of growing class inequality. The mainstream movement has paid little attention to ensuring that rights can be accessed by all parts of the community and even less attention to policy goals that might secure greater equity for poor LGBT people. The movement puts forward the optimistic message that "it gets better" to young people to offer hope, in a context where the possibility of achieving the "good life" has shrunk for most people.

The system works for some but fails most.

I'd like to conclude with three "shift ideas" that could help the LGBT movement attend more vitally to class-based differences. The first shift is conceptual and involves a change in who is included in the word *we* when it is used to define LGBT community. The second shift is institutional and involves the (heretical) idea of consolidating a wide range of currently separate organizational efforts into a more coherent force for economic justice and political power. The third shift concerns how to change current forms of financing and agenda-setting in the LGBT movement.

Having spent a lifetime pursuing formal legal equality, I clearly agree that we need to win it. And I would argue that we are a lot further from that goal than the self-congratulating tone of today's LGBT movement acknowledges. But it is neither truthful nor historically justified to assert that equality of rights will trickle down to poor queer people. Equal rights once achieved are neither equally accessible nor equally distributed. Without attention to economic justice, we risk abandoning significant segments of LGBT communities that experience profound levels of inequality to the multiple systems of exclusions that they encounter. *We* in LGBT communities must include poor and working-class queer people, and our movement must strongly advocate for them.

Conceptually, the key question for the LGBT movement in 2011 is: What will winning look like? How do we define it? A narrow view of winning frames it as the achievement of equality—defined as the achievement of legal and political non-discrimination in all aspects of life and family recognition. In other words, winning means we have the same rights as straight people. A broader view of winning frames it as equal rights accompanied by the power to enforce and experience them. Both equity and liberty are key elements of justice. Framing our goals under the rubric of liberty, rather than simple civil rights, achieves three objectives: first, such a reframing would reengage the concern with freedom that early LGBT advocates were concerned with, at a time when freedom is being diminished. Second, a focus on liberty would enable our movement to counter the economic rhetoric of the Right, which grants freedom to capital that it denies to workers, consumers, and citizens. Finally, the concept of liberty grapples with the ongoing resistance to definitions of sexual orientation and gender identity that arise out of tradition-bound notions of the gender, sexual, and reproductive order. If the LGBT coalition of movements chooses to answer the question of what winning looks like narrowly, it will limit itself to the same narrow kinds of freedom that the current political order will grant: the freedom to belong to an exhausted and failing set of institutions.

The second shift the LGBT coalition could make to address class is to consolidate the presently fractured infrastructure of progressive queer institutions. We need a new federation that unites groups working for racial, economic, sexual, and gender justice. The various queer groups now working in the arena of social service delivery, criminal law, homelessness, immigrant rights, and racial justice should come together in a new, powerful federated network that works through one institution—a new freedom-focused human rights and social justice organization, committed fully to civil, political, economic, social, and cultural rights and the political power to win these objectives. The NGLTF could offer up its elimination, to be reborn as the umbrella to this new federation, which would be owned and controlled by grassroots groups and individual members. This kind of federation would mean that progressive queers could finally be part of a genuinely democratic, multifaceted organization that would be made up of both organizational and individual members and set its agenda through a more democratic method than the selection of a self-appointed board. The federation would work—through lobbying, education, research, litigation, and grassroots organizing—to advance policies that benefit poor, working-class, middle-class, and progressive people of all kinds, including LGBT folks.

Organizations matter to any movement: they serve as a focal point for policy-oriented action. They provide a voice. Since many of the queer economic and racial justice groups are local, service-focused, or quite small, a seriously organized and funded federation would enable them to have a greater influence on the national movement agenda. Absent such a joining of forces, there will not be a shift in the voice, politics, and aspirations of LGBT political leaders.

Finally, the LGBT progressive movement must find new ways to finance its work. The existing mechanism of reliance on individual wealthy donors and foundations is not sustainable for groups working for economic security and the rights of poor and economically vulnerable populations. Foundations are dominated by the values of upper-middle-class or wealthy people. They can do a lot of good but they also extract a tacit commitment from the groups they fund not to rock the boat. Dependence on philanthropy is the antithesis of progressive politics. It invariably requires conformity to ideas, values, and practices that are in the interest of the wealthy who fund and control philanthropic institutions. It also produces vulnerability, as foundations shift according to changing fashions, changes in their leadership, or the changing interests of their donors.

Instead of relying on major donors, progressive organizations could earn revenue through benefits, social enterprises, and internet-based donations. They would turn to foundations and major donors for capital rather than operating expenses. The HRC has anchored its growth through revenue earned at expensive dinner parties; could low-cost events, held across the country on campuses, during LGBT prides, and in communities finance change? Around the world, development organizations are exploring raising money through socially beneficial businesses; could LGBT groups do something similar? What services that people currently pay for might a progressive entrepreneurial institution provide as a means for earning some of its costs?

Concluding Thoughts

The biggest form of silencing is external: the assumption of heterosexuality that pervades most institutions and experiences, and that negates so many forms of queer being. The queer embrace of the heterosexual norm—and the adoption by LGBT people of its attendant forms of domesticity, family, and sexuality—has privatized many issues that once were part of our public demands upon society. This abandonment of previous critical discourses of sexual liberation—the way the movement, since the mid-1990s, has walked away from representing non-traditional families, and its still-underdeveloped economic and racial justice politics—are examples of what Lisa Duggan has labeled homonormativity and what Jasbir Puar has named homonationalism. Homonormative framing of the LGBT agenda has grown in the movement because of two external conditions—the emergence of the anti-LGBT Right in the late 1970s, and the emergence within the LGBT movement of a queer conservative movement in the early 1990s.

Our responses to the Right's reductionism of LGBT lives have led to our own embrace of reductive logic. The Right says LGBT people want special rights; we counter that we only want equal rights. They say being gay is a choice, and we can be cured; we say we can't help ourselves, we were born this way. They say we are promiscuous and that legislating "families we choose" is dangerous to social life; we say we need marriage so we can be monogamous. They say gay people are powerful and privileged and do not deserve more rights; we counter with a victimization discourse that emphasizes LGBT marginalization and discrimination but minimizes or omits race, class, and gender differences within queer experience.

But the unconscious or conscious promotion by the LGBT movement to hetero-forms of family, or white-privileging forms of community-building, or class-informed notions of the "gay agenda" can also be seen as internally driven and desired. As a movement, we are constituted by our constitutions; we express who we are, and our desires and imagination are grounded in these material experiences of being.

As a white-dominated, couple-based, relationship-seeking, heavily middle- to upper-middle-class-led social movement that seeks affirmation, belonging, and benefits from the existing system, the norm has replaced transformation in our political imaginations.

The irony is that the world to which we seek so desperately to belong is crumbling all around us. It is too hard to explain queer diversity and deviance in a public forum, so we opt to tidy it up and portray ourselves as homogeneous. Yet in that silencing we foreclose society's access to forms of intimacy and community that could offer it sustenance. Queer practice—LGBT life in its widest range—builds curious and sometimes marvelous communities. Our subcultures turn pain into caring; our institutions deliver services, resilience, and humor instead of bitterness and violence; our extended kinship structures deliver emotional and material support, independent of blood ties. Our community is full of exceptional acts of generosity and affiliation with those who are social and political outcasts. Sadly, the LGBT movement tries to restrict these creative forms of expression, to run from the freedom we have had to build unique lives. Instead, we submit ourselves to the confining forms of propriety, adherence to tradition, and legibility that this form of capitalism demands.

I look forward to a political praxis for the queer movement that does not limit itself to a politics of inclusion—which tends to leave the limitations of the status quo in place. I look forward to the second wave of a liberation movement whose dominant symbol is not an equal sign but the greater-than sign.

10

AFTER MARRIAGE = VIRTUAL EQUALITY

These remarks were delivered at the plenary session of the Conference on LGBTQ Politics After Marriage, October 1, 2016, Center for Lesbian and Gay Studies, New York City.

In my book, *Virtual Equality*, I argued that equality could feel like appeasement. Like being bought off by the things you wanted to buy. Like living in a simulation, which feels mighty real inside its confines, but which ends in a return to life unchanged. Like declaring "Victory" and "Mission Accomplished" based on a narrow definition of what winning means.

We are living that appeasement today. Marriage embodies both all that is good and all that is insufficient about equality. Marriage matters—because it did and does deliver meaningful rights, tangible benefits, access, recognition, and social respect for those who participate in the institution. It matters—because the jurisprudence that won us the right to marry expands the Fourteenth Amendment. It concedes that we have liberty, at least a few fundamental rights, and the opportunity to challenge laws based on animus.

Marriage works culturally and legally because it makes us legible to straight people—it turns outlaws into in-laws—and because it helps straight people to be less afraid of queer sexual desire. More of those folks could grudgingly concede our "common humanity," to quote the Massachusetts Supreme Judicial Court's 2003 decision legalizing our marriages in that state.

But marriage fails for the reasons that formal legal equality as an end goal fails: it does not deliver justice, transform family or culture, or expand queer freedom for all. It does not touch, much less end, structural racism; it does not change the enforcement of the gender binary; it does not deliver reproductive justice nor end familial homophobia. It has nothing to offer about ending mass incarceration and the systemic deployment of state violence against Black and brown communities.

The queer movement's focus on marriage had the effect of delaying and slowing its work on critical problems like poverty; transphobia and violence against transgender people, transgender women of color in particular; heterosexism; bias against cis-gender women; divestment in public infrastructure; and investment in wealthy people's wealth.

Marriage is not, and never was, the only, or the most important, or even the most worked-on issue in the LGBT movement. But if you read the new triumphalist accounts of queer success, you would not know this. The narratives that center marriage reduce justice to access, liberation to liberalism, same sex to same old sex. Equality, in these narratives, is little more than a straight people's club to which the queers most willing to conform have gained admission. These new narratives erase or minimize the progressivism of the very queer movements that set the stage for marriage—and that still work, beyond marriage, to win liberation and equity for all parts of queer communities.

Straight culture's supposed newfound embrace of queerness leaves me distrustful and irritated—although sometimes that makes me wonder if I'm simply perverse. I ask myself, "Isn't this what I wanted, and what we worked for?" But there is good reason to distrust.

The Right has not disappeared. It has not stopped trying to contain, control, or convert us. Donald Trump's candidacy for president and the entire Republican Party platform attest to the sexist, racist, and homophobic right wing's power in this country.

Our supposed allies now say, "Isn't the LGBT movement remarkable?" But these same allies who now want to "learn lessons from the LGBT movement on how we won marriage" are doing *nothing* to engage with queer people's lives and movements, or to resist religious-based discrimination against us. Their new compassion reeks of yet another experience of being tokenized in a lifetime of tokenization. When they ask, "What lessons can we learn from that movement that we can apply?," I want to say: "Okay, start by reading the history of colonialism, the genocide of indigenous people, slavery, women as chattel property. Then, live as outsiders to every institution. Live being shunned and beaten and abused—by family, clergy, police, prisons, and everyone else. Try that for about a century. Then go on to dying. By the thousands. No, by the tens of thousands. No, by the hundreds of thousands." Our victory required massive sacrifice and thousands of deaths from shame and stigma, from AIDS, suicide, murder, alcoholism, drug use, and hate violence.

Victory came because we created positive, defiant queer identities—which some continue to mock as a distraction from "real" politics. We built communities and institutions (which continue to be funded at twenty-eight cents for every hundred dollars of funding from US foundations, and with less than 3 percent participation from our own communities). We created community and queer cultures. We laughed, sang, wrote, danced, and created family and sexual communities in defiance and in love.

Finally, I would advise those who ask how we did it: have a lot of people go to law school and start filing suits. Then start wearing suits and buying political favors. Then create that mythic "safe space," so that reactionary people with power can think it's safe to join you.

If you do all of this, then maybe you win.

I am also irritated because so much remains unchanged in our movement. Continued racial silo-ing renders many queer organizations still not fully engaged in the fight to end mass incarceration, police violence, and the misogyny that renders lesbians, bi, queer, and trans women irrelevant to our movement's decision-making.

The bottom line is we can put on the rainbow lip gloss and celebrate Diversity Day at the corporate and university tables, but our victories have been limited: they are still partial, still incomplete. Formal legal equality—which we have not yet won—is necessary, but it is insufficient.

Where I find home and hope, where I live today, is not in the queer movement but in a stateless place where the intersectional has replaced one-dimensional identity politics. This new space of shared analysis and common purpose can be seen in each of the progressive movements that are moving today. So, I respect and take direction from the Movement for Black Lives, a brilliant and deeply thoughtful movement, grounded in Black feminism and inclusive in profound ways. I respect and take direction from the immigrant rights movement, another intersectional and expansive movement in which queer and trans people are leaders. From other movements and organizing by transgender and gender-nonconforming people, and in the transformation of the gender binary that is underway. From the anti-criminalization and prison abolition movements. From the workers' rights Fight for Fifteen movement. From the reproductive justice movement that fights for birth control access and reproductive control, and against the ban on the public funding of abortions. From anti-poverty activism. From the global climate-justice movement, and more.

Marriage is virtual equality. The liberal movement has won mainstreaming for middle-class people, of all colors. But it has not won the same for those queer people whose lives remain constrained by economic inequality, racism, and white supremacy; by a colonialist US foreign policy; and by a brutal economic system that cannot exist without exploitation.

Real social justice, real liberation, and real freedom require structural change, not just integration.

PART 3.   TAKING STOCK

FIGURE 11.1. Urvashi, © Jurek Wajdowicz, 2011.

11

QUEER DREAMS AND NONPROFIT BLUES: THE CONTEXT IN WHICH QUEER NONPROFITS OPERATE

Remarks on nonprofit funding in the queer progressive movement are excerpted here from a 2006 Dan Bradley Award acceptance speech by Urvashi at the Lavender Law Conference and from her opening plenary remarks at a 2013 conference, Queer Dreams and Nonprofit Blues, co-convened by The Engaging Tradition Project at the Center for Gender and Sexuality Law at Columbia University Law School and the Barnard Center for Research on Women. The essay has been updated with more recent references.

[2006]

I work for a national foundation, the Arcus Foundation, that focuses on supporting LGBT human rights, and I think about money a lot. To come from the grassroots and radical margin to inside the establishment has been a strange journey, and it is amazing to me that it revolves so much around money. When I started out, the movement had no money. It was funded out of the pockets of the people who volunteered in it. Institutions were rare, and full-time jobs were a dream. Well, it is indeed true what they say about money—money changes everything. It changes people. It changes their aspirations and possibilities. Sadly, organizations also change themselves for money, and that's problematic. And in many ways, having more resources has changed our movement. Working for gay and lesbian liberation requires that leaders and organizations be brave, always critical and forward-thinking, committed to the fullness of our communities, not the narrowness of our own self-interest, and mindful of co-optation.

In the early years of our modern movement, we were all these things and more—there seemed nothing to lose and a world to gain. But as we institutionalized, as we came under attack from the right wing, as we suffered immeasurable losses due to AIDS and the violent impact of homophobia, the imperative to moderate increased. A more conservative political landscape pressured a once-radical movement to tilt itself right. And underlying it all a clear paradox has emerged: the need for institutionalization, the creation of the very institutions that, I believe, are essential to save our lives, has co-opted and limited our vision and dreams. It has presented a respectable sexuality that may be more acceptable to straight folks (the consumerism of *Queer Eye for the Straight Guy*, the titillation of *The L Word*), but it has not yet created a world that embraces, respects, and celebrates queer sexual orientation or gender variance. We are still stigmatized as sinful and immoral.

Funding and its conditions have a lot to do with the construction of the movement we have today. Institutionalization takes money—big money. Those who run the large organizations are always concerned about the survival of the institutions. The impetus is not necessarily to be brave, to be inclusive, to work on and say things that are often unpopular, but rather to advance goals and ideas that funding entities might support.

The agenda of our movement should not be set by funders, but by the urgent needs of ordinary people who are trying to live and fulfill their lives. It should be set by the artists and the visionaries, the dreamers and not the fundraisers.

[2013]

When I started working in the queer movement in Boston, formally incorporated LGBT organizations were rare. These groups had to fight to get governmental approval. Lambda Legal Defense and Education Fund's founders note that, when it was formed in 1973, Lambda had to become its own first client. A New York judicial panel rejected Lambda's application to be a nonprofit organization because, in their view, Lambda's mission was "neither benevolent nor charitable." Lambda used pro bono lawyers to appeal to New York's highest court, which ultimately allowed Lambda Legal to exist as a nonprofit organization. Almost all the groups I worked with in the late 1970s—*Gay Community News*, Lesbian and Gay Media Advocates, Allston Brighton Green Light Safe-House Project, the Feminist Caucus of the Boston Food Coop—were volunteer groups, organized around feminist goals, values, decision-making processes, and theories of governance and accountability.

According to Funders for LGBT Issues, there were about fifty LGBT organizations in 1969, while today, the formally organized sector of nonprofit organizations dominates large parts of queer work. As we think about how to build our movements, the context in which queer nonprofits operate is important for us to consider.

The conservative opposition to an expanded role for government in addressing poverty and providing for the general good has long been fueled by two things: white resentment at having to address the legacies of slavery and racism, and the anti-Communist, anti-statist ideologies that dominated US domestic and foreign policy for more than fifty years, into the 1990s.

The federal government's role in the provision of supportive services, and its reliance on voluntary associations to do this, first expanded in the aftermath of the Civil War. According to the nonprofit sector historian Peter Dobkin Hall, the period of Reconstruction saw the emergence of new parties, media, and the growth of the voluntary sector. However, this expansion was resisted strongly by political leaders from southern states.

Two other expansions of the federal role in addressing social needs emerged after the Depression through the New Deal and, in the 1960s, in President Johnson's War on Poverty. Under the New Deal, the federal government implemented programs like unemployment insurance, Social Security, and pensions; created a framework for workers' rights and labor laws; and reinstituted, in 1943, a federal income tax, the first since the Civil War. This expansion was vehemently resisted by conservatives and industrial leaders, who feared the expansion of Communism and socialism in the United States. When this framework was expanded again in the 1960s and 1970s, through the implementation of War on Poverty programs like food stamps, the VISTA service program, the US Equal Employment Opportunity Commission, and Head Start, it was resisted again by those who argued that a social safety net would create dependency, which would undermine people's willingness to work and thus undermine free enterprise.

As the government commitments and regulation grew, requiring higher taxes and deficit spending, anti-tax, anti-government, libertarian, and conservative movements began to organize more actively. Their intellectual leaders—like Lewis Powell, William Simon, and the Heritage Foundation— articulated a political and economic ideology of small government, less regulation, a big defense sector, and unfettered expansion for corporations. Their strategists forged alliances across previously isolated corners of the Right and connected economic conservatives with religious or cultural conservatives, who were worried about the demand for racial equity and redistribution, about gay rights, and about the impact of new social movements that were changing the power women had in society.

Ronald Reagan's presidency gave power to these reactionaries. His mission was to dismantle the so-called welfare state—as it had come to be known in the 1960s and 1970s—and to install the neoliberal state, built upon deregulation, free trade, less taxation for corporations, privatization, devolution of services, and aggressive use of monetary and trade policy to expand the reach of markets. Aided by technological shifts, the US economy moved away from the production of goods to the production of technology and the outsourcing of services. Presidents Bill Clinton and George W. Bush continued the work that Reagan began—cutting government social service programs and privatizing them through contracting and outsourcing, expanding criminalization and surveillance, and increasing the military and police powers of the state.

The Tea Party, a movement hatched in the corporate suites of the Koch brothers–funded think tanks and strategy firms, must be seen as just the latest manifestation of a carefully executed strategy for social dominance mapped out by right-wing funders and activists, and achieved through the systematic construction of a legal, political, intellectual, grassroots media and philanthropic infrastructure that is aimed at keeping social control for its owners. The results have been phenomenal: conservatives helped elect presidents in 1980, 1984, 1988, and 2000; repeatedly won conservative majorities in Congress, in 1994, 2002, 2004, 2006, 2008, and 2012; and won major gains in mayoral, gubernatorial, and state legislative elections.

Amid all this change, the nonprofit sector has grown dramatically, serving as what gender studies scholar Miranda Joseph has called a *metonym*—a substituted concept—for the idea of community, at the very instant that such community was being destroyed by neoliberal economic policies. The vast majority of current nonprofits were formed after 1950; most global nongovernmental organizations are about forty-five years old. As government funding for poverty alleviation, housing, social services, health, and other social systems grew, nonprofits became the means through which many of these programs were carried out. A symbiotic relationship came into being among nonprofits, government funders, and corporate and private philanthropic funders, which began to change in the 1980s and 1990s, with the devolution and privatization of government programs.

According to a report by the Urban Institute, in 2016, there were 1.54 million nonprofit organizations registered with the IRS; they contributed 5.6 percent to the US gross domestic product. Most of these nonprofits are small and receive about a third of their funding from the government and two-thirds from private sources. Nonprofits are a huge part of the workforce. In

2017, 25.1 percent of US adults volunteered, contributing an estimated 8.8 billion hours, valued at nearly $200 billion.

Neoliberal policies have had a paradoxical effect: they reduced the funding available for social services, but they increased demand for services through increased unemployment, dislocation, inequality, poverty, and the abandonment of people who had previously been supported by a social safety net (such as those with mental illness).

For me, the key issue facing all movements working under neoliberalism is how we are going to overturn these policies—it is a political question. Specifically, as we work to address the distribution of resources to our communities and improve their lived experience, there are five challenges that LGBT activists face.

1. Government at every level has less money and is often running at a deficit

At the very instant that the movement seeks to support the lives of queer seniors, queer youth, and our homeless; to de-incarcerate people, to decriminalize, to invest in workforce and employment—there is less money to go around.

We came to the funding scene very late as a community. We had no one but each other for support until the 1980s, when we started to see government funds for HIV/AIDS-related organizations. Today, funding for LGBT organizations—from both private and public sources—remains very small. For example, the Foundation Center estimates that, as of 2011, there were 81,777 private foundations, which gave away more than $49 billion. That same year, only 383 of those foundations gave funds to LGBT groups, a total of $123 million, which comprises 0.26 percent of all foundation giving. A recent report based on a comprehensive database of LGBTQ funders in the public sector notes that LGBTQ organizations received approximately $560 million in philanthropic support in 2019, which was 0.13 percent of overall charitable giving. Civil rights and advocacy nonprofit organizations received the largest portion of this philanthropic support, and transgender-specific organizations experienced the fastest growth in philanthropic support for LGBTQ nonprofits from 2015 to 2019.

2. The neoliberal mantra of "reinventing government" turned into a massive outsourcing of government services to private, often corporate, hands

As William Ryan reported in his groundbreaking 1999 article, "The New Landscape for Nonprofits," Lockheed Martin and other major contractors have developed huge divisions just to administer welfare programs for counties and states.

Michael Edwards, a researcher with the Engaging Tradition Project at the Center for Gender and Sexuality Law at Columbia University, noted in his book *Just Another Emperor: The Myths and Realities of Philanthrocapitalism* that the turn to business to do what nonprofits have done is problematic because the values of each sector are very different. He points to worrisome trends in the nonprofit sector, such as competition and financial incentives diluting "other-directed behavior," an emphasis on service provision over reform, and a loss of independence.

3. Our communities are not mobilized

A majority of the queer community is not engaged in the movement, is not mobilized politically, and is not giving. Based on data from memberships and donors to the forty national LGBT organizations, the Williams Institute estimates that there are 8.4 million LGBT people in the United States; the Movement Advancement Project (MAP) estimates that fewer than 4 percent of LGBT people actually support queer organizations. This is a challenge that many groups are addressing—through organizing and membership-based structures that foster the leadership of people in our communities and seek to give control over the decisions made by organizations to those they claim to serve.

4. The infrastructure that we have operates in undemocratic and troubling ways

Queer nonprofits are in an especially peculiar position: their infrastructures are so new, they have often turned to the professional expertise and experience of nonprofit sector consultants—but these consultants do not necessarily have a social justice vision. Indeed, the majority of LGBT nonprofits do not have a social justice mission, much less an economic analysis that might lead them to fight the Tea Party mindset.

5. Queer nonprofits must act more queerly

They must operate less like conventional corporations and more like transformation-oriented institutions. This means that they operate internally and externally with values grounded in equity and social justice; that they develop methods to increase participation, internal democracy, and greater accountability to the people the institutions purport to serve; that they pay attention to issues of workplace equity, fair pay for all, and work-life balance. Gay and lesbian philanthropy must begin to fund systemic transformation, not just piecemeal policy change to achieve nondiscrimination and equal access.

12

HOMO/MENTUM OF THE "STATUS QUEER": A CRITICAL LOOK AT THE LGBT MOVEMENT

This is a condensed version of an invited talk delivered at the Center for the Study of Women, Gender and Sexuality's Gray/Wawro Lecture Series, Rice University, February 5, 2015.

These days, I find myself in three kinds of conversations about the LGBT movement. The first is an astonished, pleased excitement at the progress we've made on marriage equality. This conversation is initiated by all sorts of people, LGBT and non-gay, family members, and allies, who marvel that the dominoes of discrimination seem to be toppling. Since the 2013 Supreme Court *Windsor* decision, every day seems to bring more good news. We smile, shake our heads incredulously and say, "Isn't it amazing, can you believe it?"

The second conversation takes place with donors, who are thrilled because, as one said to me, "When we get marriage equality, we will be pretty much done." His comment expresses a pervasive fallacy among both supporters and opponents of gay rights: that marriage is the turning point, after which all other rights will simply be undeniable, if not fully realized.

The third conversation occurs among activists, especially those working at the local level in the Midwest, Southwest, or South, and among those working with queer people of color or with social service organizations dealing with youth homelessness or bullying. In these conversations, optimism is tinged with worry at the precarious position LGBT people still occupy.

Each of these conversations exposes the opportunities and pitfalls facing the LGBT movement.

The fight for LGBT rights and liberation is far from over and it is intimately tied to a larger power struggle underway in this country and around the world. Its success requires the commitment of new generations and old. Whether the LGBT movement can secure a future free from violence, persecution, and discrimination for LGBT and queer people in the United States and around the world depends entirely on the contours of the movement we create over the next ten years.

The questions facing the LGBT movement today are not just about whether marriage or nondiscrimination laws, rights or justice, assimilation or transformation should be its goals. The questions that confront the LGBT movement today are about our understandings of community and power: For whom and against what are we fighting?

As someone who has worked in the LGBT movement for over three decades, this moment of advance feels like a miracle. Homo/momentum is undeniable. Its parameters can be sketched across five dimensions: existential, legal, cultural, religious, and political. A review of each of these dimensions illustrates the progress and peril facing the "status queer."

Existential

Queerness required consciousness to come into being. Bayard Rustin identified this aspect of the movement in a brilliant talk in 1986, "From Montgomery to Stonewall." He noted,

> There are [several] burdens which gays, along with every despised group, whether it is blacks following slavery and reconstruction, or Jews fearful of Germany, must address. The first is to recognize that one must overcome fear. The second is overcoming self-hate. The third is overcoming self-denial. The fourth burden is more political. It is to recognize that ... our job is not to get those people who dislike us to love us ... [but rather] ... to control the extent to which people can publicly manifest antigay sentiment.

Before they could transform society, queer people had to develop acceptance and self-esteem to counter the shame and stigma associated with being gay. This cultural stigmatization has not disappeared. One sees its impact in the high levels of suicide among queer youth—especially transgender youth. Indeed, a significant reason why the LGBT movement remains mobilized and active is that queer people continue to experience stigmatization, family rejection, religious intolerance, bigotry, and internalized shame.

Since the 1950s, LGBT activism has organized around three stigmatizing arguments: that queer people are sick, that they are criminal, and that they are immoral. Each argument operates against LGBT people to this day. Against each argument the movement has deployed the tactics of education, protest, litigation, research, advocacy, support, and community building.

In 1973, the US LGBT movement focused on scientific ignorance and organized to change the American Psychiatric Association's century-old characterization of homosexuality as a mental illness. Yet ideas about homosexuality as mental illness and gender identity variance as a medical disorder persist. In 2014, a global panel of mental health experts recommended to the World Health Organization that it remove five homosexuality-related classifications that still existed in the International Classification of Diseases.

The elimination of state-sanctioned anti-LGBT codes has been extremely recent in the United States, with laws criminalizing same-sex sexual behavior held unconstitutional only in 2003 and the ban on military service for gay men and lesbians eliminated only in September of 2011. It is still not eliminated for trans people. Criminal laws remain in place in seventy-eight countries and new laws continue to be enacted every year. Over-policing and harassment, over-incarceration, and abusive prosecutions continue, against trans and queer people of color in particular.

Questions about the sinfulness and immorality of homosexuality persist and are vigorously debated. Despite the efforts of an active faith-based movement, queer being is still denigrated as inherently sinful, wrong, and immoral. The airwaves in every state are filled with people condemning LGBT people and blaming them for every horrible problem in this country. This discourse defines LGBT people as dangerous and seeks to ostracize them from legal and cultural protection. Transgender people encounter even more negative attitudes than other queer people.

In short, despite coming out and the changes it has brought, the existential dimension of queerness remains contested on many levels.

Legal and Legislative

A second dimension through which change can be tracked is through laws, policies, and court decisions. The legal focus of the LGBT movement has yielded both legal and political victories. President Obama signed an executive order in 2014 that bans discrimination in federal contracts and affects millions of people; key aspects of the Federal Defense of Marriage Act were struck down by the Supreme Court; the Affordable Care Act includes provisions covering sexual orientation and gender identity; every federal agency is working to include LGBT people in its mission; and twenty-one states have nondiscrimination protections, eighteen of which include trans people.

Yet legal and legislative progress toward LGBT equality is neither comprehensive nor unidirectional. Many states have few legal protections. Ironically, fifteen of the states that recognize same-sex marriage have no other LGBT rights protections. There still is no federal law banning employment discrimination; only twenty-one states allow LGBT people to adopt; more than half the states lack any bullying protections; and despite the high incidence of documented violence against transgender people, only fifteen states have hate-crime laws that include gender identity (thirty have laws that include sexual orientation).

Clearly, legal equality remains far from achieved, and the benefits of the nondiscrimination laws that we do have are not accessible to all members of queer communities.

Cultural

To tackle prejudice, the LGBT movement has engaged in dialogue and representation that have led to changed cultural perceptions and increased visibility.

Coming out is the most successful tool we have to combat anti-gay sentiment. When people know someone who is lesbian or gay, they tend to have more positive attitudes toward us and our rights. (Fewer people are aware of knowing trans people than other queer people.) Yet public opinion gains should not obscure the fact that resistance is still present. Many people oppose consenting relations between same-sex adults and LGBT people continue to encounter high levels of violence.

The struggle to change cultural perceptions of what *same-sex love* and *gender* mean is far from over.

Religious

Another driver of homo/momentum stems from change in the attitudes of religious denominations. Every legal rights gain made by the LGBT movement has been helped by the support and mobilization of people of faith. This has been the result of massive organizing for decades by LGBT and allied people of faith. The Metropolitan Community Church, a denomination founded by LGBT people, has been a leader in this organizing.

Faith-based allies contest the denigration of homosexuality and gender variance as sinful, immoral, and unnatural, and they have engaged doctrine and tradition. As a result of this organizing, and of the larger cultural work queer people have been doing, there has been a sharp shift in attitudes about LGBT issues among members of just about every religious tradition. The pursuit of reform has led to huge changes in Christian and Jewish denominational policies toward LGBT people within Episcopal, Methodist, Unitarian Universalist, Presbyterian, Lutheran, Reform and Conservative Judaism, and even within some Catholic churches.

Today, though, all of this progress is threatened by a creative new argument by the religious Right that pits the individual exercise of religion against civil rights laws. This tactic is part of culture war declared by Pat Buchanan, in his 1992 speech to the Republican national convention, when he said, "There is a religious war going on in our country for the soul of America. It is a cultural war, as critical to the kind of nation we will one day be as was the Cold War itself."

We cannot tiptoe around this fact: the "culture war" is a fight for cultural and political control, and secular values are losing.

The First Amendment protects the exercise of religion free from government restraint and regulation. It also forbids the establishment of a particular religion by the government. Few people contest the fact that members of churches, synagogues, mosques, and religions of all kinds should have freedom to practice their faith. The First Amendment goes so far as to imply that religious institutions may even be exempt from civil rights laws, if these laws violate their faith traditions. But what has happened in recent decades is that the free exercise right is now being claimed (under the rubric of so-called "religious liberty") by non-religious institutions: by business owners and other individuals who argue they should be able to opt out of observing laws with which they disagree. In its 2014 decision in *Burwell v. Hobby Lobby Stores*, the Supreme Court held that the owners of a corporation could opt out of the Affordable Care Act's requirement to cover contraception as part of the insurance they provide their employees because of their religious beliefs. This holding, that civil rights laws must yield to religious traditions, moves society dangerously close to privileging a particular religion and recognizing the precepts of that religious tradition as law. It opens a path toward the establishment of a state-sanctioned religion.

The fight for secular, nonreligious space is a global one, and the LGBT and feminist movements are on the front lines.

Political

Globally, support for sexual orientation and gender identity has advanced through queer advocacy within the human rights framework. These breakthroughs have happened only within the past decade. Of course, backsliding is also underway in many countries that have legalized discrimination through both court decisions, as in India, and legislation, as in Russia, Nigeria, and Uganda.

In the United States, the LGBT movement has achieved power by organizing political money. Under the leadership of the Gill Action Fund, the LGBT movement has organized political giving in state elections. It has educated donors to focus their giving in states that are in play legislatively or in court cases.

Political power ebbs and flows. It cannot be taken for granted.

The Trouble with Equal

In my book *Virtual Equality*, I argued that if the LGBT movement ignored the broader dynamics of racism, economic exploitation, gender inequity, and cultural freedom, it would achieve only a partial, conditional, simulacrum of equal rights, a situation that I called *virtual equality*. Some parts of the LGBT community would enjoy legal rights and formal equality, but the institutions that repress, denigrate, and immobilize sexual and gender minorities would not be transformed.

A critical part of the queer work ahead involves enabling all parts of our communities to experience freedom, opportunity, and dignity. Right now, significant parts of the queer community experience economic hardship, over-policing, and gender-based bias.

An LGBT equality politics that ignores the economic context is, in the end, a politics of exclusion. Redistribution is, in fact, contained in every LGBT policy aspiration. Social services are urgently needed for every LGBT population that is not wealthy, from elders, to parents, to youth, to college students, to anyone accessing social service programs like drug and alcohol treatment, mental health counseling, and HIV services. Yet queer leadership is silent and absent on the tax and fiscal debates in Washington, DC, and in most state legislatures—despite the fact that the destruction of the safety net, defunding, and ever-growing privatization will have severe consequences for LGBT folks. Queer leadership has not yet used its political clout to fight back against the right wing's growth, concerned as it is with reaching across the aisle for legislative compromises.

Some ask, "What about the political diversity of LGBT people?" The LGBT movement cannot be about much more than formal equality, they argue, because it would not represent conservative people. Well, it is true that not all queers are progressive, and that anywhere from 25 to 33 percent of our vote has gone to Republican candidates in national elections over the past twenty years. But let us admit a truth: beyond a shared rights agenda, there is no political unity between progressives and conservatives in the LGBT community. LGBT conservatives may work for the same basic rights as LGBT progressives, but they stand for a very different social, economic, and political order. We are not in the same movement with each other. Rather, we are in an effective and strong coalition with each other to win equal rights.

There is also a racial and gender assumption within the mainstream LGBT movement that needs to be acknowledged and challenged. The definition of *gay, lesbian, bisexual,* or *transgender* that the mainstream LGBT movement operates from, the definition of whom it represents that it holds in its mind when it speaks of the community, is unconsciously (and at times consciously) limited to white LGBT people.

Donors often see LGBT people of color as a subset—although, of course, white LGBT people are a subset too. If funding were actually aimed at insuring queer survival, in distributing life chances and opportunity to all parts of the LGBT community, then funding people of color or poor communities would not be seen as a sideshow.

The biggest challenge the LGBT movement faces in becoming a racial justice movement of queers is its narrow understanding of who is the subject of LGBT rights.

It's time to stop making excuses and incorporate racial justice as our priority. A social justice framework that explicitly includes a commitment to racial justice is a better resource for LGBT movement organizations than a neoliberal politics of equal rights that pretends color and class and gender and other human difference somehow do not affect one's life chances as long as "everyone starts at the same line."

An LGBT movement thinking beyond marriage and toward social justice would differ from the current version. First, it would focus on inequality more than it focuses on equality. Second, its infrastructure would be decentralized and stronger in the states than at the national level, and its organizations would not just be LGBT-centered but would instead be progressive with an LGBT focus. Third, it would be oriented toward building governing power for progressive values. And fourth, it would retain a central focus on the forces on the right—religious, economic, political, and cultural—that stand for authoritarianism, fundamentalism, and political and social repression.

In the first of the "Calamus" poems in *Leaves of Grass*, the nineteenth-century American poet of the democratic imagination, Walt Whitman writes,

In paths untrodden,
In the growth by margins of pond-waters,
Escaped from the life that exhibits itself,
From all the standards hitherto publish'd—from the
pleasures, profits, conformities,
Which too long I was offering to feed my Soul;
Clear to me, now, standards not yet publish'd—clear
to me that my Soul,
That the Soul of the man I speak for, feeds, rejoices
in comrades;
Here, by myself, away from the clank of the world,
Tallying and talk'd to here by tongues aromatic,
No longer abash'd—for in this secluded spot I can
respond as I would not dare elsewhere,
Strong upon me the life that does not exhibit itself,
yet contains all the rest . . .

Using the metaphor of the calamus plant, which grows in wetlands and resembles human genitals, Whitman identifies experiences, that queer activists of each era have lived: we walk "paths untrodden," often in the "growth by the margins" of society. We are nonconformers to "the life that exhibits its self" with all its "standards hitherto publish'd," and its "pleasures, profits, [and] conformities." We follow no maps, invent the language we need, and rejoice in each other despite repression, hostile laws, and violent resistance. To refuse the compulsory heterosexuality into which we were channeled, to begin to create feminist and openly lesbian, gay, bi, and transgender lives was an act of pure invention: "Strong upon me the life that does not exhibit itself, yet/contains all the rest."

The LGBT movement needs this visionary and brave spirit today. The work ahead to achieve freedom and justice for all requires us to confront inequality, racism, and white supremacy in all its institutional manifestations in policing, criminal justice policy, employment, housing, and health. It requires us to challenge the gender binary and to resume the fight for sexual freedom and sexual health, against the assertions of government and organized religion. This is a full and urgent agenda for the future, with a place in it for everyone who cares about the achievement of human rights and justice.

I look forward to walking these untrodden paths with you.

13

IRRESISTIBLE REVOLUTION: UNDERSTANDING THE LGBT MOVEMENT

This is a condensed, edited version of an invited address given at the Global Women's Conference, Middle State Tennessee University, March 23, 2017.

Thirty years ago in this state, adults were being charged and prosecuted under the so-called "sodomy laws," which criminalized their private consensual sexual conduct. Ironically, many of the people who today rail against government intervention and claim to be for smaller government led the charge for this gross expansion of government power.

Much has changed since then. Those laws were held unconstitutional by the US Supreme Court in 2003. Since then, twenty-nine states have passed some form of nondiscrimination laws protecting people from being fired or mistreated simply because of their sexual orientation and gender identity. And marriage equality is now guaranteed to everyone, no matter where they live. There is no denying it. The LGBT movement is a revolution that has happened in our lifetimes.

In my remarks today I want to make three points about this revolution and the threats it faces: First, the LGBT revolution is real. It is one of many revolutions that are underway today. Second, the LGBT revolution is not irresistible. It has enemies. And third, the LGBT revolution is far from over. Its future depends entirely on ordinary people like you and me.

Think about it: in a world built on binary codes of zeros and ones, binaries are falling apart. They do not capture the complexity of who we are and what we believe—much less what we can imagine. The old binaries—male/female, gay/straight, immigrant/national, left/right, truth/lies, us/them, black/white—are all being questioned and challenged.

Yet the fantasy of restoring the old binary systems and hierarchies is what Donald Trump's Republicans promise America. There is a through line from Barry Goldwater, to Richard Nixon, to Ronald Reagan to George H. W. Bush, to George W. Bush, and now to Donald Trump. These leaders all promised the restoration of power to an economic, racial, and gender elite. We are in a definite counterrevolutionary moment—against civil rights for African Americans, against the idea of global peace and cooperation, against the women's movement, against the LGBT movement, and against religious pluralism.

How did we get to this moment of revolution and of backlash? It was brought about by economic policies that made rich people richer and middle-class people more vulnerable. These economic policies came about for several reasons, including advances in technology and global trade deals that make it easier for multinational corporations to take their production and manufacturing overseas and hide their profits, tax-free, in offshore accounts. These economic policies cut domestic government spending, ruining public education systems, medical and mental health care delivery systems, and roads and infrastructure. The United States began to look in places like a "third-world" country, because economic elites put into place the same neoliberal policies that destroyed "third-world" countries: so-called "structural adjustments." Such policies make it easy for banks and financiers and rich people like Trump to make billions through shady financial deals, while making it impossible for a truck driver to buy a good home and take care of their family.

Revolutions occur because people resist conditions they find oppressive. What the establishment Democrats and Republicans both failed to see—and what Donald Trump and Bernie Sanders actually did see—is how deep people's anger was at the economic destruction of our country's middle class. The policies of globalization begun by previous presidents, starting with Ronald Reagan, radicalized sixty million people in America to vote for Trump, who promised to fight against these changes.

It did not matter that he had no plan. That he is corrupt. That he lies. That he is the symbol and beneficiary of an oppressive economic system. Despite having serious misgivings about his character, people still voted for him.

Why? Because they wanted a change. One of the many tragedies of President Trump's election is that about eighty thousand more people hungry for change chose him over Hillary Clinton—and in doing so, they chose someone who will actually make the lives of white and Black and brown working- and middle-class people unbearably worse.

But economic abandonment is not the only story that we must understand to explain this revolutionary moment and how to respond to it. We must also consider non-economic forces—especially the mobilization of white racism and the technological revolution that has changed how we learn and how we experience community and identity.

The growth of political organizing by the so-called "evangelical Christian Right" is often credited to their concern about issues like abortion, homosexuality, and prayer in schools. Those certainly get a lot of air time. But the deeper truth, underscored by Donald Trump's election, is that those issues are less important to evangelical voters than racial animosity and fear.

The roots of evangelical voter mobilization lie in the mobilization of racial animosity. A 2017 article in the *New Republic* traces the mobilization of the evangelical right to the Supreme Court's 1976 decision rescinding the tax-exempt status of Bob Jones University. Founded in 1927, Bob Jones University refused to admit Black students until 1975, just before a lawsuit was filed against it, and it continued to ban interracial dating and marriage between Black and white students until 2000. The decision energized a generation of Christian activists to campaign against the federal government's enforcement of civil rights laws on religious schools like Bob Jones.

Throughout the history of the modern right wing, you can find strong evidence of how racial fears and animosities were fueled and harnessed by political and legal activists to build electoral wins.

In his 2016 book, *A Black Man in the White House*, Cornell Belcher, a brilliant pollster and political campaigner who worked on Barack Obama's 2008 presidential campaign, looked at the role of racism in modern American politics, from the "dog whistle" of the Goldwater/Nixon Southern Strategy (in which they covertly appealed to southern Democratic voters' racism to win them over to the Republican Party), to Donald Trump's clear racism. Belcher argues that white voters' resentment and negative racial attitudes toward Black people affected their voting behavior more than other factors, for many election cycles. He points out that Black voters were the key reason both Bill Clinton and Barack Obama won, and they have become the new base of power for the Democratic Party. This alienated white voters even further from the Democratic Party.

James Baldwin wrote,

> Although . . . Americans are certainly capable of precipitating Arma-
> geddon, *their most desperate desire is to make time stand still.* If time
> stands still, it can neither judge or accuse nor exact payment, and in-
> deed this is precisely the bargain the black presence was expected to
> strike in the white Republic. It is why the black face had always to be a
> happy face.

Donald Trump promises to make time stand still—to assert nationalism in an era
of global connectivity and mobility, to make it acceptable to be a male chauvin-
ist pig and roll back women's equality, to win by fomenting racial divisions and
putting white supremacists in the White House, to make America white "again"
(even though it never was), to fight for biology as destiny in an era in which gender has been shown to be much deeper and more complicated than anatomy.

The challenge of the moment is not confined to the national level. Legislatures in thirty-three states are governed by Republican governors, and sixty-
nine out of ninety-nine state legislative houses are controlled by Republicans.
This would not at all be a problem if these leaders actually listened to their
constituents and were accountable. But the leaders are bought and sold and
owned not by the people who vote them into office, but by the people who
pay them to run. And the conservative billionaires who fund their campaigns
are only interested in one goal: to get even richer. There is no holier purpose.
They don't care if pollution makes water undrinkable—they want deregulation
so they don't have to pay for clean water. They want no limits on coal digging
not because they care about coal miners but because coal mining will make
them richer in the short run. The leaders of the Republican Party are all about
the ruling class. But ordinary folks vote for them, against their own interests.

Another key aspect of the story of the past two decades is technological
transformation. It is the story of the mobile phone, of iTunes, of Google, and
of Facebook, of the decentralized dissemination of information, and of the
primacy of social media as the most trusted form of community and knowledge sharing.

Technology has contributed to this revolutionary moment in good and
bad ways. The National Women's March was organized online. Millions participated across the country. Breitbart spews lies and deliberate misinformation every day, yet is read by millions. Donald Trump uses Twitter like a
personal press release factory, brilliantly shifting the focus away from inves-
tigations that get too close to his sleazy behavior by saying something outra-
geous that changes the subject. It's right out of the Goebbels playbook.

Today we read blog posts by individuals we do not know, working for who knows whom (usually just for themselves, sometimes apparently for Russian intelligence agencies). We click on websites that look real but might be fake. We send our private information to hundreds of places each month, signing up for things, ordering stuff on the internet, and sharing documents and information. At the same time, we read traditional journalism less and less, watch the news on TV less and less (except for excerpts of funny bits from late night comedy shows), and pay attention less and less to any information that does not confirm what we already know—or think we know. Is it any wonder that we have become a nation of distrustful and ignorant people who at the same time believe we know it all?

So where does the LGBT movement find itself in this revolutionary moment? How does a movement for liberty and justice respond in a moment where the people are misinformed, lied to on a daily basis, and pitted against each other, where freedom of speech and dissent is attacked by a weak, thin-skinned, dish-it-out-but-can't-take-it Tweeter in Chief?

To understand the LGBT movement today, we have to consider its four biggest challenges. The first challenge is the reality of pervasive, legal discrimination. The second is the cultural battle for acceptance, which is far from won. The third is how to address economic and racial inequalities in our society and within LGBT communities—made worse by the Trump administration's policies of cutting health and social service programs. The final challenge is political: How do we muster the power to defeat the right wing culturally and politically?

Pervasive Legal Discrimination

LGBT people find ourselves fighting against the same enemies we have faced for centuries: sexual prejudice and gender binaries; overt legal discrimination in many aspects of our lives; violence against all women, but especially transgender and cisgender women of color; fundamentalist religious movements; and opportunistic political and religious demagogues.

The gigantic and dramatic achievement of marriage equality—something few people thought could be won even ten years ago—masks a deeper truth: discrimination against LGBT people in most aspects of our lives is still legal in most parts of this country. LGBT people can lose their jobs, be denied promotion, be banned from housing and access to public accommodations like bathrooms, and be refused to be served by public officials whose salaries we pay. They can be refused access to credit or to a safe and secure education, and can be denied the right to form their own families, to adopt, and to foster parent. Since the 2015 Supreme Court marriage decision, innumerable state anti-LGBT bills have been introduced.

This massive legal discrimination is being challenged in lawsuits, legislatures, and the court of public opinion. But turning it around will require the LGBT movement to have much more support from our friends, families, faith communities, and workplaces than we currently have: *Equality is not guaranteed just because the movement won marriage!*

Cultural Acceptance

The second reality confronting the LGBT movement today is that our fight for cultural acceptance is not won. Since its birth and even now, the LGBT movement has faced three arguments against homosexuality and gender variance: that we are sick, that we are criminal, and that we are immoral and sinful.

To counter these arguments, the LGBT movement carried out what Michel Foucault describes as an "insurrection of subjugated knowledges." Coming out, going public with something you were told should be kept shameful and private, was such an insurrection. It was about self-determination and the production of new forms of knowledge about LGBT lives. It was the most successful (if personally painful) strategy we deployed. James Baldwin wrote, "[A label] may seem to define you for others, but it does not have the power to define you to yourself."

As LGBT people came out about their sexual orientation and, more recently, about their gender identities, to their loved ones and coworkers, these people realized we were not aliens, not Other, but simply their siblings, their children, and their friends. We began to be seen as part of the diversity that constitutes *human* being.

Yet even though many people know us, deep cultural stigmatization continues. Indeed, a big reason why the LGBT movement remains mobilized and active is that LGBT people continue to experience stigmatization, family rejection, religious intolerance, government bigotry, and internalized shame. Just look at the bitter battles about the use of bathrooms and you can understand that crazy attitudes, stigma, and fear of homosexuality and of transgender people have not gone away. You can see the impact of anti-LGBT stigma, disastrously, in the high levels of suicide among queer youth—especially transgender youth.

Questions about the sinfulness and immorality of homosexuality have not gone away. While a pro-LGBT faith movement has grown and remains very strong, anti-LGBT religious movements continue to spread defamation about the intrinsic moral character of LGBT people, and about our acceptance in the eyes of whatever power we understand to be God.

Economic and Racial Inequality

Another complication for the LGBT movement today is the challenge of its own internal diversity. The movement is diverse by income, age, race, and geography. It encompasses people of all physical abilities, from all backgrounds and cultures. Not all LGBT people are white and middle-class, no matter what queer conservatives like Peter Thiel or a few television sitcoms with lesbian and gay characters might suggest.

The truth is that economic hardship and racial inequalities affect the lives of millions of LGBT people.

As a justice-seeking movement, the LGBT movement must start to focus on ensuring the survival not only of all members of our community but also of everyone in our society. To do so requires the movement to work on issues of poverty, violence, mass incarceration, over-criminalization, deportations and other harmful immigration policies, and public education.

The agenda and goals of LGBT organizations must include:

· More social services for poor people, and fewer tax breaks for the wealthy.

· Living wages for all working people. LGBT organizations must stand with unions as they work to expand workplace benefits like paid sick leave and childcare.

· Support for transgender women, especially trans women of color, and resistance against the violence, employment bias, public accommodation bias, and other problems they face.

· Absolute defense of the personhood of women, so we have the right to control our own bodies from levels of misogyny, violence, and legislative discrimination that are so high that sometimes it feels as if feminism never happened.

Political Power and Challenges

At the very moment that federal structure for a social safety net is under attack, LGBT people need it most. The Trump administration has created corporate tax cuts and breaks that it pays for by gutting social services.

The LGBT movement needs to fight these kinds of cuts to poverty programs and social services, but we do not have the power to fight these battles on our own. The only way the movement can get stronger is to join forces with others who share our vision and values—not just our identities. The remarkable progress on LGBT rights was won by a rather quirky and small movement. In 1969, there were perhaps fifty LGBT organizations in the country. Today there are hundreds more, but they still make up a tiny fraction of the millions of nonprofit organizations that exist, and the LGBT infrastructure is particularly weak at the state level. (Most data show that few LGBT people actually join or give money to queer organizations. Of the nearly ten million LGBT people estimated to be part of the US adult population, the Movement Advancement Project estimates that fewer than 4 percent of LGBT people give to the movement's organizations—yet the movement is entirely funded by these contributions; it is rarely supported by foundations or mainstream donors.)

To achieve and sustain legal and cultural change, the LGBT movement has to join forces politically with many other kinds of people to win political power. The movement created LGBT-specific social service organizations to take care of its own people because no one else was doing it. That is why HIV-services organizations came into being: *no one else* would take care of people with HIV and AIDS. Our LGBT community centers, health clinics, youth groups, suicide hotlines, legal and criminal justice organizations, and groups that advocate for homeless and transgender people exist for this same reason. These groups address the needs and lived realities of LGBT people who are not wealthy or mainstream.

But a political infrastructure that is LGBT-specific is not adequate to the task at hand. The fifty-state infrastructure needed to defeat right-wing ideas politically and culturally must be intersectional; it will need to bridge and bring together LGBT people, women, African Americans, Latinx folks, Asian and Pacific Islanders, Native Americans, immigrants, environmental advocates, workers and labor unions, and anyone else that feels this country is on the wrong track. We need a united political movement that is far bigger, more powerful, and more progressive than the traditional Democratic Party.

In my experience, it may be individual crises and desperation that fuel revolutionary change, but it is political parties, civil society, and social movements that give individual desperation some structure, goals, and leadership. Right now, progressive people do not have a party. The Democratic National Committee is a driverless car. And the Republican Party is closed to LGBT people. I don't care how many times people tell me about Republican politicians with gay or lesbian kids! Read the laws they are passing. Read their lips. They are antigay bigots.

What makes revolutions attractive—even irresistible—and what makes them complicated is that they are about power. LGBT people and our allies need to win governing power at the local, state, and national levels. Progressives are ambivalent about power; we're mealymouthed when we have it and we're afraid to use it. Yet this is what politics, law, and social change are all about. We've got to get over it. And we can no longer stand by and not vote. In the post-Trump era, we are in the streets, but we are still not voting. We have to get serious about what we believe!

The largest challenge the LGBT movement faces is the existence of an organized, anti-LGBT right wing that gained enormous support and prominence under the Trump administration. Donald Trump in his first sixty days reversed many of the gains made on LGBT rights over the past twenty years. He ran on the most antigay platform we have ever seen. Nearly every one of his cabinet members is on the record as hostile to LGBT equality and there are legions of additional zealots coming into federal government with two missions only: to destroy civil rights gains and to loot the government for their corporate masters.

Trump and his team have promised to block civil rights laws, roll back marriage equality, expand exemptions to laws granting LGBT people equal rights, reverse laws protecting transgender students from bullying, and issue executive orders that ban Muslims from entering the United States. They have launched pogroms against legal immigrants in this country that threaten millions of law-abiding permanent residents and citizens—like me!—and reversed policies of shelter for asylum seekers and refugees fleeing persecution. Assisted by the cowardly Republican puppets in Congress, Trump is not only anti-LGBT; he is the most racially divisive president of the past fifty years and the most openly sexist we have seen in my lifetime.

Our country has been taken over by mad men. We are in a battle for our lives—again.

There is a battle between the insiders who want to preserve their control and domination—and those of us who have been fighting to make America more free, more just, and more successful for all of its people.

This is a battle enabled by the rage of people who have, in fact, lost ground economically and socially, whose rage is directed at people whom they believe have unfairly benefited from their losses. That makes the battle complicated.

Trump won by the manipulation and exploitation of the pain of people he had no intention of helping. Our enemies are not most Trump voters, who are our families, neighbors, and friends. They do not have power. Our enemies are people like Donald Trump, the liars and crooks he has put in power, the Russians and corporate oligarchs who hacked this election for him, and the racists and bullies who want to silence anyone who challenges them. These people are the enemies of American values. Many are members of the evangelical Christian Right, which openly wants to create America as a Christian state.

This country is in the middle of a counterrevolution caused by a reaction to our challenge to ancient fixities—traditions—of colonialism and imperialism, of white supremacy, patriarchy and male domination, and heterosexuality as the universal and sole norm.

Against calls for human rights and tolerance, traditionalists promote nationalism, notions of "a conflict of civilizations," and racially tinged deployments of surveillance, policing, and incarceration.

Against calls to care for the poor and needy, traditionalists promote austerity and cuts in social services for those who need the most help, while lavishing benefits on those who need it least.

Against calls for gender justice, traditionalists wage a relentless war to enforce patriarchal power, to dominate women, and to condemn and ostracize transgender people. They want government to be the enforcer of gender hierarchies and binaries.

There is nothing inevitable about whether the LGBT movement or other movements for liberty and justice will win. Winning requires sacrifice, dedication, and a lot of unglamorous work. It requires faith. And it requires living with danger and threat. It requires courageous and honest dialogue across the lines that divide us in this country.

For progressives and queer people, the question is whether we are willing to step up and champion liberty and justice—sometimes even for people who have voted against us—because we see the truth of their pain. Whether we are able to fight and resist and rebuild this country despite the threats and divisions and gulags and camps that Trump and his crazy circle are planning to put us in. Whether we are able to hold true to the values that we are fighting for—and make our revolution irresistible. The decision is in each of our hands.

14

THE 22ND CENTURY INITIATIVE
TO COUNTER AUTHORITARIANISM

Cowritten with Scot Nakagawa

This initiative was created by Urvashi Vaid in collaboration with Scot Nakagawa, who currently directs it and organized its first national conference in July 2023. Its aim is to facilitate widespread opposition to authoritarian movements and ideas, and to support resource organizations and networks to build an enduring, reparative, people-powered democracy. The following is an edited version of a concept paper about the initiative, from November 2021.

A global rejection of liberal democracy and neoliberal economic solutions has created conditions that have resulted in a dramatic increase in authoritarianism in the United States and around the world. In a 2020 report, the V-Dem Institute, a global democracy watchdog organization based in Sweden, noted that—for the first time since 2001—most of the world's nations were autocracies (ninety-two countries). The institute further noted that a third of the world's nations, including the United States, are in the process of becoming autocracies, a process that is marked by the weakening of key elements of a democracy such as a free press, trust in elections, academic freedom, and the right to peacefully assemble in protest. In its 2021 report, the V-Dem Institute noted that the percentage of the world's population living under autocratic governments had grown from 54 percent to 68 percent, with India becoming the world's largest electoral autocracy, while liberal democracies declined in number in the last decade from forty-one to thirty-two nations.

In the United States, the process of "autocratization" has gone hand in hand with a rapid expansion and mainstreaming of white nationalism, anti-

Semitism, misogyny, and theocratic Christianity through the growth of Far Right movements in civil society, policymaking bodies, and the public sector. We use the term *Far Right* to mean a wide range of social movements promoting white supremacist, authoritarian, and anti-democratic values. It is our contention that the rise of the Far Right—and the associated surge in activity by the paramilitary arm of the white nationalist movement—is to be seen not merely as a criminal threat to be addressed by increased law enforcement but as an *existential challenge to democracy*. Calls for increased law enforcement in response to a fear of violence have only deepened anti-government radicalization among Far Right supporters.

On the positive side, as autocracy has been on the rise globally, so have mass-based pro-democracy movements. In the United States, this is reflected in the proliferation of several grassroots organizing efforts such as the Women's March, the Movement for Black Lives, Indivisible, MoveOn.org, and Mijente, among others. Investment into these emerging movements is critical to resisting autocracy and the threat to democracy posed by the Far Right. But more is needed. It is critical that support be channeled to groups dedicated to monitoring Far Right actors, reporting on their activities and plans, and refuting and reframing their key arguments. It is critical that an effective organizing and educational strategy be developed to counter the advancement of Far Right ideas and goals.

A strategy of investing in explicit efforts to respond to the growing appeal of Far Right and authoritarian social movements in the United States must be a priority to defend cultural norms of democracy, pluralism, equity, and social cohesion. Social justice leaders need current language, messaging, tool kits, digital training, narrative and organizing strategies, and new approaches to engagement that can address the deep polarization found within communities and even inside families.

Social justice movements must build bulwarks against authoritarianism that are both cultural and political, ideological and practical. Building capacities to decrease the impact of the Far Right will require effective and new infrastructure, new narrative and communications strategies, awareness, and leadership from all sectors of society, engaged nonprofit and academic institutions, collaborative strategies, and new communities of practice.

The mission of the 22nd Century Initiative (22CI) is to counter the influence of racial and religious nationalism, terrorism, and reactionary populism in American politics and advance a radically inclusive and equitable vision of social justice and democracy for the twenty-second century.

To be successful, our efforts must be grounded in an understanding of the cultural and identity fault lines that the Far Right is exploiting to foster societal polarization and to maintain the current alignment of economic and racial power. These fault lines include racism, anti-Semitism, xenophobia, gender and sex essentialism, misogyny, and religious chauvinism. As we build strategies to mitigate the influence of the Far Right, we must also amplify compelling, future-oriented narratives of a people-centered, equitable, plural democracy and a just economy.

We envision three goals of 22CI:

1 To identify, from activist groups' accounts of their experiences, theoretical and strategic frameworks that can support practical actions to minimize right-wing influence in US domestic and foreign policy;

2 To synthesize these frameworks and offer recommendations that cultural change agents advocating for social and economic justice can use in developing metanarrative, cross-sectoral strategies, and new infrastructure(s); and

3 To establish a think/act tank, based on the analytical frameworks and recommendations identified in this process.

To accomplish these goals we will engage in an iterative process, bringing together people from a wide range of perspectives and areas of expertise to help us answer two questions: (1) How do we build a bulwark against the influence of right-wing groups and movements in US politics? and (2) What capacities do we need to build in order for a people-centered, equitable, and inclusive democratic state to survive in a future that, we believe, will be marked by novel threats and crises that will greatly amplify the appeal of ethnic/racial/religious nationalism, authoritarianism, reactionary populism, and tribalism?

Our initiative is guided by certain assumptions: that modern politics is religion by other means, making religious nationalism a constant, looming threat, and that authoritarian movements in the United States drive their agendas down the avenues of race and gender because race and gender have, together, served to justify unjust hierarchies. They have enshrined inequality in the context of a democratic state, creating the ideological and political leverage antidemocratic movements have used to exercise popular power, even against majority opposition to their overall agendas. Over the course of history, authoritarian movements have threatened the central ethos of American nationalism: democracy founded in civic nationalism centered on the possibility that, out of many, one union, one nation under a single, consistently enforced rule of law is possible.

Plural democracies are fragile, containing within them a number of critical vulnerabilities. First, they are founded on elections as a means of democratic participation, but elections that rely on majority rule invite the tyranny of majorities, threatening freedom of speech and expression and the guarantee of democratic representation of minority groups (including ideological minorities). Second, when antidemocratic challengers to democratic states rise, values of freedom of speech and assembly and of pluralism create the opportunity for those challengers to seize power through the democratic process. Third, authoritarian regimes are grounded in appeals that speak to ordinary people's fear of economic precarity or loss of social status. But to take power, authoritarian nationalism must enlist economic elites and industrialists whose motivations are a mix of nostalgia, ego, greed, and hunger for power.

These vulnerabilities alert us to be vigilant against antidemocratic ideologies and movements and to resist white nationalism and patriarchy by fostering an educated public and public policy reforms. When the dominant ethnic/religious/racial group in a multiethnic, religiously pluralistic state goes in a nationalist direction, those states tend to fail. The failure is the result not just of the majority group's nationalism, but also of minority groups' reaction, who then tend to regard democracy as an open door to the threat of a hostile majority, causing them to demand the door be shut.

Our initiative's long-term vision is to achieve a progressive 22nd century that is grounded in equity, justice, and pluralism. We will achieve this by contributing to the growth of resilient, diverse, strategically informed, and better coordinated movements that challenge the growth of authoritarianism in the United States. A first step is to develop a more powerful and better connected national infrastructure that generates new strategies to mitigate and decrease the impact of the Far Right in the United States. We see this as a decades-long endeavor, with 22CI serving as a catalyst, convener, incubator, and partner, connecting activists working in social movements, academia, media, technology, business, philanthropy, nonprofit think tanks, and issue-based groups, among other spaces.

PART 4.   THE PROMISE — AND PRECARITY — OF JUSTICE

FIGURE 15.1. Urvashi, 1981.

15

POLITICS AS AN ACT OF FAITH:
TEN LESSONS FROM LGBT ACTIVISM

This is a condensed version of a talk presented on April 17, 2009, at the Unitarian Universalist Intergenerational Seminar, "All in the Name of Faith: Rights, Religion and Responsibility," held at Hunter College in New York and reprinted in Irresistible Revolution: Confronting Race, Class and the Assumptions of LGBT Politics *(Magnus Books, 2012).*

I offer some reflections on activism in the form of ten key lessons gleaned through my own experiences of organizing in social justice movements over many years. In the course of this work, I have been lucky enough to see enormous advances and equally devastating setbacks. From all these experiences, I have learned that social change is never linear, nor inevitable, but that it is always faith-based. It is faith-based not in the sense of being aligned with any religious tradition but simply in the sense that, to be an advocate for change, you have to have faith that change is possible. Indeed, the very act of being an advocate for justice is an act fueled by a belief in the idea that we can make a better world.

LESSON #1: TO BELIEVE THAT CHANGE IS POSSIBLE YOU HAVE TO BE ABLE TO IMAGINE THE IMPOSSIBLE. I wonder about the kind of imagination it took my predecessors, like Harry Hay, Del Martin, and Phyllis Lyon—gay activists in the 1950s who founded the modern LGBT movement in the United States. What, other than sheer faith in the human capacity to grow and change, could have emboldened these pioneers to found gay and lesbian organizations in an era when the only publicly supported spaces for gay people were prisons and mental institutions? Imagining the impossible is the first step to work toward achieving it.

LESSON #2: KNOWLEDGE GAINED—AND SHARED—IS POWERFUL. People who are outside of the power structure and are marginalized must first organize to understand themselves, in order to change the awareness of others. But self-knowledge alone is not transformative; it must also be widely shared. The LGBT activists of the 1970s prioritized a form of knowledge building in a slogan borrowed from the women's movement: "the personal is political." They transformed it into "Come out! Come out wherever you are!" Coming out was a process of self-determination, of going public with something you were told should be kept shameful and private. As people came out about their sexual orientation and, more recently, about their gender identities, to their family members and others, they began to be seen not as some dreaded Other but as part of the diversity of being human.

LESSON #3: TO WIN CHANGE YOU HAVE TO GET ORGANIZED. LGBT folks got organized as lawyers, as voters, and grassroots organizers, in our workplaces and unions, in our churches, in the media, in universities, and in political campaigns. We created institutions wherever we found resistance, made allies, and worked at local, state, and national levels to effect change and create a flourishing community, a community that—three decades ago—had practically no public visibility, few cultural spaces in which to connect, barely any political presence, and few political friends.

LESSON #4: WORKING FOR SOCIAL JUSTICE IS A MARATHON, NOT A SPRINT. The punk band Richard Hell and the Voidoids sang, "What I want, I want now, and that's a whole lot more than anyhow." In my younger days I, too, wanted it all *now*, but I have come to learn that there is no contradiction between pursuing that urgent desire and committing to disciplined organizing and keeping the long view in mind. Change involves tireless efforts to talk to people at community gatherings and building a leadership and a lasting organizational infrastructure that can be mobilized as and when needed. There is no shortcut to this process.

LESSON #5: KNOW YOUR REAL ENEMIES. They are not always who you think they are. Ordinary people all over the world are sensible and fair, especially if they can put themselves in our shoes. Even if they disagree with us, ordinary people are not the enemy. The organized, anti-democratic, authoritarian, theocratic right wing is—especially when its adherents hold positions of power.

LESSON #6: HUMAN RIGHTS HAVE A MORAL BASIS. The struggle for social justice is waged not just at the legal or political level but also at the moral one. Issues like transgender inclusion challenge fundamental assumptions about gender as an either-or; issues like same-sex marriage challenge and broaden the moral assumptions underlying ideas about human rights. Morality is about ethical choices. When do we turn to tradition and when do we turn away? The morality we need at this crucial time will not be found in the exclusionary forms of fundamentalist religions dividing the world today, even when disguised in the rhetoric of community and love. The moral values we need can be found in social movements and leaders who believe in accountability, pluralism, democratic participation, human rights, rule of law, caring, and environmental sustainability.

LESSON #7: SOCIAL JUSTICE IN THE UNITED STATES CANNOT BE ACHIEVED UNLESS WE CHALLENGE AND END RACISM. America's history of slavery created structures and residues that continue to affect us to this day. From calls for sterilization of people of color to the welfare policies of the 1990s that punish certain kinds of families and reward others—these are all deeply racist measures to regulate low-income families, and families of color in particular. These efforts to constrain and contain family forms through government policy are linked to the efforts to ban LGBT folks' access to the institutions of family formation and protection. When government can mandate one form of family as its sole, desirable form, we all suffer. Today's racism is couched as colorblindness and it has people of color tokens as its spokespersons. It is embodied in cartoons, talk-radio rants, and racist imagery denigrating President Obama and the First Lady. Today's racism poses as race-neutral and casts affirmative action policies as "reverse racism." Today's racism blames the immigrant for taking jobs and argues for closing the borders for some, even those fleeing persecution, while offering an open door to anyone with money. It is critical that the LGBT movement forge relationships with communities of color and that people of color leaders have greater power, voice, and visibility within both communities of color and within the LGBT movement to name, challenge, and end racist policies that affect our lives on so many levels.

LESSON #8: SOCIAL JUSTICE ACTIVISTS MUST HAVE BIG AND BOLD VISIONS. Politics at its most inspired is about organizing with a vision. Vision is present every time an activist imagines some goal, institution, or idea that goes against the dominant grain. Vision is found in the creative advocacy to educate and counter homophobia within religious denominations, to change school systems, and to expand family forms. It is found in the thriving cultural work of LGBT artists and poets and writers.

LESSON #9: TO BE EFFECTIVE, YOU HAVE TO HAVE COURAGE. In a historic sermon delivered at the Ebenezer Baptist Church entitled "Antidotes for Fear," Rev. Martin Luther King Jr. noted that courage, love, and faith are needed to overcome fear. For King, religious faith was essential to finding courage and the motivation to carry on a sustained political struggle. To this day, gay people confront fear at every step as they decide how out to be. Will I be understood? Will I be happy? Will the ones I respect and love accept me? Will I be attacked? Will I lose my children? But, to me, the most paralyzing fear that LGBT people face as a movement today is found in the failure of progressive LGBT people to articulate their values and vision. We are a movement afraid of owning our unique queerness, our roots in feminism, our challenge to gender roles and gender rigidity. This avoidance, ultimately, reflects a lack of faith in ourselves—in our own goodness and decency and integrity. Our sexual selves are nothing to be ashamed of. I find great courage in the leadership of grassroots activists of the 1980s during the struggle to get the government to respond to HIV/AIDS. I also see courage in that straight young person who organizes a Day of Silence against homophobia at her school and in the pastor who stands up and condemns anti-gay violence in a fundamentalist church. Finding the courage to carry on is especially hard when we experience setbacks or failure, but we must not stop trying.

LESSON #10: INTERSECTIONAL PRAXIS IS THE ONLY WAY TO ACHIEVE A MORE JUST WORLD. Progressives believe that through democratic participation, debate, and innovation, the institutions that reproduce inequality can be transformed. They also believe that justice is not severable: we cannot get ours without standing up for and beside others seeking theirs. Any sober assessment of the status of LGBT people, of women, of people of color, of poor people, of immigrants, of those dispossessed of economic power reveals that justice is an ideal we have not achieved. I believe that pursuing this ideal cannot be done piecemeal, with a single-issue, identity-based focus, but has to take a more expansive view that sees that race, sex, class, and power are inextricably linked in shaping the vision of the kind of world we want to live in. As hard as it seems in the present to imagine that the ideal of justice will ever be realized, I choose, nevertheless, to believe in the existence of a spiritual justice, beyond nation, or law, or police state. That keeps me believing that I can, in my lifetime, live to see a society where all people have affordable health care, food, work, shelter, access to education, and freedom.

16

FORWARD-LOOKING 377 ORDER HOLDS LESSONS FOR THE WORLD

In 2018, the Supreme Court of India overturned Section 377 of the Indian Penal Code, which had made sexual acts "against the order of nature" illegal, and criminalized consensual sex between same-sex adults. The law dated from 1861, during the period of British colonial rule of India, and was based on the British Buggery Act of 1533. Its repeal was the result of a two-decade-long campaign by Indian LGBTQ activists. This invited opinion piece about the significance of the repeal appeared in the Times of India *on September 9, 2018. It is reprinted here with permission.*

Supporters of equality and justice around the world celebrated the decision of the Supreme Court of India affirming the fundamental rights, dignity, and equality of LGBTQ people in India. Thursday's verdict strikes a blow against every colonial-era sodomy law and strengthens the ongoing efforts of reformers working to overturn anti-LGBTQ criminal laws in more than seventy countries.

For LGBTQ activists in the United States, the court's eloquent articulation of transformational constitutionalism and its forward-looking reasoning stand in stark contrast to the regressive politics on issues of gender and sexuality prevalent in America. It is hard to imagine a US Supreme Court majority affirming so clearly that "The Constitution protects the fluidities of sexual experience. It leaves it to consenting adults to find fulfillment in their relationships, in a diversity of cultures, among plural ways of life and in infinite shades of love and longing."

This victory is the achievement of a diverse, brilliant Indian LGBTQ movement. It is a testament to so many people's courage and decades of effort to build intellectual, cultural, legal, and political space; to forge positive identities despite stigmatization; to support each other, to create and engage families, to build alliances, and to sacrifice a great deal to bring change. The long struggle suggests that the promise of justice expressed in this decision will require persistent, broad-based, inclusive action to be realized.

Court decisions declare what is lawful, but extra-judicial organizing, education, and political engagement will be needed to extend rights and realize equality for all LGBTQ people, not just a privileged few. Greater resources will be needed for groups working to ensure that LGBTQ people (especially the working class, marginalized castes, sex workers, and trans people) have access to justice. The International Commission of Jurists outlined in its 2017 report, titled *Unnatural Offences: Obstacles to Justice in India Based on Sexual Orientation and Gender Identity*, that reforms in police procedures, courtrooms, and the entire legal profession are urgently needed to combat bias, misinformation, violence, and police abuse.

This decision underscores the truth that changing law and policy is tied to changing culture, behavior, and attitudes. Groundbreaking work by Indian legal scholars, writers, and think tanks to analyze homosexuality from an Indian cultural and constitutional context set a strong foundation for the Supreme Court verdict. Changing cultural norms requires greater support for research, as well as for media, educational, artistic, and community outreach, and other creative projects.

Alliances across civil society are essential to the project of cultural, policy, and attitudinal change. Indeed, every advance for LGBTQ rights around the world has been built on a foundation of activist leadership's forging hard-fought and at times uneasy alliances across social movements and civil society: transgender, caste, HIV/AIDS, women, progressive legal reform, business sector groups, civil rights, racial justice, progressive faith, workers, and minority rights groups, to name just some.

The Supreme Court's powerful articulation of the difference between social morality and constitutional morality may well be tested in the months to come. Reactionary forces manipulate fear and misinformation about sexuality and gender identity to build a political base, as movements in Russia and the United States can attest. Gains in LGBTQ rights are followed by backlash, often fomented by a specific, globally connected network of anti-LGBTQ organizations and donors. Some of these groups claim the mantle of religious expression, but are not representative of religious traditions; pro-LGBTQ voices exist in every religious tradition. In this context, the Supreme Court's statement that "identity is equivalent to divinity" is a profound affirmation of sexual and gender identity.

Finally, the court's ruling suggests what experience reveals: equal rights and access to justice will require government action. And ensuring that this action is unbiased requires mobilization of a political infrastructure. The US movement still lacks political power, but through education, advocacy, and engagement with all parties, especially at the local (municipal) and state level, it has increased political support significantly. Non-LGBTQ allies have been especially important in the process of educating public officials, as have parents and family members. Still, the political challenges to LGBTQ equality remain significant.

The Supreme Court offered a clear vision of full citizenship for LGBTQ people. Under the continued leadership of India's activists, lawyers, and movements, this promise of justice will ultimately be fulfilled.

17

IT'S TIME TO RE-EMBRACE A POLITICS
OF RADICAL, QUEER, OUTSIDER ACTIVISM

This article was published in The Nation *on July 15, 2019, as part of its "Reclaiming Stonewall 50" series in honor of the fiftieth anniversary of the Stonewall Rebellion.*

The commemoration of Stonewall by the very institutions that have generally ignored LGBTQ people for the past five decades—by museums and corporations, banks and media companies—is noteworthy. But it also risks becoming a parody.

Stonewall's fiftieth anniversary presents the LGBTQ movement with a choice: merely to celebrate this sanitized, marketed reenactment of a revolutionary moment or to remember and rebuild our movement on Stonewall's militant foundation—on fierce protest against the state, and as outsiders to a system with little to lose and everything to gain.

Direct action has always been our first and most urgent strategy: messy, massive, persistent protest anchors every gain. Stonewall itself was a protest against police violence and harassment. It challenged laws that criminalized and limited our freedom of assembly and expression and sought to control our sexual and reproductive lives. Similar forms of state repression exist today. Senseless laws criminalize people with HIV, immigrants, women, transgender people, and protesters against the Trump regime; they prevent people of color from voting; and new court decisions rig the system to maintain control for an oligarchy. This moment requires an escalated response from us, one grounded in protest.

It is true that the LGBTQ movement's relationship to the state has evolved over the past five decades. We have gone from wanting government out of our lives in the 1950s and 1960s to urging that government recognize our lives through equal rights in the 1970s, to demanding government save our lives in the 1980s, to insisting government affirm our lives through marriage equality in the 1990s and 2000s, to believing that the state would be best if it were governed by us, as the candidacy of an openly gay man for president promises today.

Still, it bears remembering that the state has been the enemy of LGBTQ people more often than it has been our friend. Again and again, it has targeted queer people for punishment—from the Lavender Scare that purged gay people from federal jobs in the 1950s to the use of criminal laws against us today; and from the use of medical classifications to stigmatize queer and trans bodies to the disparaging clause stating that "nothing in this Act shall be construed . . . to promote or encourage homosexuality" that is still codified in federal law. Even now, the granting of marriage equality sits alongside the refusal of equal protection in employment, public accommodation, family law, and access to services for queer and trans people.

In an era in which the state is captive to capital, in which it serves as a cudgel for the moneyed class, a skeptical stance toward state power is essential for our survival. The access provided by queer money is not enough to secure rights or justice for all our people. Instead, LGBTQ futures depend on the political and cultural victory of a broad progressive alliance in which we play a leadership role and in its creation of more accountable forms of governing power.

Outside is where queer began—not as a meme, but as the deep experience and memory of being different because of gender identity or sexual orientation. LGBTQ people remain outsiders to racist patriarchy and its economic and gender values. This outsider frame is a potent resource in an era of autocracy, reaction, conformity, and social control. A queer future rests on remembering our difference, in the critical perspective it provides and in the possibility of radical solidarity it affords with other outsiders. As Audre Lorde wrote, "There is no separate survival."

As marriage turned us from outlaws into in-laws, a compliant politics glorifying sameness replaced the more radical political goal we once had: that of building a society that secured justice for all. We have an opportunity and an obligation to recommit to that goal. The celebration of Stonewall 50 grounds us in our movement's urgent and fearless roots, reminding us that transformation, not accommodation, is Stonewall's true legacy.

18

CHEMO KILLED THE SMALL-TALK GENE

Urvashi was first diagnosed with breast cancer in 2012. This 2014 essay recounts her experience following that diagnosis.

Cancer surprised me twice: first, thyroid cancer, and just last year, breast cancer. My journey through diagnosis, treatment, and recovery struck me at first review to be a depoliticized experience, yet everything about my cancer journey was profoundly about power—which is what defines the political. I'm a feminist activist who came to consciousness in the 1970s and a lesbian who has worked in the queer movement since 1979. My formative experiences included the women's self-help movement, which empowered women to know our bodies, to ask questions and to consider ourselves experts. I also witnessed the urgency and life-saving value of building a lesbian community: I worked on that through the women's culture movement. Musicians, poets, and writers were our leaders in the 1970s and 1980s, not politicians. And I spent more than a decade as an AIDS activist, organizing media coverage, protests, legislative campaigns, institutions, and funding to demand a

© 2014 from *Journal of Lesbian Studies* 18 (31–42), by Urvashi Vaid, interviewed by Nanette Gartrell. Reproduced by permission of Taylor and Francis Group, LLC, a division of Informa PLC.

response from cultural, medical, and research establishments to an epidemic and to people living with HIV/AIDS, which these institutions did not want to address.

These experiences with both lesbian feminist activism and AIDS activism taught me to advocate for myself, to not be intimidated by an expert presence in the room, and to value my lived experience as expertise. Yet both times, cancer—the ugly specifics of its physical devastation, the mechanics of surviving it, and the structure of the industry that surrounds it—rendered me politically disempowered and personally immobilized. The two cancers left me at the mercy of medical technologies that could not guarantee my health, much less limit their own negative effects. They shrunk my world down to a small sphere of medical appointments, caregivers, and tasks. And they also reminded me of the transformational power of love and community in any struggle to survive.

Even though I've had close friends with cancer, including various kinds of breast cancer, I knew very little about cancer treatment before my diagnosis. That's quite amazing given that more than 1.6 million cases of cancer were diagnosed in 2012 and that 226,000 of these were breast cancer. My ignorance left me scrambling—calling friends, reading websites, devouring books, and, most importantly, talking to women who had gone through the experience I was facing.

Both cancers were detected only because I had excellent health providers and great health insurance. With the thyroid cancer, I felt a weird swallowing blockage in my throat that came and went. I thought it was swollen glands, and my partner Kate Clinton said I should just have our doctor look at it. My brilliant general practitioner/internist, Dr. Michael Liguori, examined me and found nodules on the thyroid. He recommended me to an endocrinologist, who ordered sonograms and then sonogram-guided biopsies, and the confirmation of cancer. Dr. Luguori referred me to a surgeon and I had the thyroid removed; they found cancer was in my lymph nodes, so I had radiation. They give you a pill instead of beam radiation; you have to be isolated for a couple of days while you're nuclear. You're actually radioactive for a while afterward and they tell you to stay away from children. I asked about Kate, and the medical technician asked her, "How old are you?" She told her age (in her fifties) and he said, "Oh it won't matter." That callous calculus made me wonder at the ethics of medical treatment and the number of people walking around with nuclear medicine in their bodies, irradiating everyone.

With breast cancer, it was once again Dr. Liguori, whose insistence on annual mammograms got me detected early. When the mammogram revealed more calcifications than the prior year, we all thought it was nothing, since I have no family history of breast cancer. My doctor referred me to a very skilled breast surgeon at Beth Israel Medical Center. He took a lot of time and care, even reviewed old films for comparison, and concluded there were two spots that looked suspicious, one more so than the other, so he performed a biopsy of that spot.

That first biopsy revealed ductal carcinoma in situ (DCIS). The breast surgeon told me that some people don't even consider this cancer; it's bad news but not as bad as it could be. The treatment program for this is lumpectomy and possible radiation. But the good news about DCIS is that the cancer cells haven't breached the cell wall.

I asked about the other spot. The surgeon replied that he would check it out when he did the lumpectomy. I said, "Don't you want to do an MRI? Wouldn't it tell you more about what's going on in this breast?" I was worried also about the other breast though nothing had turned up on it. The surgeon agreed that an MRI is a more precise test, but insurance companies sometimes do not pay for it, so it's not routinely ordered. Kate said, "I will write you a check." And we insisted on the test.

The MRI revealed definite activity at the opposite side of the breast, including a node that looked suspicious. I had three biopsies done in one day and that pathology report came back showing invasive breast cancer. I'll never forget that when we walked in to see the surgeon. We thought I had breast cancer, Stage 0 (DCIS); by the time we walked out of that appointment, I had Stage III—tiny tumors, but designated so because it was invasive and because of the lymph involvement.

A couple of things stood out for me in that whole experience. One, you have to be your own strongest advocate. I wasn't particularly well informed about any of this before I went into it beyond the fact that I knew that there something called an MRI. It seemed reasonable to insist that before anybody did surgery on my body there should be a more accurate mapping of what was going on. My insistence on an MRI changed the whole treatment recommendation, because when they found multi-focal breast cancer with lymph node involvement, the recommended treatment was mastectomy and chemo.

The second thing that stands out is how valuable it was to talk to people who have gone through this experience to anticipate what to expect. With something as major as this, you need information and practical advice—doctors do not give you that. For me it was reaching out to friends involved in breast cancer work and people referred to me by others who had dealt with cancer. They told me very useful things, like to make sure to gather copies of

Chemo Killed the Small-Talk Gene · 193

every test result as you have them done. They told me to take my time and talk to different doctors till I found one I liked. They discussed their experience with different hospitals, and their strengths and weaknesses. They told me to take the time to get a second opinion.

The second opinion process was nerve wracking—you want to move quickly to get the cancer out, but you also want someone to tell you it's been a terrible mistake. The process involved deciding where to get the opinion; collecting all the test results, biopsy slides, and data from various labs; waiting for an appointment; waiting for the retesting to confirm what you fear. I got the second opinion at Memorial Sloan Kettering Cancer Center—it was an in-plan hospital on my health plan (which makes coverage cheaper). The breast surgeon I selected was busy, brilliant, and efficient. She recommended a mastectomy to remove the tumors and chemotherapy as a systemic treatment. She told me that radiation might be needed because there could be some errant cancer cell in the skin.

Then the big question arose: whether to have a single or double mastectomy, and whether or not to have breast reconstruction. That was an interesting decision-making process. After asking around, I quickly found women who had breast implants and reconstruction and who were willing to talk. Two good friends who had that procedure said they would never do it again because it was so painful. There was a very funny moment when a social worker connected me to a lesbian I had never met to discuss the reconstruction surgery she had. The very first time I met her, within five minutes, she said, "Do you want to feel my breasts?" And I did! It was quite odd and tender to be feeling up the body of a woman I had just met: cancer creates immediate intimacy. You share at a level that propriety avoids.

It was harder for the hospital to connect me to people who had not done reconstruction. The medical providers make an assumption that women will all want reconstruction to feel "whole." The breast cancer medical machinery pushes you to consider plastic surgery and reconstruction. It is bundled with the mastectomies because it's easier (and probably less costly) for them and the insurance companies. They push for simultaneous reconstruction even though it is a harder and more complex surgery for the patient, makes the recovery time longer, the mobility more constricted, and the risk of complications higher. The resulting implants do not look or feel like a breast. I know many women want that breast reconstruction conversation, but I found it all profoundly heteronormative. In fact, the whole experience of breast cancer treatment was infused with heterosexual norms that Kate's presence and our overt queerness challenged.

Ultimately, I decided on a double mastectomy—without reconstruction. I did both breasts because I wanted to minimize the chance of recurrence of breast cancer in the right breast. I am very glad I made that decision.

After surgery, you have to find an oncologist to work with you on drug treatment and follow-up care. Kate and I had also been collecting information on oncologists at Sloan Kettering, and we ended up with an amazing one. It was the old-dyke network and my surgeon who came through with the connection. Two activist lesbian friends urged me to see Dr. Larry Norton, who had treated the sister of one my friends. He's a renowned oncologist, head of the Evelyn H. Lauder Breast Center at Sloan Kettering, so I thought the chances of getting an appointment with him were low, but my surgeon said it was worth an ask. The friend whose sister had been treated by Larry called him and urged him to see me, and he did.

What I love about my oncologist is that he actually likes his patients and doing clinical practice, and he spends all the time that I need with him. He and his team are amazing. They do a good physical exam, from the start and each time we meet, which I appreciate because it means he is examining my body and not just the paperwork.

During the initial conversation, he recommended sixteen weeks of chemotherapy, eight infusions every two weeks. He was the first doctor to say that it was very curious that I had no family history yet ended up with two bouts of cancer, and he theorized it may be exposure related. He was careful to note this was speculation, but he was really interested in epidemiology of cancer, not just the treatment. It was quite reassuring to Kate and me that he was engaging in a conversation about my specific history and cancer. Most doctors just look at you clinically and technically, like a specimen, and don't engage with the human story you bring.

Dr. Norton's second recommendation was harder to hear. He found huge uterine fibroids during the physical exam. He wanted me to see a gynecological surgeon, because he was worried about the possibility of excessive bleeding during chemotherapy. So I went to a gynecological surgeon at Sloan Kettering and also called my old friend, Dr. Kate O'Hanlan, a dyke doctor, and the most experienced and brilliant gynecological oncological surgeon around for advice. It was clear I had large fibroids—the size of grapefruits and oranges (they always use fruit imagery). So, six weeks after my breast surgery was done, I had to have a laparoscopic hysterectomy. It was truly awful. It felt much harder and more invasive than the mastectomies. And the recovery was tough. But the body is amazing and resilient and five weeks after that second surgery, I was ready for chemo.

Eventually, they say, they will know the genetic make-up of the cancers we get and be able to target drugs to particular forms of cancer (there are something like twelve kinds of breast cancer, for example). But right now, it's all about the odds—like a casino. The goal of chemo treatment currently is nothing more precise than reducing the odds of recurrence. They use a set of drugs that have been clinically shown to destroy cancer cells without destroying you. Chemo is usually a drug combination—mine was ACT: Adriamycin, Cytoxan, and Taxol.

Adriamycin was terrifying—I made the mistake of reading about it before the first infusion. Don't read too much on the internet. It's bright red, like Red Dye #2, and so toxic the nurse has to wear hazard protection to infuse you so she does not get any on her. Yet, it went into my system four times, in combination with the Cytoxan. The last four treatments were with Taxol—a monstrous drug that is so bad for your white blood cells that you have to get a shot of another drug called Neulasta each time you get infused, so your white blood cells don't completely disappear! Taxol also has the lovely side effects of neuropathy, horrible aches, and ickiness.

Chemotherapy was an endurance test. Some of the infusions were four hours long, and sometimes waiting for a room took hours as well. Kate and I prepared ourselves in different ways. We got a juicer, we bought bland and salty crackers, we got lots of anti-nausea pills, and special home remedies from friends to deal with the binding constipation the drugs produce. We bought lots of greens and coconut water to hydrate and keep flushing the poisons out. My sister sent me a pile of very useful books including one about how to survive and thrive during chemo. I did not have terrible nausea because I changed the way I ate. Sadly, I couldn't eat my favorite spicy Indian food during chemo.

The best thing I did for myself during this whole process was to start seeing a highly skilled medical massage therapist affiliated with Sloan Kettering's integrative medicine services center. The surgery messes with all your muscles and nerves—especially since they removed lymph nodes. And radiation inflames tissues and makes things tight as well—so massage and physical therapy to maintain mobility and looseness is essential. This amazing woman insured that I could move. Many people also recommended exercise, and so Kate and I walked religiously every morning. At first (after surgeries or after chemo) I could only walk one block with Kate's help. But we persisted. And our morning walks in Riverside Park were deeply healing and important to both of us.

My hair started falling out after the second treatment, so I had it buzzed very close to my head and eventually shaved off. It came back about three months after treatment ended, and it came back curly—totally different from my old hair. I never wore a wig, just hats and scarves. Being bald was interesting—my one-year-old neighbor across the hall, who was shy with everyone else, suddenly loved seeing me—I think because I reminded her of her bald dad.

Toward the end of chemotherapy—around the seventh or eighth session—we began preparing for radiation. That involves going to a new set of doctors and labs, getting your breast "mapped" for the radiation field, getting a mold made of your body in the position they want you in for the treatment—so you will be positioned the same each time you go. I waited about a month to recover from the chemo. Then I had radiation for five weeks.

For me, beam radiation was the worst of the year-long medical treatments. It does not hurt and the actual beam is only about ten or so minutes in duration, but the tension of that experience was daily and exhausting (as was the side effect of the radiation itself). It was just a wretched experience, awful in a whole different way from chemotherapy. Partly this was because radiation was every day—so it's always present in your life. I felt like a slab of meat on a table, probed and positioned by an ever-changing team of technicians who seemed to have more work than they could handle, like workers on an assembly line. They line you up on the table, in your mold, with a huge machine over you and target the beam radiation onto a field mapped out for your body by a specialist.

It was also hard because Sloan Kettering's radiation center is hideous. The radiation facility was under construction at the time I went, impersonal, ugly, institutional, and unpleasant. Everyone had to wait hours for appointments—and when you go five days a week, that is a lot of time in a waiting room. The other cancer patients waiting were fantastic. You get to know everybody, women and men and even some kids, all waiting for their radiation treatments. There is instant camaraderie and storytelling.

One of the saddest aspects of the radiation treatments, though, was the unexpected presence of three of my friends from the queer movement who turned out to be in cancer treatment there, at the same time, in the same facility. Two of them had breast cancer and one had an unusual cancer on his arm. It was surreal to be together in that place.

Radiation left me with a large blotchy patch of discolored skin on my chest—like a sideways map of Maine. Fortunately, my skin did not blister too badly, but I was proactive and went to a great cancer-specializing dermatologist who gave me several different kinds of cream and lotions to help. Again, if I had not been proactive, I am not sure I would have gotten the additional salves.

The final step in treatment for me is the daily pill that I take—called an aromatase inhibitor. I think of it as aroma therapy. The drug I am on has side effects (of course)—it destroys your bones and leaves you aching and moving stiffly like you are eighty-five years old and arthritic. I may have to change it if it gets impossible. So far, I am trying to stay active and manage the painful joints and aches.

When this journal asked me to share my experience of cancer, I found myself sharing a lot of details—a catalog of the medical treatments—and not as much of an evaluation of or reflection on the experience. I'm still newly emerging from this experience, so it's hard to be detached. But I chose to tell the story in this way in case it helps someone facing breast cancer to learn a few specifics about what it's like to go through the treatments—there are so many more details that could be shared at each stage.

The story would be incomplete without a discussion of the support I had that got me through. I am profoundly lucky to have had my partner in life, Kate, go through this with me at every step. I cannot imagine having gone through this without her. We shared the terror, absurdity, sadness, laughs, and pain.

My cancer—from the conversations, to medical and doctor-related research, to going for tests, doctors' appointments, treatment appointments—became a second part-time job for Kate and me. We kept a daily pill log, along with little notebooks on our dresser, writing down what was happening every day, which was really helpful. Having somebody in the room with me during appointments was extraordinarily important. Sometimes it was even good to have two people in the room, because there were moments when it was hard for Kate to hear some of what was being said.

The intimacy of any ill person with their caregivers is hard to describe. This cancer experience brought intensely personal, quiet moments of connection with Kate. She did it all, from handling my bodily fluids, including changing my drains, and as she says, when you change someone's drains after breast surgery, that's real intimacy. She gave me the shots of Neulasta each week, massaged my aching back and neuropathy-tinged feet and legs, propped me up in pillows at night, dealt with the night sweats, shared the anxiety-ridden moments, and helped me stay positive throughout. This year marked our twenty-fifth anniversary. And we celebrated it by formally getting married on our anniversary date.

Our family of origin and community of close friends were also strongly present throughout. Support also came from my work colleagues, people in my apartment building, business owners in the block I live on who saw me go bald and figured out what was happening, and total strangers who were incredibly kind. One of my sisters lives in New York, and she and her husband were there for every surgery with Kate. My other sister came and cooked for a week! Friends from out of town came and stayed with me during Kate's work trips. Local friends came and cooked dinners, sat with me when I was just stupid from the chemo or tired from radiation.

We watched endless hours of T V shows—Netflix streaming service should be prescribed as an anti-anxiety drug for every person with cancer. Kate and I watched television series and movies during this past year—in waiting rooms on my iPad, in the hospital rooms after surgeries, and at home, several episodes a day. *The Wire, Friday Night Lights, Game of Thrones, 24, Damages, Mad Men, Lip Service, M15, Downton Abbey*—the narcotic effect of these television series matched that of the best drugs.

When I first got diagnosed, two friends in DC encouraged us to consider using a website that they had used to manage support during one of their breast cancer treatment years called MyLifeLine.org. The site allows you to create a private, personal Facebook-like website on which you can post information and photos and receive messages. We used Mylifeline.org throughout the year to keep in close contact with a large circle of families and friends. It was incredibly helpful. We posted updates—sometimes several times a day—described different procedures, results of tests, and posted pictures of ourselves in the experience. In turn, our friends posted their encouraging messages—we loved them all, even the repetitive, "go Urvashi," "go Kate," or "thinking of you, sending love"—I mean there's only so much people can say after a point. The site cheered us up throughout this ordeal. And it helped our national circle of friends feel like they could provide some support, even long-distance.

A friend gave me a button at the start of my treatments that read, "I may not look like I'm doing much, but at the cellular level I'm very busy." I worked throughout. Again I was lucky. My work right now involves research, writing, and convening—not a lot of travel or management or running an organization, as I have done in the past. Cancer made it hard to concentrate, and it was tough physically at times, but I worked steadily. Throughout the year, I went regularly to my office at Columbia. I took my full vacation and sick days, but I actually wanted to work—because going to work in my office was usefully distracting. I had decided to publish a book of essays before I got diagnosed and I worked on that book throughout the year. It makes me very happy that the book came out in November of 2012, at the end of my chemo treatments. It's titled *Irresistible Revolution: Confronting Race, Class and the Assumptions of Lesbian, Gay, Bisexual, and Transgender Politics.*

During chemo I also cotaught a class called "Queer Theory Workshop" with my colleague Katherine Franke at Columbia Law School. We planned something called "Theory Meets Practice" where she was the queer theory part and I was the queer practice part. Chemo was on the same day as class so every two weeks I would end my chemo, and then Kate and I would take a cab to Columbia. Kate went to every one of those classes with me—so sweet—just to make sure I was okay. They pump you full of steroids during chemo, so I had lots of energy, but on some days in class I looked green, on others I looked yellow, and sometimes I was white. A few days later I would crash after the steroids ran their course. I went to every class except one when chemo took longer than usual.

And on my other volunteer commitments, my colleagues were also incredibly supportive. I continued to participate on the board of the Gill Foundation. They were so good to me and arranged to have meetings in New York for a whole year because I couldn't fly. The lesbian SuperPAC board I'm on—LPAC—was also incredible. Work was a great distraction.

This whole experience left me furious at the epidemic incidence of breast cancer and at the current state of breast cancer diagnosis, care, and treatment. The field is ripe for militant action and yet, for the most part, this kind of activism is not taking place.

Breast cancer is a raging and deadly epidemic—yet it's treated in the media and by the breast cancer-industrial complex as if it's just a chronic, normal condition that one can "manage" and "survive." I certainly intend to survive, but breast cancer kills some 40,000 people annually in the United States and affects over 230,000 new people each year. During my year of cancer treatment, I learned of more than a dozen close friends who had also been diagnosed.

At every stage of cancer—the diagnosis stage, the surgery stage, the chemo and radiation stages—there are differences in how a woman is treated depending upon where she happens to go for treatment. The treatment varies not because of the specifics of the cancers, but because of the quirks of the doctors, their knowledge or lack of it, the insurance regimes that they operate under, and the hospital policies and protocols they follow. There's no national best practice or standard of care that I can discern. If I were to be diagnosed with breast cancer in a small town like Provincetown and seek treatment at

Cape Cod Hospital, I would not get the same quality of care or even the same protocols of treatment, and I think that's preposterous. Given how much information is available and the ubiquity of this disease, how can there not be a best practice?

Suppose I had not insisted on the MRI and just gone with the advice of my initial capable surgeon. Without the MRI, I would have had a lumpectomy, and then I would have had to go back for another procedure, the mastectomy, because he hopefully would have found the invasive cancer and lymph involvement during the lumpectomy. Friends I know have had to keep going back after their lumpectomy to have more surgeries to ensure that the margins between the tumor and the cell wall are wide enough. And they must go for MRIS and mammograms every six months. Is the extra strain of that continuous monitoring, the multiple trips to the surgeon to whittle away at cancer as it is discovered—is it worth "breast-preserving surgery"—which is supposed to be the big innovation in cancer treatment?

One would suppose that after they sandblast you in this primitive way with chemo drugs, they could tell you at the end of it all that the cancer is actually gone. They cannot. What they can tell you are probabilities, and these are not yet tailored to one's particular chemistry or cancer. Similarly, with radiation: the experience varies drastically depending on which hospital you go to. And again, when it is over, they cannot tell you much about a prognosis.

How much money is being thrown at breast cancer research? Billions upon billions. And yet, there is not a great deal of coordination of that research— no overall strategic game plans to pursue cures or even causes. Research institutions compete and do not share information. Trials are taking place, and I don't know if there is a central repository for patients to access. Scientists make fortunes selling their marginally effective treatments to drug companies. And drug companies in turn make fortunes marketing toxic and relatively useless drugs. They have no incentive to stop cancer—just to maintain us on their drips.

The drug development process seems actually counter to the best interests of the patient. If researchers can clinically prove that a drug is going to kill cancer cells for twelve weeks versus six weeks, that's considered a success. What happens after the twelfth week to the body of the patient? We don't know. The pharmaceutical company is delighted because they have a new drug in the pipeline, and the researchers are delighted because they get kudos for extending something by six weeks. The academic researcher gets tenure, but the patient doesn't have an improved quality of life or get an improved prognosis.

There's a clear need for an ACT UP–type direct action movement organized around diagnosis, treatment, and care for breast cancer. Wonderful groups exist for advocacy, education, and support—the Breast Cancer Fund and Breast Cancer Action, for example. But they are not organized to mobilize the anger and energy of breast cancer survivors and our families to pressure and demand an improvement in diagnostic technologies, in drug development, in standards of care and treatment, or in health insurance coverage, for example.

Power yields to demands and demanding requires us to take it to the corporate suites, the staid university research centers, the oncology conferences, and the governmental bodies that are not exercising their clout enough. I see so many sites of potential engagement to challenge the hideous machinery of drug development, the lack of coordination among researchers, and the lack of patient-centered care and treatment—like we did during the AIDS epidemic.

One of the strangest side effects of this whole experience has been its impact on my ability to make chit chat. A lot of time in nonprofit-based political activism is spent in small talk—the fundraiser is ubiquitous because it is essential. Yet chemo seems to have killed my small-talk gene. I find myself standing awkward and mute in situations in which I normally thrived. My tolerance for small talk and my filter are off. Some unsuspecting person comes up to me and asks the common question, *How are you doing?* And instead of the expected answer, *Just great, how are you?*, I find myself launching into a detailed explanation of how I am really feeling. Even the mortified look on their faces does not stop me. The best resolution has been to not go to places where small talk is required.

I finally have the time to feel and to mourn now that treatments are done. I also am quite exhausted. Certainly I'm relieved it is over, but that feeling is laced with uncertainty about the future. I guess I'll feel more confident after the five-year marker or whatever marker puts you in another category statistically. I wish they could tell me more precisely. Two things I feel very clear about, though: both material and immaterial things matter in dealing with cancer. Health insurance must be universal, and we cannot let it be deprived to anyone. And creating loving communities around people dealing with illness is essential for anyone dealing with cancer.

Urvashi's cancer recurred in the summer of 2020, after she and her partner, Kate Clinton, had moved to Provincetown to ride out the pandemic. She underwent several rounds of chemo at Dana Farber and later at Sloan Kettering. She kept in active touch with her circle of friends through MyLifeLine.org and continued to work on multiple initiatives until just weeks before she died, in May 2022.

FIGURE 18.1. Urvashi and her life partner, humorist Kate Clinton, 1990. Photograph by Tim Francis.

19

LONGEVITY IS A PRECARIOUS DREAM

These remarks were given as an acceptance speech for the 2022 Susan J. Hyde Award for Longevity in the Movement. They were delivered via Zoom at the Creating Change Conference in March 2022. The award was introduced by Sue Hyde and presented to Urvashi by Kate Clinton.

I'm so grateful and moved to accept this award because of my own love and passion for this wild, ever-changing, magnificent movement that each of you at this conference and thousands of others have helped to create. I've organized for LGBTQ rights and liberation since the late 1970s. While we've been through so much over the past six or seven decades in this movement's life, we're still in the early stages of our struggle for freedom and dignity.

The four arguments that we had to overcome to arrive at the current, still uneven, level of freedom we've achieved continue to be encountered in the United States and around the world. The arguments are that we're sinful, that we're criminal, that we're immoral, and that we're dangerous. From the anti-transgender bills that have been proposed and passed across this country, to the pervasive violence against transgender women of color, lesbians, and bisexual people; from the governmental homophobia and violence of the regimes of Hungary and Poland and Russia to the hostile stance of the US Republican Party's platform, which still calls for an overturning of the freedom to marry; from the inability of state legislatures to pass pro-LGBT laws, to the presence in courts across this country of so-called justices who will recognize the freedom of men to go unmasked during a life-threatening epidemic, but will not respect the freedom of women to determine what to do with their own bodies, even when their lives are put at risk.

The truth is that the struggle for queer dignity and rights is not over. Indeed, the opposition to the recognition of our full humanity remains the same opposition it has always been: religious orthodoxy, patriarchal and supremacist traditions, political opportunism, gender binaries, and hostile ideas of human deservedness that come from a failing economic system. A system that every day proves itself unable and unwilling to meet the biggest challenges of our time—challenges like climate destruction, global health crises, and meeting human needs with caregiving and caretaking instead of division and destruction. Achieving a feminist, anti-supremacist, multiracial, queer, loving democracy is the challenge that lies ahead of us, of each of us, in the LGBTQ rights and liberation movements.

Plural and free democracy is not guaranteed at all. The enemies of freedom posture as its defenders but, as always, they lie. Look under the attacks on feminism, on social justice, on critical race theory, on Black Lives Matter, on all that they call "cancel culture." Look underneath their slick ads and rhetoric. Can you see the guns? Can you see the murders? Can you see the violence? Can you see the bullying and hostility to difference? Can't you hear their repeated expressed desire for the annihilation of strong women, of queer people, of Jews, and anyone who disagrees with them? Listen closely and tell me who the real cancellers are! Donald Trump and the Republican Party establishment today do not represent freedom. They represent tyranny. Their rhetoric bears echoes of final solutions. Their base is fear.

The LGBTQ movement is not just in a fight for a federal equality act. It's in a fight for the survival of freedom and pluralism. We are facing an existential threat. Our response must be strong, militant, and much more aggressive than it's been so far.

What tools do we have at our disposal? Creativity! It's creativity that enabled us to build self-esteem, to build power and our own institutions, despite rejection and hatred and fear. We have the tools of the vote, which they're doing their best to eliminate, but which we must deploy in the next election to vote every one of these monsters out of power. Don't forget, to paraphrase Jim Morrison and the Doors, that while they may have the guns, we've got the numbers.

As a person living with Stage IV metastatic breast cancer, longevity is a precarious dream. The longevity I hope to contribute to is the survival of our movement and its values of freedom, human dignity, justice, and love.

Thank you again to the Task Force for this award, and thank you to Sue Hyde.

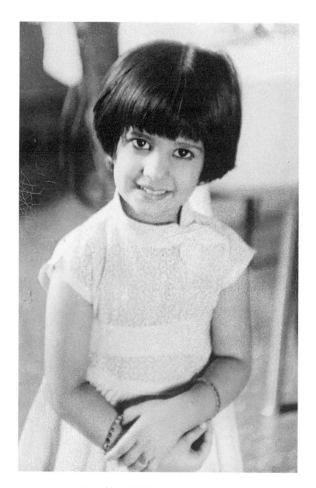

FIGURE 20.1. Urvashi in Delhi, circa 1960.

URVASHI VAID — A BIOGRAPHY

Early History

Jyotsna Vaid and Amy Hoffman

Urvashi Vaid was born in New Delhi, India, on October 8, 1958. She was the youngest of three daughters. Urvashi's father, Krishna Baldev Vaid, was a prominent writer of experimental fiction in Hindi and a professor of English literature. Her mother, Champa Vaid, was a schoolteacher who much later in life became a published poet in Hindi and then an abstract expressionist painter. Urvashi's parents and extended family were among the millions of displaced refugees whose lives had been profoundly shaped by the trauma of Hindu/Muslim violence as a result of India's Partition in 1947.

When Urvashi was six months old, she was left in the care of her maternal grandparents in Delhi, while her sisters, Rachna and Jyotsna, then five and three, accompanied their mother to the United States, to join their father, who was working on his Ph D at Harvard. Raised by devoted grandparents for the first four or so years of her life, Urvashi developed a deep connection to her Indian roots and a strong sense of self. "Intelligent, quick and [with] the quality of leadership" is how her kindergarten teacher from Ragubir Singh Junior Modern School in New Delhi described her.

In 1963, Urvashi's parents relocated to Chandigarh. Urvashi and her sisters attended Carmel Convent School, where she accumulated Certificates of Merit in arithmetic, Hindi, general science, and moral science, and became a favorite of the nuns who ran the school. In 1966, the family left Chandigarh for America, as Urvashi's father had accepted a faculty position at the State University of New York at Potsdam. With her mother and sisters, Urvashi arrived in Potsdam in November 1966, having just turned eight. As the first school-aged children from India in that small upstate college town, the Vaid sisters' arrival was eagerly anticipated by their soon-to-be classmates at Con-

FIGURE 20.2. The three Vaid sisters (left to right) Jyotsna Vaid, Urvashi, and Rachna Vaid, circa 1964.

gdon Campus School, an innovative school affiliated with the State University. Urvashi would fit right in and quickly distinguish herself as a leader. She performed at the highest levels in her class, was active in sports, and played the lead role in her school's production of the Broadway musical *Guys and Dolls*.

The Potsdam years coincided with political and cultural upheavals in many parts of the world (the Prague Spring, the formation of Bangladesh) and with massive anti–Vietnam War protests at US college campuses. Urvashi and her sisters participated in some of these protests and rallies and actively followed the televised news coverage of the turbulent political events around the civil rights struggle. At her junior high graduation ceremony in May 1972, Urvashi gave her first political speech, titled "Election '72," in which she made the case for George McGovern for President.

The Potsdam years were also a time when Urvashi developed a keen interest in music. Jazz (Dave Brubeck, John Coltrane), Indian classical instrumental music (Ali Akbar Khan, Ravi Shankar), and *ghazals* (Urdu poetry put

FIGURE 20.3. (left to right) Krishna Baldev Vaid (Urvashi's father), Kate Clinton, Champa Vaid (Urvashi's mother), Urvashi. Provincetown, Massachusetts, at an exhibition of Champa Vaid's artwork, July 2012.

to music) sung by Begum Akhtar were staples in the Vaid household. Urvashi discovered a taste for the music of Bob Dylan, the Beatles, the Rolling Stones, Ten Years After, and many emerging rock groups of the time.

Urvashi graduated from Potsdam Central High School in her junior year in June 1975, as salutatorian of her class. In fall 1975 she started college at Vassar, while only sixteen years old. Her sister Rachna had already graduated from Vassar by the time Urvashi joined, and her other sister, Jyotsna, was by then in her final year there. From the start of her college years, Urvashi was active in joining and leading initiatives, and organizing rallies and protests. On February 24, 1978, for example, in a letter published in the Vassar *Miscellany*, she urged her fellow students to "Take a position / End high tuition." That same year she represented a large coalition of student groups demanding the trustees of Vassar include student representatives on an Ad Hoc Committee on Investor Responsibility to divest funds from the apartheid government of South Africa. She also helped bring women musicians to perform on campus, organized several feminist conferences, and was involved

Urvashi Vaid—A Biography · 211

with community organizing around poverty in Poughkeepsie. In January 1979 Urvashi became a naturalized US citizen.

At Vassar, Urvashi was first introduced to the writings of feminist poets, writers, and musicians (Patti Smith, June Jordan, Adrienne Rich, Audre Lorde, Barbara Smith, Angela Davis, and Lauren Berlant, among others). It was also at Vassar where Urvashi came out as a lesbian. On graduating in June 1979 with a double major in English and political science, Urvashi moved to Boston to participate more actively in the women's liberation movement. She worked for a year while cofounding local grassroots feminist projects (the Allston-Brighton Greenlight-Safehouse Network, the Boston Lesbian and Gay Political Alliance). She also worked as a volunteer at the influential weekly *Gay Community News*, which further developed her political sensibility. On May 29, 1983, Urvashi earned a JD from Northeastern University School of Law, with a focus on gender and sexuality law.

Career

Urvashi started her working career in 1983 as a staff attorney at the National Prison Project of the American Civil Liberties Union (ACLU) in Washington, DC. She worked in this position for three years, conducting the first survey of HIV/AIDS policies in US prisons in 1984. In Washington, she was introduced to activists working in the National Gay and Lesbian Task Force (NGLTF, now the National LGBTQ Task Force) and decided that she wanted to work full time as a gay rights activist.

Over the next forty years, Urvashi would hold leadership roles in advocacy, philanthropy, academia, and community-based organizations. She cofounded several initiatives, including the National Religious Leadership Roundtable and the Federation of Statewide LGBTQ Organizations (which became Equality Federation), and served on the boards of numerous organizations, including the Roadwork Foundation (1984–87), National Board of the Planned Parenthood Action Fund, the ACLU (2000–4), *Ms. Magazine* (2002–6), the Provincetown Commons, and the American Museum of LGBTQ History and Culture, to name just a few.

In the domain of advocacy, Urvashi worked for several years and in different roles at the NGLTF in Washington, DC, serving first as its Public Information Director (1986–89), then as its Executive Director (1989–92). She led the NGLTF to achieve major policy wins on HIV, anti-violence, and LGBTQ rights at the national level; refocused organization on state-level advocacy, organizing, and training programs; cofounded the national Creating Change

Conference; and initiated work on religion, military reform, family policy, sodomy repeal, racial justice, and progressive alliance building.

In 1988, Urvashi met activist and political humorist Kate Clinton, and after a period of long-distance relationship they became partners for life. Urvashi left the NGLTF in early 1993 and moved to Provincetown, Massachusetts, to live with Clinton and work on *Virtual Equality: The Mainstreaming of Gay and Lesbian Liberation* (Anchor Books, 1995).

After a fifteen-city national speaking tour to publicize the book, she moved to New York City to direct the NGLTF's Policy Institute (1997–2000) and coedited *Creating Change* (St. Martin's Press, 2000). She also began a speaking and consulting practice for nonprofits on program development and strategy, fundraising, leadership development, coalition building, and management. In 2010, she formalized this practice as The Vaid Group, LLC. She continued to speak extensively at colleges and universities and other venues on LGBTQ, civil rights, social justice, and public policy issues, giving well over 250 invited talks. She also wrote a column for *The Advocate*, and contributed op-ed essays to other progressive publications.

For ten years, Urvashi worked in philanthropy, first as the deputy director of the Governance and Civil Society Unit of the Ford Foundation, shaping funding initiatives in social justice (2001–5), and then as executive director of the Arcus Foundation, which she transformed from a small institution to a leading global funder of social justice and great ape conservation (2005–10). She also served on the board of the Gill Foundation for several years.

Urvashi spent a year as a visiting scholar in sociology at the Graduate Center of the City University of New York (2010–11), where she advised the Sexuality and Social Justice Project on a research initiative on LGBTQ communities of color and wrote and developed an outline for her book, *Irresistible Revolution: Confronting Race, Class and the Assumptions of LGBT Politics* (2012, Magnus). From 2011 to 2015, she was a senior fellow and director of the Engaging Tradition Project at Columbia University Law School's Center for Gender and Sexuality Law. There, she explored how tradition-based resistance inhibited projects to advance gender, sexual, and racial equity. She had planned to write a book on this topic, tentatively titled *Against Tradition*, but was unable to complete it for various reasons.

Over the course of her career, Urvashi received numerous awards and accolades. In 1990 she was named Woman of the Year by *The Advocate* magazine. That same year, she received an inaugural Stonewall Prize by the Paul Anderson Foundation, for outstanding work in LGBTQ rights. The prize came with a $25,000 check. In a letter to Paul Anderson in February 1991, Urvashi expressed her gratitude, noting:

> Like most political activists, I have never been recognized in this manner before. . . . Until I received your award, I owned the standard activist property—lots of books, fraying clothes, a pull-out couch, and an aging record collection; no house, no car, no computer, no fancy stereo. I wanted you to know that I have bought a computer. Because of this prize, I may actually write the book that I have been dreaming of writing for some time.

In 1992, when Urvashi left the Task Force to work on her first book, it was major news. The Mayor of the city of Seattle, Norman B. Rice, issued a proclamation, declaring October 2, 1992, to be *Urvashi Vaid Day*, in recognition of her tireless work and accomplishments to promote civil rights and provide a positive voice for gays and lesbians, and "continually giv[ing] of her time, spirit, intellect, energy and heart to those around her."

In September-October 1993, Urvashi was featured on the cover of *Ms.* magazine, in conversation with Gloria Steinem, bell hooks, and Naomi Wolf. In its December 5, 1994, issue, *Time* magazine named her as one of Fifty for the Future (nationally), and Hundred for the Future (internationally) most promising leaders under the age of forty. (She was the only out lesbian in the national list and the only Indian American.) In April 2009, *Out* magazine named her one of the fifty most influential LGBTQ people in the United States.

Urvashi was honored by numerous organizations: she received the Lambda Liberty Award from Lambda Legal (1996), the Civil Rights Leadership Award from the Asian American Legal Defense and Education Fund (1997), the American Foundation for AIDS Research Honoring with Pride Award (2002), the Dan Bradley Award from the National Lesbian and Gay Law Association (2006), a Lifetime Achievement Award from the Gay Men's Health Crisis Center in New York (2008), the Ken Dawson Advocacy Award from Advocacy and Services for LGBTQ+ Elders (2010), and the Kessler Award from the CLAGS Center, New York, for Lifetime Contributions to LGBTQ Studies (2010).

Urvashi's book, *Virtual Equality: The Mainstreaming of Gay and Lesbian Liberation*, won the Stonewall Book Award and the American Library Association's Gay, Lesbian and Bisexual Book Award in Non-Fiction in 1996. In 1997, Urvashi was featured in a National Film Board of Canada documentary, *My Feminism*. In 1999, she received an honorary degree from Queens College of

Law, City University of New York, and in 2015, she received an honorary degree from Kalamazoo College. Her book *Irresistible Revolution: Confronting Race, Class and the Assumptions of LGBT Politics* was awarded the American Library Association's Over the Rainbow award in 2013.

In 2014, Urvashi received the Social Justice Action Award from Teachers College, Columbia University, and the Spirit of Justice Award from GLAD. The following year, Harvard Law School awarded her the Women Inspiring Change Award, for "representing the best of where the queer legal movement has been and of where it might go next" and for "challenging all of the many movements of which she is a part to strive for greater inclusivity, class consciousness, and radicalism." In 2021, Urvashi was selected by the Auburn Seminary's Lives of Commitment as a Woman of Moral Courage. In 2022, she was featured on the cover of *Queer Forty* as Woman of the Year, in an article titled, "Our Very Own Wonder Woman." And in spring 2022, Urvashi received the Susan J. Hyde Award for Longevity in the LGBTQ movement. The honors and recognitions have continued even after her death.

From 2015 to 2022, Urvashi worked full-time as president of The Vaid Group, LLC, a consulting and innovation firm working for racial, gender, and economic equity for innovators in government, nonprofit, and philanthropic sectors seeking to develop intersectional projects that advance social justice. The Vaid Group partnered with groups working for education reform and international human rights, ending hunger, advancing LGBTQ rights, addressing climate change and advocating for environmental justice, deepening democracy and civic engagement, increasing the scope of philanthropy to advance racial and gender equity, and engaging in deep community development. With its affiliated 501(c)(3) think tank Justice Work, the group incubated projects that included national research initiatives, networks and coalitions, and new organizations and programs.

As part of this work, Urvashi authored, coauthored, or served on advisory boards of projects that led to important research reports. These include the first national policy agenda on criminalization of LGBTQ people, *A Roadmap for Change: Federal Policy Recommendations Addressing the Criminalization of LGBT People and People Living with HIV* (Columbia University Law School, 2014); a participatory research project to develop a national agenda addressing LGBTQ poverty called *Intersecting Injustice: Addressing LGBTQ Poverty and Economic Justice for All* (2018); and the first report on engaging high-net-worth donors of color, titled *The Apparitional Donor: Understanding and Engaging High Net Worth Donors of Color* (Advancement Project and Donors of Color Network, 2017). A large-scale, national LGBTQ+ Women's

Community Survey that she helped spearhead released its detailed findings in a report published in October 2023 (*We Never Give up the Fight* by Jaime Grant and Alyasah Ali Sewell).

Through Justice Work, Urvashi was actively organizing new initiatives right up to the final months of her life. Aside from the National LGBTQ+ Women's Community Survey (2021), she helped found the Donors of Color Network (2019), the first multiracial network connecting individuals of color to leverage their giving for racial equity; LPAC, the first national lesbian political action committee for queer and progressive women running for office (2012); and the 22nd Century Initiative to Counter Authoritarianism (2021). It is a testament to the power of the relationships she developed over her lifetime that these initiatives are continuing and are bearing fruit.

BIBLIOGRAPHY OF WORKS BY
AND ON URVASHI VAID

Writings by Urvashi Vaid

Books

Vaid, Urvashi. *Virtual Equality: The Mainstreaming of Gay and Lesbian Liberation.* New York: Anchor/Doubleday Books, 1995.

D'Emilio, John, William B. Turner, and Urvashi Vaid, eds. *Creating Change: Sexuality, Public Policy, and Civil Rights.* New York: St. Martin's Press, 2000.

Vaid, Urvashi. *Irresistible Revolution: Confronting Race, Class and the Assumptions of LGBT Politics.* New York: Magnus Books, 2012.

Book Chapters

Vaid, Urvashi. "Prisons." In *AIDS and the Law,* edited by Harlon Dalton, 235–50. New Haven, CT: Yale University Press, 1987.

Vaid, Urvashi. "To Dare to Dream." In *Long Road to Freedom: The Advocate History of the Gay and Lesbian Movement,* edited by Mark Thompson, 391–93. New York: St. Martin's Press, 1994.

Vaid, Urvashi. Preface to *My American History: Lesbian and Gay Life during the Reagan and Bush Years,* 1st ed., by Sarah Schulman, xi–xiii. New York: Routledge, 1994.

Vaid, Urvashi. Foreword to *Hospital Time,* by Amy Hoffman, ix–xv. Durham, NC: Duke University Press, 1997.

Vaid, Urvashi. "Sex, Love and Birth Control in the 21st Century." In *This Is What Lesbian Looks Like: Dyke Activists Take on the 21st Century,* edited by Kris Kleindienst, 259–67. Ithaca, NY: Firebrand Books, 1999.

D'Emilio, John, William B. Turner, and Urvashi Vaid. Introduction to *Creating Change: Sexuality, Public Policy, and Civil Rights,* edited by John D'Emilio, William B. Turner, and Urvashi Vaid, vii–xii. New York: St. Martin's Press, 2000.

Vaid, Urvashi. "Getting There Means Mapping Here: Challenges to Collaborations between a GLBT and Labor Movement." In *Out at Work: Building a Gay-Labor Alli-*

ance, edited by Kitty Krupat and Patrick McCreery, 232–35. Minneapolis: University of Minnesota Press, 2001.

Vaid, Urvashi. "What's Sexuality Got to Do with It?" In *Race in 21st Century America*, edited by Curtis Stokes, Theresa Meléndez, and Genice Rhodes-Reed, 423–34. East Lansing: Michigan State University Press, 2001.

Vaid, Urvashi. "Speech at the March on Washington, April 25, 1993." In *Great Speeches on Gay Rights*, edited by James Daly, 81–84. Mineola, NY: Dover Thrift Editions, 2010.

Vaid, Urvashi. Foreword to *My American History: Lesbian and Gay Life during the Reagan and Bush Years*, 2nd ed., by Sarah Schulman, xv–xvii. New York: Routledge, 2018.

Vaid, Urvashi. Preface to *My American History: Lesbian and Gay Life during the Reagan and Bush Years*, 2nd ed., by Sarah Schulman, x–xv. New York: Routledge, 2018.

Vaid, Urvashi. "What Can Brown Do for You? Race, Sexuality, and the Future of LGBT Politics." In *Queer Then and Now: The David R. Kessler Lectures 2002–2020*, edited by Debanuj Dasgupta, Joseph V. Donica, and Margot Weiss, 147–83. New York: Feminist Press, 2023.

Vaid-Menon, Alok, and Urvashi Vaid. "Feminist Coalition and Queer Movements across Time: A Conversation between Alok Vaid-Menon and Urvashi Vaid." In *FUTURE/PRESENT: Arts in a Changing America*, edited by Daniela Alvarez, Roberta Uno, and Elizabeth M. Webb, 504–15. Durham, NC: Duke University Press, 2024.

Selected Research Reports and Briefs

Vaid, Urvashi. "Media Skills Workshop for Gay and Lesbian Activists and Organizations." National Gay and Lesbian Task Force, 1988.

Vaid, Urvashi. "Testimony on the Nomination of Judge David Souter." Testimony submitted by National Gay and Lesbian Task Force to US Senate Judiciary Committee, opposing nomination of Judge Souter to the Supreme Court." Washington, DC, September 1990.

Vaid, Urvashi. *Selected Bibliography of Resources on Gay and Lesbian and AIDS Issues in South Asia*. National Gay and Lesbian Task Force Policy Institute, April 1992.

Vaid, Urvashi. "Testimony on Homophobia." Presentation at meeting organized by the Women's Environment and Development Organization, at the Fourth UN World Conference on Women, Beijing, September 1995.

Hanssens, Catherine, Aisha C. Moodie Mills, Andrea Ritchie, Dean Spade, and Urvashi Vaid. *A Roadmap for Change: Federal Policy Recommendations Addressing the Criminalization of LGBT People and People Living with HIV*. Center for Gender and Sexuality Law, Columbia University Law School, 2014.

Vaid, Urvashi, and Ashindi Maxton. *The Apparitional Donor. Understanding and Engaging High Net Worth Donors of Color*. 2017. DOI: 10.13140/RG.2.2.18700.77448.

Hunter, Lourdes A., Guillaume R. Bagal III, Juan Battle, Frank J. Bewkes, Sasha Buchert, Tyrone Hanley, Meghan Maury, Ashe McGovern, Taissa Morimoto, Carla Sutherland, and Urvashi Vaid. *Intersecting Injustice: Addressing LGBTQ Poverty and*

Economic Justice for All: A National Call to Action (New York: Social Justice Sexuality Project, Graduate Center, City University of New York, March 2018). https://socialjusticesexuality.com/files/2018/04/Poverty-Reports-Exec-Summary.pdf.

Articles, Essays, and Opinion Pieces

Vaid, Urvashi. "NPP Gathers the Facts on AIDS in Prisons." *National Prison Project Journal* 6 (Winter 1985).

Vaid, Urvashi. "Balanced Response Needed to AIDS in Prison." *National Prison Project Journal* 7 (Spring 1986).

Vaid, Urvashi. "Out of the Closet and into the Fray: Three Views on Outing." *On the Issues Magazine*, November 4, 1990. https://ontheissuesmagazine.com/gender/out-of-the-closet-and-into-the-fray-three-views-on-outing/.

Vaid, Urvashi. "Outing Is Coercion Not Liberation." *Gauntlet: Exploring the Limits of Free Speech* 2 (1991): 290–93.

Vaid, Urvashi. "Funding Lesbian Organizations." *Women in Foundations Newsletter*, Fall 1992.

Vaid, Urvashi. "After Identity." *New Republic* 208, no. 19 (May 10, 1993): 28.

Vaid, Urvashi. "Compromising Positions." *The Advocate* 63 (June 26, 1993): 96.

Vaid, Urvashi. "A Queer Nation." *The Nation* 25, no. 1 (July 5, 1993): 3.

Vaid, Urvashi. "Alien Nation." *The Advocate* 638 (September 21, 1993): 80.

Vaid, Urvashi. "What's New?" *The Advocate* 644 (December 13, 1993): 80.

Vaid, Urvashi. "The Status Quo of the Status Queer." *Gay Community News* 20, nos. 1–2 (June 1994): 16–18.

Vaid, Urvashi. "Gay Lobbyists Arrived on Capitol Hill in 70s." *New York Times*, February 21, 1995, Section A, 18.

Vaid, Urvashi. "Building Bridges: Thoughts on Identity and South Asian G/L/B/T Organizing." From Keynote Address at the Pride Utsav Conference, June 17, 1995, San Francisco, CA. Reprinted in *Trikone Magazine* 11, no. 1 (1996): 64–65.

Vaid, Urvashi. "As for Welfare, Where Have the Liberals Gone?" *New York Times*, July 25, 1996. Gale OneFile: News, link.gale.com/apps/doc/A150492498/STND?u=txshracd2898&sid=bookmark-STND&xid=364de818. Accessed July 11, 2024.

Vaid, Urvashi. "Real Life Scary Stories." *The Advocate* 719 (October 29, 1996): 80.

Vaid, Urvashi. "Hope versus Hype." *The Advocate* 723 (December 24, 1996): 80.

Vaid, Urvashi. "Identity." *Trikone Magazine* (January 1997): 8.

Vaid, Urvashi. "Coalition as Goal Not Process." *Gay Community News* 22, no. 4 (Spring 1997): 6–9.

Vaid, Urvashi. "Activism Phobia." *The Advocate* 735 (June 10, 1997): 88.

Vaid, Urvashi. "Calling All Lesbians." *The Advocate* 742 (September 16, 1997): 88.

Vaid, Urvashi. "Panic or Panacea?" *The Advocate* (December 8, 1997): 88.

Vaid, Urvashi. "Status Quo or Queer." *The Advocate* 755 (March 17, 1998): 72.

Vaid, Urvashi. "We Are Devo." *The Advocate* 761 (June 9, 1998): 80.

Vaid, Urvashi. "Playing the Ex-Gay Games." *The Advocate* 768 (September 15, 1998): 72.

Vaid, Urvashi. "Inclusion, Exclusion and Occlusion: The Queer Idea of Asian Pacific American-ness." *Amerasia Journal* 25, no. 3 (1999): 1–16.

Vaid, Urvashi. "The Politics of Intersection." *Off Our Backs* 29, no. 6 (June 1999): 9–11.

Vaid, Urvashi. "Linking Arms and Movements." *The Advocate* 787 (June 8, 1999): 88.

Vaid, Urvashi. "SLOTH." *The Stranger*, June 17, 1999. https://www.thestranger.com /pullout/1999/06/17/1307/sloth.

Weiser, Jay, and Urvashi Vaid. "The Myth of Gay and Lesbian Affluence." *In These Times* (June 27, 1999): 20–21.

Vaid, Urvashi. "C-Span vs. the Kitchen Table." *The Advocate* 794 (September 14, 1999): 96.

Vaid, Urvashi. "Guess Who Isn't Coming to Dinner?" *The Advocate* 800 (December 7, 1999): 104.

Vaid, Urvashi. "Public Speech and Private Chats." *The Advocate* 807 (March 14, 2000): 65.

Vaid, Urvashi. "Testosterone Poisoning." *The Advocate* 813 (June 6, 2000): 88.

Vaid, Urvashi. "It's the Ideology, Stupid." *The Advocate* 820 (September 12, 2000): 72.

Vaid, Urvashi. "Bridging the Political Gap." *The Advocate* 826 (December 5, 2000): 72.

Vaid, Urvashi. "Rage against the Silence." *The Advocate* 833 (March 13, 2001): 72.

Vaid, Urvashi. "Sick of Being Pacified." *The Advocate* 839 (June 5, 2001): 80.

Vaid, Urvashi. "It's a Small Homophobic World." *The Advocate* 846 (September 11, 2001): 72.

Vaid, Urvashi. "A Member of the Tribe." *The Advocate* 852 (December 4, 2001): 80.

Vaid, Urvashi. "Pro-Marriage and Antigay." *The Advocate* 861 (April 16, 2002): 72.

Vaid, Urvashi. "Watching the Watchers." *The Advocate* 868 (July 23, 2002): 72.

Vaid, Urvashi. "Separate and Unequal" *The Advocate* 875 (October 29, 2002): 72.

Vaid, Urvashi. "Bring Back the Coffee Klatch." *The Advocate*, no. 884 (March 4, 2003): 80.

Vaid, Urvashi. Foreword to *Journal of Gay and Lesbian Social Services* 16, nos. 3–4 (2004): xxvii–xxx.

Vaid, Urvashi. "Wagging the Dog." *The Advocate* 972 (October 10, 2006): 10.

Vaid, Urvashi. "Still Ain't Satisfied: LGBT Politics and the Limits of Equality." *American Prospect* 23, no. 4 (May 2012): 38–43.

Vaid, Urvashi. "Be Transformative, Not Transfixed." *The Nation* (June 17, 2013).

Vaid, Urvashi. "Now You Get What You Want, Do You Want More? Symposium Issue: Making Constitutional Change: The Past, Present and Future of Perry v. Brown." *NYU Review of Law and Social Change* 37, no. 1 (2013): 101–11.

Vaid, Urvashi. "Chemo Killed the Small-Talk Gene." *Journal of Lesbian Studies* 18, no. 1 (2014): 31–42. https://doi.org/10.1080/10894160.2013.836433.

Vaid, Urvashi. "What's Liberation Got to Do with It?" In *Transformations*, Open Democracy website, June 10, 2014. https://www.opendemocracy.net/en/transformation /whats-liberation-got-to-do-with-it/.

Vaid, Urvashi. "Forward-Looking 377 Order Holds Lessons for the World." *Times of India*, September 9, 2018. Sunday Edition.

Vaid, Urvashi. "It's Time to Re-embrace a Politics of Radical, Queer, Outsider Activism." Reclaiming Stonewall 50. *The Nation* 309, no. 1 (July 15, 2019): 12–19.

Selected Award Acceptance Speeches (with Video Links)

Susan M. Love Award, Fenway Health Women's Dinner Party, March 31, 2012. https:// www.youtube.com/watch?v=K4O7nWnj-zc.

GLAD Law. "Urvashi Vaid Receives the 2014 GLAD Spirit of Justice Award," Fifteenth Annual Spirit of Justice Award Dinner, October 24, 2014. https://www.youtube.com /watch?v=Q83aPP85vRg.

Auburn Theological Seminary, Lives of Commitment—Women of Moral Courage Honorees, 2021. https://www.youtube.com/watch?v=d-8RI_MFG5s.

Susan J. Hyde Award for Longevity in the Movement, Creating Change Conference. March 19, 2022. https://www.youtube.com/watch?v=rj7xnzNtnfo/.

Selected Writings and Resources on Urvashi Vaid

Book Reviews

Aptheker, Bettina. "Imagining the Impossible." Review of *Irresistible Revolution: Confronting Race, Class and the Assumptions of LGBT Politics*, by Urvashi Vaid. *Women's Review of Books* (May–June 2013), 5–7.

Goldstein, Richard. "Virtual Reality." Review of *Virtually Normal: An Argument about Homosexuality*, by Andrew Sullivan, and *Virtual Equality: The Mainstreaming of Gay and Lesbian Liberation*, by Urvashi Vaid. *The Village Voice* (September 19, 1995), 85–87.

Goodheart, Adam. "Gay Rights: Wrong Strategy?" Review of *Virtual Equality: The Mainstreaming of Gay and Lesbian Liberation*, by Urvashi Vaid. *Washington Post*, November 21, 1995, E2.

Howard, John. Review of *Creating Change: Sexuality, Public Policy, and Civil Rights*, edited by John D'Emilio, William B. Turner, and Urvashi Vaid. *Journal of American History* (March 2002): 1623–24.

Maran, Meredith. "One Woman's State of the Union Address to Gays." Review of *Virtual Equality: The Mainstreaming of Gay and Lesbian Liberation*, by Urvashi Vaid. *San Francisco Chronicle*, September 24, 1995. https://www.sfgate.com/books /article/one-woman-s-statte-of-the-union-address-to-gays-3023780.php.

Murrell, Nancy. "Two Books on Gays like Night and Day." Review of *Virtual Equality: The Mainstreaming of Gay and Lesbian Liberation*, by Urvashi Vaid, and *Virtually Normal: An Argument about Homosexuality*, by Andrew Sullivan. *San Jose Mercury News*, October 29, 1995.

Owen, Sally. "Divided We Stand." Review of *Virtual Equality: Mainstreaming of Gay and Lesbian Liberation*, by Urvashi Vaid. *On the Issues: The Progressive Woman's Quarterly* (May 7, 1996). https://ontheissuesmagazine.com/gender/virtual-equality -the-mainstreaming-of-gay-lesbian-liberation-by-urvashi-vaid/.

Schacter, Jane S. "Skepticism, Culture and the Gay Civil Rights Debate in a Post–Civil-Rights Era." Review of *Virtual Equality*, by Urvashi Vaid. *Harvard Law Review* 110, no. 3 (1997): 684–731.

Sengupta, Shivaji. "'Virtual Equality' Holds Advice for Homosexuals." Review of *Virtual*

Equality: The Mainstreaming of Gay and Lesbian Liberation, by Urvashi Vaid. *India Abroad*, November 17, 1995, 52.

Stoddard, Tom. "She's Vaid." Review of *Virtual Equality: The Mainstreaming of Gay and Lesbian Liberation*, by Urvashi Vaid. *The Advocate* 692 (October 17, 1995): 66–68.

Stroud, Irene Elizabeth. "Practical Radical." Review of *Virtual Equality: The Mainstreaming of Gay and Lesbian Liberation*, by Urvashi Vaid. *Women's Review of Books* (January 1996): 5.

Vaillancourt, Daniel. "Manifesto for the Millennium." Review of *Virtual Equality: The Mainstreaming of Gay and Lesbian Liberation*, by Urvashi Vaid. *The Front Page*, October 13, 1995.

Selected Interviews (Print, Online, Audio, or Video)

The Advocate. "Creator of Change—Urvashi Vaid." *The Advocate* (June 28, 2022).

The Advocate. "The Return of Urvashi." *The Advocate* (October 3, 1995).

Athena Art Project. Excerpt of video interview with Urvashi Vaid, from Republican National Convention, Houston, August 17–20, 1992. https://www.youtube.com /watch?v=Df_8zatuBVk.

Barsamian, David. "A Shared Politics of Social Justice: Interview with Urvashi Vaid." In *Talking about a Revolution*, edited by the South End Press Collective, 95–112. Cambridge, MA: South End Press, 1999.

Battle, Juan. "Interview with Urvashi Vaid." City University of New York. Interview conducted via Zoom. November 14, 2020. See also https://socialjusticesexuality.com /publications/.

Billard, Betsy. Moderator. "The State of the Struggle. A Roundtable Discussion with Martin Duberman, Michelangelo Signorile, and Urvashi Vaid." *The Harvard Gay and Lesbian Review* 6, no. 3 (Summer 1999).

Brownworth, Victoria. "Irresistible Revolutionary: An Interview with Urvashi Vaid." *Curve* (March 2013): 45–46.

Chang, Alisa. "Critics of President George H. W. Bush Reflect on His Handling of the AIDS Crisis—An Interview with Urvashi Vaid." Interview on *All Things Considered*, National Public Radio, December 4, 2018. https://www.npr.org/2018/12/04 /673398013/critics-of-president-george-h-w-bush-reflect-on-his-handling-of-the -aids-crisis.

Chideya, Faria. "A 2014 Interview with Urvashi Vaid." *Our Body Politic* podcast. Aired June 17, 2022. https://cdn.simplecast.com/audio/5b658519-aa12–46c1-ac12 -a4cc142c6ac3/episodes/0028f351–0b86–49cc-89ea-67140cf52ab2/audio/8b1babc5 –0d094-f7e-b889–8920e2719207/default_tc.mp3.

Coffin, Alice. "If You Leave Me . . . I'm Coming Too: An Interview with Urvashi Vaid." EuroCentralAsian Lesbian Conference [EL*C], 2018, New York City. Published online on May 16, 2022, at https://europeanlesbianconference.org/remembering -urvashi-vaid/.

Colbert, Chuck. "Seeing a Future Beyond Formal LGBT Equality: Talking with Urvashi Vaid." *Windy City Times*, January 16, 2013, 4–5.

Cusac, Anne-Marie. "Urvashi Vaid: Interview." *The Progressive* 60, no. 3 (March 1996): 34–39.

Flanders, Laura. "Kate Clinton and Urvashi Vaid: Revolutionaries—What Makes Them Irresistible?" *The Laura Flanders Show*, 2014. https://www.youtube.com/watch?v =rj7xnzNtnfo.

Flanders, Laura. "We Need Progressive, Multi-Issue Movements—Interview with Urvashi Vaid." Grit TV, August 6, 2014. https://web.archive.org/web/20140806074912 /http://blip.tv/grittv/grittv-urvashi-vaid-we-need-progressive-multi-issue -movements-4569390.

Gessen, Masha. "Coming Out, and Rising Up, in the Fifty Years after Stonewall." *New Yorker*, June 28, 2019.

Goodman, Amy, and Sharif Abdel Kouddous. "The Fight for Equality: A Look at the State of the Gay Rights Movement." Audio and video interview, *Democracy Now*, October 13, 2009. https://www.democracynow.org/2009/10/13/the_fight_for _equality_a_look.

Hayes, Chris. "Urvashi Vaid 'Still a Great Deal of Negative Feeling.'" Video interview, *Up with Chris Hayes*, NBC News, May 12, 2012. https://www.nbcnews.com/news /world/urvashi-vaid-still-great-deal-negative-feeling-flna768485.

Houdart, Fabrice. "Interview with Urvashi Vaid." Video interview, July 15, 2020. https:// www.youtube.com/watch?v=kzHa8hlmUiA.

Isom, Darren. "Urvashi Vaid: The Relay Race of Liberation." *Dreaming in Color*, episode 2. audio interview. Aired June 23, 2022. https://www.bridgespan.org/dreaming -in-color-urvashi-vaid.

Johns, Merryn. "Urvashi Vaid Is Our Very Own Wonder Woman." *Queer Forty*, April 1, 2022. https://queerforty.com/urvashi-vaid-is-our-very-own-wonder-woman.

Khan, Surina. "Good Luck to Urvashi." *Metroline Magazine* (June 19, 1992): 18–19.

Khan, Surina. "Still Out Front: Urvashi Vaid." *Metroline Magazine* (June 10, 1993): 22–24.

Khan, Surina. "'We're Engaged in a Cultural Transformation'—An Interview with Urvashi Vaid." *The Harvard Gay and Lesbian Review* (Fall 1995): 5–8.

Kuehl, Sheila James. "Voices of Our Lives: Kate Clinton and Urvashi Vaid." *Get Used to It*, episode 10. Outfest UCLA Legacy Project. Video interview. August 1993. https:// www.youtube.com/watch?v=yyYbttW307w.

La Marche, Gara. "Navigating Philanthropy: An Interview with Bill Vandenberg, Jee Kim, and Urvashi Vaid." *Forge*, June 17, 2021. https://forgeorganizing.org/article /navigating-philanthropy.

Lewis, Valda. "Interview with Urvashi Vaid." Video interview and footage, Republican National Convention, 1988, New Orleans. From the Valda Lewis Collection, LGBT Legacy Project.

Lewis, Valda. Video footage of interview of Urvashi Vaid and remarks at "Celebration— The Louisiana State Lesbian and Gay Conference." New Orleans, 1990. https://www .youtube.com/watch?app=desktop&v=KOJl7MxQQbk.

Marcus, Eric. "An Interview with Urvashi—1989." *Making Gay History* podcast. Aired November 2022. https://makinggayhistory.com/podcast/urvashi-vaid/.

McHugh, E. (May, J., photographs). *The L Life: Extraordinary Lesbians Making a Differ-ence*. New York: Stewart, Tabori and Chang, 2011.

Meera. "Dynamic Leader, Fearless Advocate Urvashi Vaid Heads National Gay and Les-bian Task Force." *Trikone Newsletter* 4, no. 5 (September–October 1989): 1–4.

Meera. "Working Together: An Interview with Urvashi Vaid." In *A Lotus of Another Color*, edited by Rakesh Ratti, 103–12. New York: Alyson Publications, 1993.

Melwani, Lavina. "AIDS Shattered Many Myths: Interview with Urvashi Vaid." *India Today*, January 1995.

Messman, Terry. "Impossible Dream or Irresistible Revolution? The Street Spirit Inter-view with Urvashi Vaid." *The Street Spirit*, November 8, 2013. https://thestreetspirit .org/2013/11/06/impossible-dream-or-irresistible-revolution-the-street-spirit -interview-with-urvashi-vaid/.

Morgan, Robin. "Live with Robin Morgan: Interview with Urvashi Vaid." https:// music.amazon.co.uk/podcasts/7b0a260a-d409–459e-847c-4ea5b3514e6a/episodes /cf63c4d4–6ecb-4f25-a2c2–0a623cc8a3aa/women's-media-center-live-with-robin -morgan-wmc-live-30-urvashi-vaid-helen-zia-jennifer-freyd-stephanie-gilmore -original-airdate-3–16–2013.

Ms. Magazine. "Let's Get Real about Feminism: The Backlash, the Myths, the Move-ment." A discussion between Urvashi Vaid, Gloria Steinem, Naomi Wolf, and bell hooks. *Ms.* 4, no. 2 (September–October 1993): 34–43.

Pastrana, Antonio. "The Intersectional Imagination: What Do Lesbian and Gay Leaders of Color Have to Do with It?" *Race, Gender, and Class* 13, nos. 3–4 (2006): 218–38.

Peterson, Andrew L. T. "The Dubious Merits of Mainstreaming." Interview with Ur-vashi Vaid. *The Front Page*, October 13, 1995.

Priyamvada, Sunita, and Vinita Srivastava. "More than Virtual Vaid." Interview with Ur-vashi Vaid. *Trikone Magazine* (October 1995): 7–9.

Pugh, Clifford. "Rights Advocate Sees 'Two Realities' about Homosexual Issues." *Hous-ton Chronicle*, November 7, 1995, 1D, 12D.

Robinson, Charlotte. "Urvashi Vaid Talks Future of LGBT Equality and Being Honored by GLAD." Audio interview. *Huffington Post*, October 17, 2014; updated December 6, 2017. https://www.huffpost.com/entry/urvashi-vaid-talks-future_b_5996938.

Rose, Charlie. "Gay Rights March." A televised interview with Urvashi Vaid and An-drew Sullivan, *The Charlie Rose Show*, April 23, 1993.

Roy-Chowdhury, Sandip. "Beyond Legitimation, towards Liberation." Interview with Urvashi Vaid. *India Currents* (October 1995): 24–25.

Smalls, Shante Paradigm (moderator). "Queer Then and Now: CLAGS Kessler Award Winners Amber Hollibaugh, Dean Spade, and Urvashi Vaid Reflect on Queer/Trans Activism and Scholarship." Cosponsored by Center for Lesbian and Gay Studies, City University of New York, and the Center for Feminist Futures, University of Cal-ifornia, Santa Barbara, Zoom interview, February 18, 2021.

Spade, Dean, and Hope Dector. "Queer Dreams and Nonprofit Blue: Understanding the Nonprofit Industrial Complex." Six-part video interview series featuring Urvashi Vaid and other speakers, October 2013 conference co-convened by Barnard Cen-ter for Research on Women and Engaging Tradition Project at Columbia University

Gender and Sexuality Law, February 28, 2016. https://www.deanspade.net/2016 /02/28/queer-dreams-and-nonprofit-blues/. Also available at *The Scholar and Feminist* online issue "Activism and the Academy," 12.1–12.2. http://sfonline .barnard.edu/activism-and-the-academy.

Stack, Liam. "'He Did Not Lead on AIDS': With Bush, Activists See a Mixed Legacy." *New York Times*, December 3, 2018. The print version appeared in New York edition, December 5, 2018, Section A18, titled, "Activists Remember Man Who Did Not Lead in Deadly Days of Crisis."

"Stonewall Portraits: An Interview with Urvashi Vaid." Video interview, Provincetown Community Television, 2009. https://archive.org/details/Stonewall_Portraits _-_An_Interview_with_Urvashi_Vaid.

Sundaram, Viji. "Gay Rights Activist Vaid Devoted to Her Cause." *India West*, June 23, 1995, C7.

Torregrosa, Luisita Lopez. "The Gay Nineties: Interview with Urvashi Vaid." *Vanity Fair*, April, 1993, 122–26, 178–83.

Woubshet, Dagmawi. Moderator, "Saving Sex: Urvashi Vaid, Susie Bright, and David France, in Conversation." Opening Lecture at Human Sexuality Collection exhibition, Cornell University, March 18, 2014. https://events.cornell.edu/event /human_sexuality_exhibition_opening_lecture_with_susie_bright_and_david _france.

Wolf, Brandon. "After Gay Marriage, What?" Interview with Urvashi Vaid. *Outsmart* Magazine (January 1, 2015). https://www.outsmartmagazine.com/2015/01/gay -marriage/.

Selected Video Footage and Documentaries

Cardona, Dominique, and Laurie Colbert. *My Feminism*. 1997. National Film Board of Canada. https://www.wmm.com/catalog/film/my-feminism/. This film features interviews with Urvashi Vaid, bell hooks, Gloria Steinem, and Urvashi Butalia on the past, present, and future status of the women's movement and its racial, economic, and ideological diversity.

Creating Change Conference: 1992–1995. Video footage, from the Valda G. Lewis Collection, LGBT Legacy Project. https://lgbtlegacyproject.org/filmmaker.

Kates, Nancy, director. Forthcoming documentary of Urvashi Vaid, in progress, July 2024.

Syers, Mike. Director. *There Are Things to Do*. 2023. Produced by Fermin Rojas. https:// www.therearethingstodo.com/. This eighteen-minute film about Urvashi Vaid explores Urvashi's ties to Provincetown, Massachusetts, and her thirty-four-year relationship with partner Kate Clinton. The film's title comes from the last section of *Virtual Equality: The Mainstreaming of Gay and Lesbian Liberation*, the book Urvashi moved to Provincetown to work on.

Tributes

American LGBTQ Museum. "The American LGBTQ Museum Mourns the Loss and Celebrates the Life of Urvashi Vaid." New York, May 2023. https://americanlgbtq museum.org/2022/08/memorial-to-urvashi-vaid/.

"Arcus Foundation Mourns Loss and Celebrates Legacy of Urvashi Vaid." New York, May 16, 2022. https://www.arcusfoundation.org/arcus-mourns-loss-and-celebrates -legacy-of-urvashi-vaid/.

Arora, Priya. "In Urvashi Vaid's World All Were Welcome." *The Juggernaut*, May 17, 2022.

Boston Spirit Magazine. "LGBTQ Activist, Part-Time Provincetown Resident Urvashi Vaid Dies at 63." *Boston Spirit Magazine*, May 17, 2022.

Brownworth, Victoria A. "Activist Urvashi Vaid's Immeasurable Impact on the LGBTQ Rights Movement." LGBTQ Nation, October 10, 2022. https://www.lgbtqnation .com/2022/10/activist-urvashi-vaids-immeasurable-impact-lgbtq-rights-movement/.

Burns, Richard. "Remembering Urvashi Vaid." American LGBTQ+ Museum, New York, May 2023.

Cassell, Heather. "Urvashi Vaid, Noted LGBTQ Leader, Dies." *Bay Area Reporter*, San Francisco, May 16, 2022. https://www.ebar.com/story.php?ch=news&sc=latest_news &id=315610.

D'Emilio, John. "A Leader in the Fight for Social Justice: Lessons from the Career of Ur-vashi Vaid." Remarks given at Symposium on Social Movements and the Politics of Law in Honor of Urvashi Vaid. Emory University School of Law, October 6, 2023.

D'Emilio, John. "Remembering Urvashi Vaid." *Democratic Left*, June 9, 2022. https:// www.dsausa.org/democratic-left/remembering-urvashi-vaid/.

The Fight. "Los Angeles LGBT Center Mourns the Passing of Legendary LGBT Activist and Leader Urvashi Vaid." *The Fight*, May 16, 2022. https://thefightmag.com /2022/05/los-angeles-lgbt-center-mourns-the-passing-of-legendary-lgbt-activist -and-leader-urvashi-vaid/.

Flanders, Laura. "Urvashi Vaid, 1958–2022: Telling the Truth, Standing Together, and Fighting for Liberation." *The Nation*, May 26, 2022. https://www.thenation.com /article/activism/urvashi-vaid-obituary-lgbtq/.

Funders for LGBTQ Staff. "We Honor the Life and Legacy of Urvashi Vaid." May 17, 2022. https://lgbtfunders.org/newsposts/we-honor-the-life-and-legacy-of -urvashi-vaid/.

Gessen, Masha. "The Prolific Activism of Urvashi Vaid." *New Yorker*, May 24, 2022. https://www.newyorker.com/news/postscript/the-prolific-activism-of-urvashi-vaid.

Green, Andrew. "Urvashi Vaid: LGBTQ and Health Activist, Lawyer and Writer." *The Lancet* 400, no. 10349 (July 30, 2022): 354. https://doi.org/10.1016/S0140 -6736(22)01393-9.

Jean, Lorrie L. "Rest in Power: Urvashi Vaid—The Queer Movement's Legendary Fire-brand." *Ms.*, August 16, 2022. https://msmagazine.com/2022/08/16/urvashi-vaid/.

Marble, Steve. "Urvashi Vaid, Pioneering LGBTQ Activist and Author, Dies at 63." *Los Angeles Times*, May 18, 2022.

Marcus, Eric. "Remembering Urvashi Vaid '79." *Vassar Quarterly* (Summer 2022). https://read.nxtbook.com/vassar/vq/summer_2022/remembering_urvashi_vaid _79_1.html.

Marquard, Bryan. "Urvashi Vaid, LGBTQ Activist from Boston to the National Stage." *Boston Globe*, June 8, 2022. https://www.bostonglobe.com/2022/06/08/metro /urvashi-vaid-lgbtq-activist-boston-national-stage/.

National LGBTQ Task Force. "Statement on the Passing of Urvashi Vaid, Activist, Author, Attorney, and Past Task Force Executive Director." Washington, DC, May 14, 2022. https://www.thetaskforce.org/news/passing-of-urvashi-vaid-activist-author-attorney-and-past-task-force-executive-director/.

Noyce, Eleanor. "Renowned LGBTQ Activist Urvashi Vaid Has Died at 63." *DIVA*, May 15, 2022. https://diva-magazine.com/2022/05/15/renowned-lgbtqi-activist-urvashi-vaid-has-died-at-63%EF%BF%BC/.

Recchio, Tom. "Urvashi Vaid, Tireless Fighter for Gay Equality, Dies at 63." *Provincetown Independent*, May 18, 2022. https://provincetownindependent.org/obituaries/2022/05/18/urvashi-vaid-tireless-fighter-for-gay-equality-dies-at-63/.

Risen, Clay. "Urvashi Vaid, an L.G.B.T.Q. Activist Hailed as 'a Revelation,' Dies at 63." *New York Times*, May 18, 2022, A21. https://www.nytimes.com/2022/05/17/us/urvashi-vaid-dead.html.

Rupert-Gordon, Imani. "To Honor a Legend, Continue Her Legacy: Urvashi Vaid, 1958–2022." National Center for Lesbian Rights, May 25, 2022. https://www.nclrights.org/to-honor-a-legend-continue-her-legacy-urvashi-vaid-1958-2022/.

Smith, Harrison. "Urvashi Vaid, Forward Thinking Rights Activist, Dies at 63." *Washington Post*, May 16, 2022. https://www.washingtonpost.com/obituaries/2022/05/16/lgbtq-activist-urvashi-vaid-dead/.

Sutherland, Carla. "The National LGBTQ+ Women's Community Survey—Unfinished Business." Justice Work, New York City, May 20, 2022. https://mailchi.mp/fc36ca809e30/unfinished-business?e=dfddccb2fd.

TAG—Treatment Action Group. "Treatment Action Group Mourns Urvashi Vaid, Celebrates Her Life and Legacy." Treatment Action Group, May 17, 2022. https://www.treatmentactiongroup.org/statement/treatment-action-group-mourns-urvashi-vaid-celebrates-her-life-and-legacy/.

Treisman, Rachel. "Remembering Urvashi Vaid, an LGBTQ Activist Who Spent Decades Fighting for Equality." National Public Radio, May 18, 2022. https://www.nprillinois.org/2022-05-18/remembering-urvashi-vaid-an-lgbtq-activist-who-spent-decades-fighting-for-equality.

Vaid, Rachna. "Urvashi Vaid—A Remembrance." Unpublished remarks delivered at Funeral Service, New York City, May 18, 2023. Available from the editors on request.

Vaid-Menon, Alok B. "Urvash Masi—A Tribute." Unpublished remarks at Memorial Celebration, New York City, November 3, 2022. Available from the editors on request.

Exhibits, Commemorative Events, Impact

Peter, Gio Black. "Fire in the Night: A Celebration of Queer Tenacity." A commissioned installation of portrait paintings on New York City subway maps of Marsha P. Johnson and iconic queer thought leaders James Baldwin, Ceyenne Doroshow, Félix González-Torres, Journey Forrester Streams, Amanda Lepore, and Urvashi Vaid, June 16–August 22, 2022.

Urvashi Vaid—One of Five 2022 Honorees Added to the Stonewall Inn's "Wall of

Honor: Honoring Our Pioneers, Trail-Blazers and Heroes." Sponsored by the Task Force and the Imperial Court, New York City, June 23, 2022.

The Urvies Project. A set of six posters of images and sayings of Urvashi Vaid produced by Sue J. Hyde and Susan Fleischmann for display at Dyke Marches in different cities. The New York City Dyke March was organized by Johanna Sanders, June 25, 2022.

The History Project. Urvashi Vaid—Memorial Gathering, Boston, September 28, 2022. Featuring tributes by Amy Hoffman, Richard Burns, and others. https://www.you tube.com/watch?v=J8uCo5U-YbQ.

"Celebrating the Life and Impact of Urvashi Vaid, '83, LGBTQ Activist and Trailblazer." Panel at Northeastern University Law School Reunion, Boston, October 21, 2022.

"A Celebration of the Life of Urvashi Vaid." B'Nai Jeshurun, New York City, November 3, 2022. Remarks by Tony Kushner, Kate Clinton, Alok B. Vaid-Menon, Gloria Steinem, Natalia Kanem, Trishala Deb, Rabbi Sharon Kleinbaum, and Richard Burns. https://americanlgbtqmuseum.org/2022/08/memorial-to-urvashi-vaid/.

"I Still Love You: Queerness, Ancestors, and the Places That Made Us." Exhibit held at James B. Hormel LGBTQIA Center, San Francisco Public Library, March–June 2023. https://sfpl.org/exhibits/2023/03/18/i-still-love-you.

Cristi, A. A. "Performance Space New York Presents a Marathon Reading of Late Activist + Writer Urvashi Vaid's *Virtual Equality*." Organized by Sarah Schulman, April 10, 2023. https://www.broadwayworld.com/off-off-broadway/article/Performance -Space-New-York-Presents-A-Marathon-Reading-Of-Late-Activist-Writer-Urvashi -Vaids-VIRTUAL-EQUALITY-20230410.

"A Celebration of the Life and Legacy of Urvashi Vaid." Organized by Roadwork and Mary Farmer, All Souls Church, Washington, DC, May 14, 2023.

"Urvashi Vaid's Extraordinary Legacy at Justice Work." Justice Work, June 2023. https:// lgbtqwomensurvey.org/wp-content/uploads/2023/06/Resource_Urvashi-Vaids -Extraordinary-Legacy-at-Justice-Work.pdf.

"Kevin Cathcart Movement Leader Award" was given to Urvashi Vaid posthumously at Lambda Legal's fiftieth anniversary Liberty Awards Dinner, New York, June 2023.

Roldan, Bec. "Many LGBTQ+ Women Face Discrimination and Violence, but Find Support in Friendships." National Public Radio, July 1, 2023. https://www.npr.org /sections/health-shots/2023/07/01/1185536324/many-lgbtq-women-face -discrimination-and-violence-but-find-support-in-friendship.

Hunter, Nan, Darren Hutchinson, and Nancy Marcus, co-convenors. "Social Movements and the Politics of Law—A Symposium Honoring Urvashi Vaid's Life's Work," Center for Civil Rights and Social Justice, Emory University School of Law, October 5–6, 2023.

"Urvashi Vaid Changemakers Fund," Provincetown Commons, October 7, 2023. https:// www.provincetowncommons.org/contribute/urvashivaid.

Stein, Marc. "Urvashi Vaid: The Vassar and Boston Years, 1975–1983." *OutHistory*, November 2023. https://outhistory.org/exhibits/show/urv/urvintro.

"Urvashi Vaid Planned Parenthood Fund to Further the Mission of Planned Parenthood Federation of America for Future Generations." November–December 2023.

Tracy, Matt. "Fire Island's Trailblazers' Park Set to Showcase 16 LGBTQ Icons." May 24, 2024. https://gaycitynews.com/fire-islands-trailblazers-park-pride-16-lgbtq-icons/.

Bench with memorial plaque dedicated to Urvashi Vaid in AIDS Memorial Park, New York City, June 2024.

The Urvashi Vaid '79, Fellowship for Social Justice. Endowed fellowship, Vassar College, established in July 2024.

EDITOR AND CONTRIBUTOR BIOGRAPHIES

JYOTSNA VAID earned her doctorate in experimental psychology at McGill University and joined Texas A&M University in 1986, where she is currently Professor of Psychological and Brain Sciences and Women's and Gender Studies. She directs the Language and Cognition Lab, is a founding member of the Diversity Science Research Cluster, and convenor of the South Asia Studies Working Group. Vaid has published extensively on cognitive and neural aspects of bilingualism, literacy, and creativity, and the impact of gender and race on professional visibility in academia. In addition to numerous scholarly articles and book chapters, she edited *Language Processing in Bilinguals: Psycholinguistic and Neuropsychological Perspectives* (Erlbaum, 1986/2014), and co-edited *Creative Thought: An Investigation of Conceptual Structures and Processes* (American Psychological Association, 1997). Her research has been supported by the Fulbright Foundation, the National Science Foundation, and the Melbern G. Glasscock Center for Humanities Research. For several years, Vaid edited the journal *Writing Systems Research* (2009–20), and was founding editor of the *Committee on South Asian Women Bulletin* (1983–96). She is an elected Fellow of the American Association for the Advancement of Science, the Association for Psychological Science, the Psychonomic Society, and the American Psychological Association.

AMY HOFFMAN is the author of five books: *Hospital Time* (Duke University Press, 1997), *An Army of Ex-Lovers: My Life at the* Gay Community News (University of Massachusetts Press, 2007), *Lies about My Family* (University of Massachusetts Press, 2013), *The Off Season: A Novel* (University of Wisconsin Press, 2017), and *Dot & Ralfie: A Novel* (University of Wisconsin Press, 2022). She was managing editor of *Gay Community News* for four years and editor in chief of the *Women's Review of Books* for fourteen years. She also worked at South End Press, the Women's Lunch Place, the Unitarian Universalist *World* magazine, and the Massachusetts Foundation for the Humanities. In addition to her career as a writer, editor, and fundraiser, she has taught creative writing and literature at Emerson College and the University of Massachusetts, and is on the faculty of the Solstice Low-residency MFA Program. Her activism over the years includes, most recently, volunteering with the Boston LGBTQ History Project.

TONY KUSHNER (b. 1956) is a playwright and screenwriter. His plays include *A Bright Room Called Day, Angels in America, Homebody/Kabul*, the musical *Caroline or Change* (with composer Jeanine Tesori), and *The Intelligent Homosexual's Guide to Capitalism and Socialism with a Key to the Scriptures.* He wrote the screenplay for HBO's film version of *Angels in America*, directed by Mike Nichols, and the screenplays for Steven Spielberg's films *Munich* (with Eric Roth), *Lincoln, West Side Story*, and *The Fabelmans*. His books include *Brundibar*, with pictures by Maurice Sendak; *The Art of Maurice Sendak, 1980–The Present*; and *Wrestling with Zion: Progressive Jewish-American Responses to the Israeli-Palestinian Conflict*, co-edited with Alisa Solomon (2003). Kushner is the recipient of two Tony Awards, an Emmy, an Olivier Award, four Oscar nominations, and the Pulitzer Prize in Drama. In 2013 Kushner received the National Medal of Arts from President Barack Obama. He lives in Manhattan with his husband, the writer Mark Harris.

ACKNOWLEDGMENTS

This book could not have come into being without the access to Urvashi's archives provided by Kate Clinton. Thank you, Kate, for believing in this project and in us.

Kate, Susan Allee, Richard Burns, and Charles Flowers provided feedback in the early stages and were encouraging and supportive throughout the project.

We are grateful to Ken Wissoker, senior editor at Duke University Press, for recognizing the significance of this collection of writings; assistant editor Ryan Kendall and books project editor Bird Williams were extremely helpful in guiding us through the publication process.

We thank Tony Kushner for writing a foreword that articulates so beautifully who Urvashi was and what she stood for.

We are grateful to Rachna Vaid and Alka Vaid Menon for helping us arrive at a framing of the introduction to the book, and Alok Vaid-Menon for sharing video clips and their own writings on Urvashi's impact.

Several people in Urvashi's vast personal and professional network shared photos, articles, interviews, and memories that gave us a fuller picture of her life and work. In particular, we thank John D'Emilio for sending us his 2023 Emory conference remarks on Urvashi's legacy; Eric Marcus for sharing an early interview with Urvashi that was aired on his podcast, *Making Gay History*; and Jaime Grant for sending us regular updates on the national LGBTQ+ women's community survey that culminated in a book (this was a project that Urvashi had initiated). Marc Stein, director of Outhistory.org, published an illuminating roundtable conversation by Urvashi's friends and college roommates about her years at Vassar and in Boston. Rebecca Hankins, curator and archivist at Texas A&M University, was enormously helpful in finding early writings by Urvashi that enriched the bibliography.

Ritu Menon and Mannika Chopra put us in touch with the *Times of India* editors who gave us permission to reprint Urvashi's 2018 invited essay. Scot Nakagawa shared archival drafts on the 22nd Century Project that Urvashi and he started, and updates on the inaugural 22CI conference. Nan Hunter of Georgetown Law put us in touch with Darren Hutchinson at Emory Law, who invited us to the October 2023 symposium at Emory honoring Urvashi's life and work. Filmmakers Mike Syers, Nancy Kates, and Valda Lewis were generous in sharing links and video footage of Urvashi. We appreciate the generosity of Jurek Wajdowicz, Donna Aceto, the Associated Press, *OutWeek* magazine, and the estate of Ellen Shub for sharing their photos of Urvashi.

Amy would like to thank her longtime writing buddies, Anita Diamant and Stephen McCauley; Richard Burns; the members of her Girlzzz Group; and especially her wife, Roberta Stone—whose writing smarts, general wisdom, and love continue to enhance her literary endeavors and her life.

Jyotsna thanks her family, friends, and colleagues in College Station, New York, Montreal, San Diego, and elsewhere, and her COSAW buddies, conference buddies, and students for their support, solidarity, friendship, and community.

Jyotsna and Amy thank each other for being patient, meticulous, diligent, resourceful, and generally wonderful colleagues as we put together this book over many drafts, emails, and Zoom calls.

And of course, we are both deeply grateful to all those in Urvashi's queer family—and in her family of origin—who surrounded her with love and gave her a sense of belonging and purpose.

NOTES

Foreword

Epigraph 1. Urvashi Vaid, "Race, Power, Sex, Citizenship, and the LGBT Movement," 2008,

xiv BERTOLT BRECHT "And I Always Thought," *From Bertolt Brecht Poems 1913–1956*, edited by John Willet and Ralph Manheim with the cooperation of Erich Fried. London: Methuen, 1979.

Introduction

1 CATAPULTED URVASHI VAID ONTO THE NATIONAL STAGE Shortly after the incident, on April 10, 1990, the NGLTF issued a press release in the form of an editorial by Geni Cowan and John D'Emilio, then cochairs of the task force's board of directors, titled, "Mr. President, May We Have Your Attention? Why Urvashi Vaid Stood Up to Speak to George Bush." A copy of the press release is available here: https://digital.library.unt.edu/ark:/67531/metadc916378/.

2 LAUNCHING SEVERAL IMPORTANT INITIATIVES AND NETWORKS See "Urvashi Vaid's Extraordinary Legacy at Justice Work," *JusticeWork*, June 2023. https://lgbtqwomensurvey.org/wp-content/uploads/2023/06/Resource_Urvashi-Vaids -Extraordinary-Legacy-at-Justice-Work.pdf.

2 "MOST PROLIFIC" ORGANIZER IN THE LGBTQ MOVEMENT'S HISTORY See Masha Gessen, "The Prolific Activism of Urvashi Vaid," *New Yorker*, May 24, 2022, https://www.newyorker.com/news/postscript/the-prolific-activism-of-urvashi -vaid.

3 CRITICALLY IMPORTANT ROLE AT A CRITICALLY IMPORTANT HISTORIC MOMENT John D'Emilio, "A Leader in the Fight for Social Justice: Lessons from the Career of Urvashi Vaid," October 2023, Social Movements and the Politics of Law—A Symposium in Honor of Urvashi Vaid, Center for Civil Rights and Social Justice, Emory University School of Law.

3 "ORGANIZE, ORGANIZE, ORGANIZE, AND CONNECT, CONNECT, CONNECT."
D'Emilio, "A Leader in the Fight for Social Justice: Lessons from the Career of Urvashi Vaid."

3 CREATING CHANGE CONFERENCE At the 2022 Creating Change Conference, Urvashi was awarded the Susan J. Hyde Award for Longevity in the Movement. In introducing Urvashi and her impact on the movement, Sue Hyde recounted how they cofounded Creating Change in 1987. See https://www.youtube.com/watch?v=rj7xnzNtnfo.

3 MILLIONS MORE HAVE VIEWED AND HEARD THE LIVE VIDEO For a video clip of the 1993 remarks by Urvashi Vaid, see https://www.c-span.org/video/?c5040679/user-clip-urvashi-vaid-speech-1993-march-washington-lesbian-gay-bi-equal-rights-liberation.

4 THINGS TO DO "There Are Things to Do" was the title of the concluding chapter of *Virtual Equality.*

5 MAXIMIZING THE LIFE-CHANCES, FREEDOM, AND SELF-DETERMINATION OF ALL LGBT PEOPLE Urvashi Vaid. *Irresistible Revolution: Confronting Race, Class and the Assumptions of LGBT Politics* (2012, Magnus Books), xi.

6 BUILD RELATIONSHIPS WITH PROGRESSIVE, FAITH-BASED ORGANIZATIONS Urvashi received the Auburn Seminary's 2021 Lives of Commitment Award Celebrating Women of Moral Courage. The award citation noted that "[her] decades of investment in, and cultivation of, people of faith working on behalf of LGBTQ justice is instrumental in shaping so much of how we understand social justice, activism, and advocacy."

8 LATER INTERVIEWS Urvashi Vaid. "Dreaming in Color Podcast," Episode 2, 43 min. Interview with Urvashi Vaid in early 2022 by Darren Isom, June 23, 2022. https://bridgespan.org/dreaming-in-color-urvashi-vaid/.

10 ONE OF URVASHI'S MOST IMPORTANT AND NUANCED ESSAYS "What Can Brown Do for You?" was published in Urvashi Vaid's *Irresistible Revolution* (2012) and has been reprinted in a 2023 compilation of Kessler talks from 2022 to 2020, titled *Queer Then and Now*, edited by Debanuj Dasgupta, Joseph Donica, and Margot Weiss (New York: Feminist Press).

14 URVASHI WAS ALL IN For a video recording of remarks by Urvashi's nibling, Alok, at the memorial celebration held for her in New York City, November 3, 2022, see https://americanlgbtqmuseum.org/2022/08/memorial-to-urvashi-vaid/.

16 "REALISTIC OPTIMISM" "Realistic optimism" was a phrase that Urvashi began using toward the end of her life, to describe her own struggle to survive.

16 BUILD ANEW "Keep Your Eyes on the Prize" was a folk song that became influential during the American civil rights movement. For a 1963 rendition by Pete Seeger, see https://www.youtube.com/watch?v=AdJhoF_vYs8.

17 THEY LIGHT THE PATH FOR US There are many translations from the Hebrew of this poem. One, titled "Stars Up Above," can be found at "Sermons," https://www.centralsynagogue.org/worship/sermons/stars-up-above.

21 *VIRTUAL EQUALITY: THE MAINSTREAMING OF GAY & LESBIAN LIBERATION*
Urvashi Vaid, *Virtual Equality: The Mainstreaming of Gay and Lesbian Liberation*
(New York: Anchor Books, 1995), xiii–xvii.

21 GAY PEOPLE TOOK TO THE STREETS OUTSIDE THE STONEWALL INN The beginning of the contemporary LGBTQ movement is usually traced to the Stonewall Inn bar in New York City in 1969, when patrons, many of whom were drag queens, lesbians, and street people, rebelled against a police raid. https://guides.loc.gov/lgbtq-studies/stonewall-era.

21 KRISHNA BALDEV VAID Krishna Baldev Vaid (1927–2020) was a prominent Hindi writer born in Dinga and educated in Lahore (in what is now Pakistan). He witnessed the violence and mass displacement created by the Partition of India in 1947, when he fled with his family to the Indian side. An experimental fiction writer in Hindi from an early age, Vaid was the author of two Partition novels (*Steps in Darkness, The Broken Mirror*) and several other works (novels, short stories, plays, and memoirs, as well as translations into English of his own and others' work). He also published a Hindi translation of *Waiting for Godot* and *Alice in Wonderland*. Vaid married Champa Vaid in 1952 and they had three daughters (Rachna, Jyotsna, and Urvashi). In 1958, he went on a Fulbright to Harvard University, where he completed a PhD in English in 1961. He subsequently taught at Panjab University in Chandigarh before taking up a faculty position at SUNY Potsdam in 1966. In the early 1980s, he and Champa moved back to India, where they stayed until the mid-2000s, when they moved in with their daughter, Jyotsna, in Texas. See https://www.andrewwhitehead.net/partition-voices-kb-vaid.html; https://lithub.com/in-memory-of-krishna-baldev-vaid-pioneer-of-modern-hindi-fiction/.

21 CHAMPA RANI VAID Champa Rani Vaid (1930–2017) was born in Jhang province (in what is now Pakistan) and moved with her family to Delhi around the time of Partition. Going against the Indian norm of arranged marriages, she and her husband, Hindi writer Krishna B. Vaid, had a "love marriage," in 1952. She held an MA in Hindi literature from Panjab University and an MA in education from Boston University and taught at a convent in Chandigarh. In 1966, she joined her husband in Potsdam, NY, along with their three children (Rachna, Jyotsna, and Urvashi). She began writing poetry in her sixties, in India, publishing four books (*Ab Sab Kuch*, 1993; *Sannatay Ke Ird Gird*, 1997; *Swapan Mein Ghar*, 2001; *Aawaazen*, 2011) and a fifth one in English translation (*The Music of Bones*, 2011). In her mid-seventies, she started painting and had four solo exhibitions in India and one in the United States (in Provincetown, MA, in 2012). See https://www.wickedlocal.com/storyprovincetown-banner/2012/07/20/translating-poetry-brush/39904486007/; http://www.artmarketprovincetown.com/archive/2012–17.php.

21 THREE DAUGHTERS All three sisters studied at Vassar. Rachna Vaid (b. 1953) completed a law degree at the University of San Diego and is an attorney at New York University. Jyotsna Vaid (b. 1955), completed a PhD at McGill University and is a professor of psychology and women's and gender studies at Texas A&M University.

21 PRO-MCGOVERN VALEDICTORY TALK George McGovern (1922–2012) was a liberal US senator from South Dakota who ran as an anti–Vietnam War candidate in 1972 against Richard Nixon. He lost every state but Massachusetts. https://www .nytimes.com/2012/10/22/us/politics/george-mcgovern-a-democratic-presidential -nominee-and-liberal-stalwart-dies-at-90.html.

2`1 JIM FOSTER Jim Foster (1934–1990) was a founder, in 1964, of the early LGBTQ rights organization the Society for Individual Rights (SIR) and, in 1972, of the first LGBTQ democratic club, the Alice B. Toklas Democratic Club. He addressed the 1972 Democratic Convention. https://www.lgbtqnation.com/2019/10/in-1972-gay -people-spoke-at-the-democratic-national-convention-for-the-first-time/.

23 FRANK KAMENEY After losing a government job in the 1950s, Frank Kameny (1925–2011) became an early and dedicated crusader for LGBTQ rights. https:// www.newyorker.com/magazine/2020/06/29/frank-kamenys-orderly-square gay-rights-activism.

23 SUSAN ALLEE After graduating from Vassar, Susan Allee began her longtime service in international relations, working in several capacities at the United Nations. https://www.choices.edu/scholar/susan-allee/.

23 BETSY RINGEL Betsy Ringel's career encompasses several nonprofit organizations, including Oxfam America and the National AIDS Network. She was a program officer and the executive director of the Blaustein Philanthropic Group beginning in 1995.

23 AMY HOROWITZ OF ROADWORK Amy Horowitz was a founder of the women's cultural production company Roadwork in 1978. https://amyhorowitz.org /roadwork/.

23 VARIED VOICES OF WOMEN BLACK TOUR Olivia Records was founded in 1973 to promote music by feminists and lesbians. https://www.theguardian.com/music /2020/jul/19/lesbian-record-label-olivia-linda-tillery-californian-feminists-death -threat-music.

23 MICHIGAN WOMYN'S MUSIC FESTIVAL The Michigan Womyn's Music Festival was founded in 1976. It later became controversial because of its policy of admitting only "womyn-born-womyn" and excluding trans women. https://afterellen .com/setting-the-record-straight-about-michfest/.

23 FIRST NATIONAL MARCH ON WASHINGTON FOR LESBIAN AND GAY RIGHTS The First National March on Washington for Lesbian and Gay Rights was held on October 4, 1979. https://go.gale.com/ps/i.do?id=GALE%7CA130244942&sid =googleScholar&v=2.1&it=r&linkaccess=abs&issn=15321118&p=LitRC&sw =w&userGroupName=mlin_oweb&isGeoAuthType=true&aty=geo.

23 SEABROOK NUCLEAR PLANT There were protests against the construction of a nuclear power plant in Seabrook, New Hampshire, organized by the Clamshell Alliance, from 1976 until its construction in 1990. https://nvdatabase.swarthmore.edu /content/clamshell-alliance-campaigns-against-seabrook-nuclear-power-plant -new-hampshire-1976–1989.

25 MIKE RIEGLE, NATIONAL PRISON PROJECT Mike Riegle (1943–1992) was GCN's office manager from 1979 until shortly before his death. At GCN he expanded the

Prison Project, which sent books, articles, and helpful pamphlets to LGBTQ prisoners, and he carried on an extensive correspondence with many of them. https://www.historyproject.org/sites/default/files/2018–01/Coll01MikeRiegle.pdf.

25 JEFF LEVI Jeff Levi was Director of Governmental and Political Affairs at the NGLTF during the 1980s. https://publichealth.gwu.edu/professor-jeff-levi-retires-after-distinguished-career-public-health.

25 GINNY APUZZO Ginny Apuzzo (b. 1941) was a director of the NGLTF, whom Urvashi considered a mentor. https://lgbthistorymonth.com/virginia-apuzzo?tab=biography.

25 KATE [CLINTON] Kate Clinton (b. 1947) is one of the first openly lesbian comedians, performing from the 1980s through the 2000s throughout the United States. She and Urvashi were partners from 1987 until Urvashi's death, in 2022. https://www.aclu.org/kate-clinton.

27 "AMERICA, I'M PUTTING MY QUEER SHOULDER TO THE WHEEL." "America" by Allen Ginsberg. https://www.poetryfoundation.org/poems/49305/america-56d22b41f119f.

2. A National Lesbian Agenda

41 NATIONAL LESBIAN CONFERENCE IN ATLANTA, GEORGIA Robert B. Ridinger, *Speaking for Our Lives—Historic Speeches and Rhetoric for Gay and Lesbian Rights: 1892–2000* (Philadelphia: Routledge, 2004).

41 KAREN THOMPSON GUARDIANSHIP OF SHARON KOWALSKI Karen Thompson and Sharon Kowalski had been together for four years when Kowalski was badly injured in a car crash in 1983. Her conservative parents took control of her life and refused to let Thompson see her, which resulted in a long court battle, which Thompson won in 1991. Once Kowalski was home, her health improved dramatically. http://www.glbtqarchive.com/ssh/kowalski_thompson_S.pdf. See also Karen Thompson and Julie Andrzejewski, *Why Can't Sharon Kowalski Come Home?* (Tallahassee, FL: Spinsters Ink, 1988).

41 REBECCA WIGHT, AND WOUNDED HER LOVER, CLAUDIA BRENNER Rebecca Wight and Claudia Brenner were hiking on the Appalachian Trail in 1998 when both were shot by a local man living in the area, Stephen Ray Carr. Wright died but Brenner survived. https://www.advocate.com/arts-entertainment/advocate-45/2012/05/07/12-crimes-changed-lgbt-world. Brenner later told her story in Claudia Brenner with Hannah Ashley, *Eight Bullets: One Woman's Story of Surviving Anti-Gay Violence* (Ithaca, NY: Firebrand Books, 1995).

42 KATE CLINTON Urvashi's partner and wife, Kate Clinton (b. 1947) was one of the first out lesbian comedians, starting her career in coffeehouses and church basements. She went on to perform for wide audiences in theaters and on television. Her writings appear in her books *Don't Get Me Started* (New York: Ballantine, 1998) and *What the L?* (New York: DaCapo, 2005) and in columns for the *Advocate* and the *Progressive*. She has received numerous awards, including from the ACLU and NGLTF. https://www.aclu.org/kate-clinton.

42 ORCHESTRATED RACIST CAMPAIGN Urvashi is referring here to Ronald Reagan and the Southern Strategy, a Republican tactic to appeal to racism, misogyny, and other bigotry to gain votes in the South. https://www.washingtonpost.com /outlook/2019/07/26/what-we-get-wrong-about-southern-strategy/.

42 JESSE HELMS Jesse Helms (1921–2008) was senator from North Carolina for fifty-two years. He opposed LGBTQ rights, international treaties, and the National Endowment for the Arts, and was in general a powerful voice for conservative causes. https://www.nytimes.com/2008/07/05/us/politics/05helms.html.

43 AUDRE LORDE Audre Lorde, "Power," https://www.poetryfoundation.org/poems /53918/power-56d233adafeb3.

43 NATIONAL CENTER FOR LESBIAN RIGHTS National Center for Lesbian Rights, https://www.nclrights.org/.

3. We Stand for Freedom as We Have Yet to Know It

47 URVASHI For a live video of this speech, as shown on C-SPAN, see https://www .c-span.org/video/?c4443798/urvashi-vaid-1993-mow-speech.

48 BILL BENNETT William J. Bennett (b. 1943) was secretary of education under Ronald Reagan and went on to become a prominent right-wing writer and spokesperson. https://www.edweek.org/policy-politics/william-j-bennett-third-u-s -education-secretary-biography-and-achievements/2017/08.

48 PAT ROBERTSON Pat Robertson (1930–2023) was a Baptist minister, one-time presidential candidate, and founder of the Christian Broadcasting Network, which gave him a powerful platform for his extremist pronouncements.

48 LOU SHELDON Louis P. Sheldon (1934–2020) was a founder of the Traditional Values Coalition, a network of conservative churches dedicated to opposing LGBTQ rights. https://www.nytimes.com/2020/06/05/us/politics/louis-sheldon-anti-gay -dead.html.

48 PAT BUCHANAN Patrick J. Buchanan (b. 1938) is a longtime conservative commentator, advocate of the "culture war" (a term he coined), and consultant to US presidents including Richard Nixon, Gerald Ford, and Ronald Reagan, whom he served as communications director. https://nymag.com/intelligencer/2023/01 /pat-buchanan-a-vindicated-extremist-packs-it-in.html.

48 PHYLLIS SCHLAFLY Phyllis Schlafly (1924–2016) was a conservative activist who campaigned against the Equal Rights Amendment of the 1970s and also opposed LGBT rights, international arms treaties, and immigration. https://www.womens history.org/education-resources/biographies/phyllis-schlafly.

48 RALPH REED Ralph Reed Jr. (b. 1961) is best known as the first executive director, in the 1990s, of the Christian Coalition. He also founded the Faith and Freedom Coalition and Students for America. https://www.wabe.org/this-conservative -leader-is-trying-to-make-white-evangelical-politics-less-white/.

48 BILL KRISTOL William Kristol (b. 1952) founded the conservative magazine the *Weekly Standard* and comments widely on political events. He is currently known as a right-wing, Republican "Never Trumper." https://archive.nytimes.com/www .nytimes.com/ref/opinion/kristol-bio.html.

48 R. J. RUSHDOONY The writer and philosopher R. J. Rushdoony (1916–2001) was known as the founder of Christian Reconstructionism, a belief that the laws of scripture should be applied to modern society. https://en.wikipedia.org /wiki/R._J._Rushdoony.

49 ANTI-GAY MEASURE Measure 8, a 1987 ballot referendum in Oregon, in response to an antidiscrimination executive order by Governor Neil Goldschmidt, would have prohibited state officials from requiring nondiscrimination against LGBTQ state employees. It passed but was ruled unconstitutional by the Oregon Court of Appeals.

49 LOST A BIG FIGHT IN COLORADO Colorado's Amendment 2, prohibiting the state from enacting laws against LGBTQ discrimination, passed in 1992 but was declared unconstitutional by the US Supreme Court in *Romer v. Evans* in 1995. https://coloradoencyclopedia.org/article/amendment-2.

4. A Shared Politics of Social Justice

51 *TALKING ABOUT A REVOLUTION* South End Press Collective, editor, *Talking about a Revolution: Interviews with Michael Albert, Noam Chomsky, Barbara Ehrenreich, bell hooks, Peter Kwong, Winona LaDuke, Manning Marable, Urvashi Vaid, and Howard Zinn* (Boston: South End Press, 1999).

51 ALTERNATIVE RADIO David Barsamian, https://www.alternativeradio.org /barsamian/about-barsamian/.

52 THE CHRISTIAN COALITION The Christian Coalition was founded by the conservative Baptist minister Pat Robertson in 1987 after his unsuccessful presidential run. Its original purpose was to encourage Christians of all denominations to vote and to become politically active in advocating for conservative religious causes. https://www.influencewatch.org/non-profit/christian-coalition-of -america/.

52 PAT BUCHANAN Pat Buchanan (b. 1938) is a longtime conservative commentator, advocate of the "culture war" (a term he coined), and consultant to US presidents including Richard Nixon, Gerald Ford, and Ronald Reagan, whom he served as communications director. https://nymag.com/intelligencer/2023/01/pat-buchanan -a-vindicated-extremist-packs-it-in.html.

53 LOUIS FARRAKHAN Louis Farrakhan (b. 1933) is the NOI minister. In the late 1970s, when one faction of the NOI split and became more like Sunni Islam, Farrakhan revived the NOI according to its original principles. Often called antisemitic, he advocated for a strong, unified Black community. https://www.thehistory makers.org/biography/honorable-minister-louis-farrakhan.

53 NATION OF ISLAM (NOI) The NOI, founded in the 1930s, promotes Black pride and self-sufficiency, but has also been accused of promoting hatred of whites and of antisemitism. Its most well-known adherent was probably Malcolm X, although before his assassination he began to question some of the NOI's separatist ideology and deviations from traditional Muslim thought and practice. The NOI split after Malcolm's death and was revived by Louis Farrakhan. https://en.wikipedia.org /wiki/Nation_of_Islam.

58 **PHYLLIS SCHLAFLY** Phyllis Schlafly (1924–2016) was a conservative activist who campaigned against the Equal Rights Amendment of the 1970s and also opposed LGBT rights, international arms treaties, and immigration. https://www.women shistory.org/education-resources/biographies/phyllis-schlafly.

5. Awakened Activism

61 Epigraph 1: New Gingrich, "Newt Sets Strategy for Religious Right—10 Years Ago." *Freedom Writer*, February 1995, p. 2. (*Freedom Writer* was the newsletter of the Institute for First Amendment Studies, a pro-democracy think tank that operated from 1989 to 2001).

62 **GAY COMMUNITY NEWS** *Gay Community News* (*GCN*) was a weekly newspaper published in Boston from 1973 to 1999. Distributed nationally, it had a small staff and was written and produced mostly by volunteers. Before computers, email, and the internet, it was a major source of news and ideas for the LGBTQ community.

62 **WALTA BORAWSKI** A widely published poet, Walta Borawski (1947–1992) also wrote for many LGBTQ publications, including *GCN* and *FagRag*. https://wgs .fas.harvard.edu/news/michael-bronski-co-edits-invisible-history-collected -poems-walta-borawski.

62 **MICHAEL BRONSKI** Michael Bronski (b. 1949) has been writing about LGBTQ culture and politics since 1970; he was a mainstay of *GCN* throughout its history and he continues to write prolifically and to teach. https://wgs.fas.harvard.edu /people/michael-bronski.

63 **JOHN MITZEL** John Mitzel (1948–2013) was a founding member of *FagRag* and writer about LGBTQ culture. He ran the Boston bookstores Glad Day Books, until 2000, and Calamus Books, until his death. https://en.wikipedia.org/wiki /John_Mitzel.

63 **CHARLEY SHIVELY** Charley Shively (1937–2017) was a founder of *FagRag* and a prolific writer and theorist, author of the classic essay, "Cocksucking as an Act of Revolution," published in *FagRag* in 1971. He became notorious for a speech at the Boston Gay Pride March in 1977, during which he burned a Bible, his Harvard PhD, and his insurance policies. https://slate.com/human-interest/2017/10 /remembering-charley-shively-a-gay-liberation-activist-who-rejected-equality.html.

63 **ANITA BRYANT** Anita Bryant (b. 1940), a popular singer and orange juice promoter, became involved in the Save Our Children campaign to repeal the Dade County, Florida, ordinance banning LGBTQ discrimination, which succeeded in 1977. She subsequently became a well-known speaker against gay rights. https:// en.wikipedia.org/wiki/Anita_Bryant and https://www.nbcnews.com/nbc-out/out -news/1970s-christian-crusader-anita-bryant-helped-spawn-floridas-lgbtq-cult -rcna24215.

63 **AMY HOFFMAN** Amy Hoffman (b. 1952) worked at *GCN* from 1978 to 1982, an experience that she wrote about in her book *An Army of Ex-Lovers: My Life at the Gay Community News* (University of Massachusetts Press, 2007). Her books also include *Hospital Time* (Duke University Press, 1997) and other memoirs, and two

novels. She was editor of *Women's Review of Books* and teaches creative writing and literature. www.amyhoffman.net.

63 ERIC ROFES Eric Rofes (1954–2006) was a prolific gay and men's health activist, teacher, and writer. In the 1970s, he worked at GCN and founded the Boston Lesbian and Gay Political Alliance. He became executive director of the Los Angeles Gay and Lesbian Center in 1985, and went on to direct the San Francisco's AIDS service group, the Shanti Project, in 1989. https://en.wikipedia.org/wiki/Eric_Rofes.

63 RICHARD BURNS Richard Burns (b. 1955) was managing editor of GCN from 1978 to 1982 and went on to found several organizations, including GLAD (Gay and Lesbian Advocates and Defenders), the New York City AIDS memorial, and the American LGBTQ+ Museum. He was executive director of the New York LGBT Community Center from 1986 to 2009 and continues to consult with numerous nonprofit organizations. https://lgbthistorymonth.com/sites/default/files/icon _multimedia_pdfs/2018/Burns-Bio7.pdf.

63 NATIONAL LESBIAN AND GAY MARCH ON WASHINGTON The first National March on Washington for Lesbian and Gay Rights took place on October 14, 1979, the first national gathering of its kind. https://en.wikipedia.org/wiki /National_March_on_Washington_for_Lesbian_and_Gay_Rights.

64 KEVIN CATHCART Kevin Cathcart (b. 1953) was executive director of GLAD from 1984 to 1992 and of Lambda Legal Defense from 1992 through 2016.

64 CATHERINE HANSSENS Catherine Hanssens was founder of the Center for HIV Law and Policy, executive director from 2006 to 2022, and continued to serve as chief strategy advisor until 2023. https://www.nycaidsmemorial.org/interviews /catherine-hanssens.

64 JESSE HELMS Jesse Helms (1921–2008) was a leader in the conservative movement and served as senator from North Carolina from 1978 to 2003. He not only was known for curtailing LGBTQ rights but was also notorious for trying to defund the National Endowment for the Arts. https://en.wikipedia.org/wiki/Jesse_Helms.

64 BOB ANDREWS Bob Andrews was a GCN volunteer and early AIDS activist. He died of AIDS in 1999.

64 STEVE ANSOLOBEHERE Steve Ansolobehere was a lawyer and activist with GLAD, who died in the late 1990s of AIDS.

64 MIKE RIEGLE Mike Riegle (1943–1992) was the longtime office manager, writer, and director of the Prison Project for GCN. He was the subject of Amy Hoffman's AIDS memoir, *Hospital Time* (Duke University Press, 1997). He died of AIDS in 1992.

65 BEN SCHATZ Ben Schatz was executive director of the Gay and Lesbian Medical Association and a member of President Clinton's Advisory Council on AIDS—and went on to perform with the Kinsey Sicks, a drag singing group. https://www.the crimson.com/article/2018/9/20/ben-schatz-dragapella/.

65 ERIC ROFES Eric Rofes, "Gay Groups vs. AIDS Groups: Averting Civil War in the 1990s." *Outlook National Lesbian & Gay Quarterly*, no. 8 (Spring 1990): 13–14.

66 OUTLOOK MAGAZINE IN 1989 Rofes, "Gay Groups vs. AIDS Groups: Averting Civil War in the 1990s."

66 PEOPLE WITH AIDS COALITION The People with AIDS Coalition was founded in 1983 in New York City by a group of people with AIDS who had been inspired by the Denver Principles. They advocated for better treatment for people with AIDS, educated the public, ran a hotline, and provided access to AIDS drugs. https://snaccooperative.org/view/44555590.

66 *COALITION NEWSLINE* Michael Callen, *PWA Coalition Newsline*, March 1989.

68 NGLTF The National Gay and Lesbian Task Force (NGLTF, now the National LGBTQ Task Force) was founded in 1973 and continues to train and mobilize LGBTQ activists. Urvashi was public information director and then executive director of the task force from 1986 to 1992. https://www.thetaskforce.org/about/mission-history/.

68 HOMOSEXUAL The *New York Times Style Guide* forbid the use of the word *gay* until 1987. https://www.nytimes.com/2017/06/19/us/gay-pride-lgbtq-new-york-times.html.

68 DENVER PRINCIPLES The text of the Denver Principles can be seen here: https://data.unaids.org/pub/externaldocument/2007/gipa1983denverprinciples_en.pdf.

68 AIDS COALITION TO UNLEASH POWER (ACT UP) ACT UP was founded in New York in 1987. It organizes direct actions to demand services and research on AIDS and provides support for people with AIDS and the LGBTQ community. https://en.wikipedia.org/wiki/ACT_UP.

68 *AND THE BAND PLAYED ON* Randy Shilts, *And the Band Played On: Politics, People, and the AIDS Epidemic* (New York: St. Martin's Press, 1987).

70 JEFF LEVI Jeff Levi was executive director of the NGLTF from 1986 to 1989. He was a member of President Obama's National Advisory Group on Prevention, Health Promotion, and Integrative and Public Health and continues to be a public health and AIDS advocate. https://accountablehealth.gwu.edu/directory/jeff-levi.

70 TOM STODDARD Tom Stoddard (1949–1997) was executive director of Lambda Legal from 1986 to 1992. He directed the Campaign for Military Service and pressured President Bill Clinton to end the ban on LGBTQ people in the military. He died of AIDS. https://lgbthistorymonth.com/tom-stoddard?tab=biography.

71 NATIONAL LESBIAN AND GAY HEALTH ASSOCIATION The National Lesbian and Gay Health Foundation was founded in 1977 and merged with the Alliance of Lesbian and Gay Health Clinics in 1994 to form the National Lesbian and Gay Health Association. https://rmc.library.cornell.edu/EAD/htmldocs/RMM07613.html.

72 LAMBDA LEGAL DEFENSE AND EDUCATION FUND Lambda Legal Defense and Education Fund (now Lambda Legal) was founded in 1973 as an organization of volunteer lawyers to fight for LGBTQ rights in the courts. https://lambdalegal.org/history/.

73 PWA COALITION, VENEREAL DISEASE CLINICS *Venereal disease* is now more commonly referred to as *sexually transmitted disease* (STD).

74 RODGER MCFARLANE Rodger McFarlane (1955–2009) began volunteering for the Gay Men's Health Crisis shortly after it was founded in 1982 and quickly became its first executive director. He served from 1982 to 1985 and went on to direct Broadway Cares/Equity Fights AIDS from 1989 to 1994. He continued to advocate for

people with AIDS throughout his life. https://www.nytimes.com/2009/05/19/
nyregion/19mcfarlane.html.

74 GAY MEN'S HEALTH CRISIS (GMHC) Gay Men's Health Crisis (GMHC) was
founded in 1981 in New York by playwright Larry Kramer and five of his friends, all
of whom understood that the new disease, which the Centers for Disease Control
had warned about earlier that year, could become a major disaster for the gay male
community. https://www.gmhc.org/history/.

75 LARRY KRAMER Larry Kramer (1935–2020) was a playwright and film producer
who was one of the founders of GMHC and a fiery speaker about the dangers of
AIDS. His passionate speech at the New York Lesbian and Gay Community
Center in 1987, calling for LGBTQ people to take action against AIDS, inspired
the founding of ACT UP. https://en.wikipedia.org/wiki/Larry_Kramer. At a
recent memorial gathering for Larry Kramer, Anthony Fauci recalls their thirty-
three-year-long, complicated relationship. https://www.nytimes.com/2023/06
/27/style/larry-kramer-memorial.html. See also https://www.nbcnews.com
/feature/nbc-out/hiv-covid-19-dr-fauci-his-complicated-relationship-larry
-kramer-n1241684.

75 NEW YORK CITY LESBIAN AND GAY COMMUNITY SERVICES CENTER The
New York City Lesbian and Gay Community Services Center (now the Center) was
founded in 1984, one of the oldest LGBTQ centers in the world. It provides meeting
space for a huge diversity of LGBTQ groups as well as social services and support
for youth, elders, and others. https://gaycenter.org/about/history/.

76 ACT UP MEMBER DAVID BARR David Barr (b. 1956) was an early ACT UP member who now works on international AIDS issues. https://static1.squarespace.com
/static/6075fe20d281ea3f320a7be9/t/60e3cbbac9dcc410ce234850/1625541563344
/073+-+David+Barr.pdf.

77 MORAL MAJORITY Founded by Baptist minister Jerry Falwell Sr. in 1979, the
Moral Majority became a powerful force on the Christian Right during the 1980s.
It expanded the participation of conservative Christians in politics, in part by its
innovative use of direct mail and public rallies. https://en.wikipedia.org/wiki
/Moral_Majority.

77 AIDS MEMORIAL QUILT The Names Project AIDS Memorial Quilt was conceived
by LGBTQ activist Cleve Jones in 1985. They organized people to sew quilt squares
in remembrance of loved ones who had died of AIDS. The quilt was displayed for
the first time during the second LGBT March on Washington in 1987, where it covered the National Mall. https://www.aidsmemorial.org/quilt-history.

78 ANN NORTHROP Ann Northrop (b. 1948) was a journalist and veteran anti-war,
feminist activist, and AIDS educator when she became involved in ACT UP in 1988.
She went on to cohost the *Gay USA* cable TV program. https://gayusatv.org
/ann-northrop/.

78 MICHELANGELO SIGNORILE Michelangelo Signorile (b. 1960) is a journalist,
author, and talk radio host, most notorious for promoting the outing of public
figures, especially those who are anti-gay. https://en.wikipedia.org/wiki
/Michelangelo_Signorile.

78 KEITH HARING Keith Haring (1958–1990) was known for his distinctive political art. In addition to public art projects, he created posters, flyers, and publicity material for ACT UP and other AIDS groups. https://www.haring.com/!/about-haring/bio.

78 GRAN FURY COLLECTIVE Gran Fury was a collective of eleven artists that formed in ACT UP in 1988. They created many of ACT UP's most memorable images, including the Silence = Death graphic. https://hyperallergic.com/42085/aids-art-activism-gran-fury/.

78 TESTING THE LIMITS The Testing the Limits Collective emerged out of ACT UP to record the group's direct actions and aimed to empower people to make their own films and educate the public about AIDS. https://scribe.org/wetell/makers/testing-limits-collective.

79 BARNEY FRANK Barney Frank (b. 1940) was a US congressional representative from Massachusetts from 1981 to 2013. He was known for his liberal stands, eloquence, and humor. He was closeted until the mid-1980s, when there was an investigation and congressional effort to expel him because of his relationship with a young man who was accused of operating a prostitution ring out of Frank's home. Frank was re-elected to Congress and continued to serve as an out gay man until his retirement in 2011. https://en.wikipedia.org/wiki/Barney_Frank.

80 QUEER NATION Queer Nation was a direct-action group founded in New York City in 1990 by ACT UP members who wanted to work on LGBT issues beyond AIDS, especially anti-gay violence. https://queernationny.org/history.

80 HUMAN RIGHTS CAMPAIGN FUND Human Rights Campaign Fund (now the Human Rights Campaign, HRC) was founded to fund pro-LGBT candidates in 1980 and expanded its mission in 1995, dropping the word "fund" and reorganizing as a lobbying group that also encouraged electoral activism among LGBT people. https://www.hrc.org/about.

80 LOG CABIN REPUBLICANS The Log Cabin Republicans were founded in California in the late 1970s as a grassroots advocacy group that aims to make the Republican Party more responsive to LGBT issues. https://logcabin.org/about-us/.

80 MAXINE WOOLFE Maxine Wolfe (b. 1941) is a feminist and reproductive rights activist who became involved in ACT UP to advocate for additional attention to lesbian issues. She was also a founder of the lesbian direct-action group Lesbian Avengers. https://en.wikipedia.org/wiki/Maxine_Wolfe.

81 WOMEN'S ACTION COALITION (WAC) Women's Action Coalition (WAC) was inspired by ACT UP to organize direct actions to promote feminist causes. https://en.wikipedia.org/wiki/Women%27s_Action_Coalition.

81 WOMEN'S HEALTH ACTION MOBILIZATION (WHAM) Women's Health Action Mobilization (WHAM) was founded after the Supreme Court's *Webster* decision in 1989, which curtailed reproductive rights. Inspired by ACT UP, WHAM's actions targeted officials and institutions whose policies they believed hurt women. http://dlib.nyu.edu/findingaids/html/tamwag/tam_162/bioghist.html.

81 LESBIAN AVENGERS Lesbian Avengers was founded in 1992 to increase lesbian visibility and support lesbian survival. A direct-action group, they were known for

drawing media attention by eating fire at their demonstrations, and for their bomb logo. http://www.lesbianavengers.com/about.shtml.

82 NATIONAL ORGANIZATION FOR WOMEN (NOW) The National Organization for Women (NOW) was founded in 1966 to fight for equality for women. It is the largest women's rights organization in the United States and has evolved to work on today's issues. https://now.org/about/history/.

6. Inclusion, Exclusion, and Occlusion

86 "MAIDEN VOYAGE" Dana Y. Takagi, "Maiden Voyage: Excursion into Sexuality and Identity Politics in Asian America," in *Asian-American Sexualities: Dimensions of the Gay and Lesbian Experience*, ed. Russell Leong (New York: Routledge, 1996), 21–35. For other readings in this field, see also Connie Chung, Alison Kim, and A. K. Lemeshewsky, eds., *Between the Lines: An Anthology of Pacific/Asian Lesbians* (Santa Cruz, CA: Dancing Bird, 1987); Karen Aguilar-San Juan, ed., *The State of Asian America: Activism and Resistance in the 1990s* (Boston: South End Press, 1994).

87 LIFELONG LESSONS ABOUT RACE AND GENDER See Urvashi Vaid, "What's Liberation Got to Do with It?," Transformation Series, Open Democracy, 2014. https://www.opendemocracy.net/en/transformation/whats-liberation-got-to -do-with-it/.

87 OUR OWN (RACIST) DIFFICULTY IN IDENTIFYING AS PEOPLE OF COLOR Sucheta Mazumdar, "Race and Racism: South Asians in the United States," *Frontiers of Asian American Studies: Writing, Research, and Commentary*, ed. Gail Nomura et al. (Pullman: Washington State University Press, 1989), 25–38.

88 WHAT RACE WE WERE Ronald Takaki (1939–2009), author of *Strangers from a Different Shore: A History of Asian Americans* (Penguin, 1989), was a historian, author, and activist credited with founding ethnic studies.

88 SOUTH ASIAN FEMINIST ACTIVISTS AND WRITERS IN THE SUBCONTINENT See, for example, Radha Kumar, *The History of Doing: An Illustrated Account of Movements for Women's Rights and Feminism in India, 1800–1990* (New Delhi: Kali for Women, 1993); Kum Kum Sangari and Sudesh Vaid, eds., *Recasting Women: Essays in Colonial History* (New Delhi: Kali for Women, 1989); Shahnaz Rouse, *Shifting Body Politics: Gender, Nation, State in Pakistan* (New Delhi: Women Unlimited, 2004); Rubina Saigol, "The Past, Present, and Future of Feminist Activism in Pakistan," *Herald*, July 15, 2019, https://herald.dawn.com/ news/1398878); and Naisargi N. Dave, *Queer Activism in India* (Durham, NC: Duke University Press, 2012).

88 DIASPORA See, for example, the *Committee on South Asian Women Bulletin* (1983–1996) and Jyotsna Vaid, "Beyond a Space of Our Own: South Asian Women's Groups in the US," *Amerasia Journal* 25, no. 3 (2000): 111–26. See also Sunaina Maira and Rajini Srikanth, eds., *Contours of the Heart: South Asians Map North America* (New York: Asian American Writers' Workshop, 1996); Chandra Talpade Mohanty, *Feminism without Borders: Decolonizing Theory, Practicing Solidarity* (Durham, NC: Duke University Press, 2003).

88 **WHAT, AFTER ALL, DID BEING A SOUTH ASIAN MEAN** See, for example, Chandra T. Mohanty, "Defining Genealogies: Feminist Reflections on Being South Asian in North America," in *Our Feet Walk the Sky: Women of the South Asian Diaspora*, edited by the Women of South Asian Descent Collective (San Francisco, CA: Aunt Lute Books, 1993), 351–58.

88 **TRIKONE** Founded in 1986 in San Francisco, Trikone is a nonprofit support organization for South Asian lesbian, gay, bisexual, and transgender people. From 1986 to 2014, it published a newsletter by the same name. https://en.wikipedia.org /wiki/Trikone. Other queer South Asian newsletters that emerged were Anamika, Sangat, and Rungh. For scholarly works, see Shweta M. Adur, "Memories and Apprehensions: Temporalities of Queer South Asian Belonging and Activism in the Diaspora," in *Routledge Handbook of the Indian Diaspora*, edited by Radha Hegde and Ajaya Sahoo (New York: Routledge, 2017), 304–14; Gayatri Gopinath, *Impossible Desires: Queer Diasporas and South Asian Public Cultures* (Durham, NC: Duke University Press, 2005).

88 *A LOTUS OF ANOTHER COLOR* Rakesh Ratti, ed., *A Lotus of Another Color: An Unfolding of the South Asian Gay and Lesbian Experience* (Boston: Alyson Publications, 1993).

88 **DESH PARDESH** Sharon Fernandez, "More than Just an Arts Festival: Communities, Resistance, and the Story of Desh Pardesh," *Canadian Journal of Communication* 31, no. 1 (2006): 17–34; see also Urvashi Vaid, *Queer Politics/Queer Vision*. Speech given at Desh Pardesh, Toronto, June 14, 1997.

90 **RALPH REED** Ralph Reed is an American politician and lobbyist who served as the first executive director (from 1989 to 1997) of the Christian Coalition.

90 **THE PROMISE KEEPERS** The Promise Keepers are an evangelical Christian men's organization, founded by Bill McCarney in 1990, to "call men back to courageous, bold leadership." They held enormous rallies of men during the 1990s, including a march on Washington in 1997 that drew 700,000 participants, but their influence waned afterward. They were revived in the 2020s. https://religionispatches.org /satanic-or-systemic-promise-keepers-are-back-and-looking-toend-racism-via -trickle-down-racial-reconciliation/ and https://religionnews.com/2021/07/16 /promise-keepers-says-it-has-changed-the-times-have-changed-more/.

94 **RICH TRADITION OF SAME-SEX LOVE AND EXPERIENCE IN EVERY CULTURE AND CONTINENT OF THE WORLD** See, for example, Giti Thadani, *Sakhiyani: Lesbian Desire in Ancient and Modern India* (New York: Cassell, 1996); Ruth Vanita and Saleem Kidwai, eds., *Same-sex Love in India: Readings from Literature and History* (New York: Palgrave-Macmillan, 2000).

7. Race, Power, Sex, Citizenship, and the LGBT Movement

98 **POWER YIELDS NOTHING WITHOUT A DEMAND** This phrase, now reprinted on T-shirts, was part of a speech by Frederick Douglass. https://www.blackpast.org /african-american-history/1857-frederick-douglass-if-there-no-struggle-there-no -progress/.

98 "TALENTED TENTH" The *talented tenth* is a term associated with W. E. B. Du Bois, designating the leadership class of Black Americans in the early twentieth century. https://www.britannica.com/topic/Talented-Tenth.

98 H-1B VISA The H-1B visa is a temporary work visa that allows US employers to hire foreign workers in specialty occupations that require specialized knowledge. https://en.wikipedia.org/wiki/H-1B_visa.

98 KARMA OF BROWN FOLK Vijay Prashad, *The Karma of Brown Folk* (Minneapolis: University of Minnesota Press, 2001).

99 JEREMIAH WRIGHT Jeremiah Wright was a pastor of then-presidential candidate Barack Obama. In March 2008, he drew national media attention for controversial remarks excerpted from earlier sermons. See https://en.wikipedia.org/wiki /Jeremiah_Wright_controversy.

99 THE NAMESAKE *The Namesake*, directed by Mira Nair, written by Sooni Taraporevala and Jhumpa Lahiri (2006, Fox Searchlight Pictures).

100 MOST RESPECTABLE, RICH, AND BRILLIANT PERSON IN THE WORLD This dynamic is what Billie Holiday was referring to in a famous anecdote: "In 1944, a naval officer called her a nigger and, her eyes hot with tears, she smashed a beer bottle against a table and lunged at him with the serrated glass. A little while later, a friend spotted her wandering down 52nd Street and called out, 'How are you doing, Lady Day?' Her reply was viciously blunt: 'Well, you know, I'm still a nigger.'" https://www.theguardian.com/music/2011/feb/16/protest-songs-billie-holiday -strange-fruit.

102 BARBARA SMITH Barbara Smith (b. 1946) was a leading figure in the Black feminist and LGBT movement from the 1970s onward; she helped establish the Combahee River Collective and Kitchen Table: Women of Color Press. Disillusioned with the white male face of the mainstream queer movement, she focuses her organizing instead on multi-issue politics around race, gender, and class.

103 MARRIAGE CASE IN HAWAII IN 1992 In May 1993, the Supreme Court of Hawaii was the first court anywhere to rule that the right to marriage could extend to same-sex couples.

103 SHANE PHELAN Shane Phelan, *Sexual Strangers: Gays, Lesbians and the Dilemmas of Citizenship* (Philadelphia: Temple University Press, 2001), 14.

8. What Can Brown Do for You?

105 QUEER THEN AND NOW: THE DAVID KESSLER LECTURES 2002–2020 Urvashi Vaid, *Irresistible Revolution: Confronting Race, Class and the Assumptions of LGBT Politics* (New York: Magnus Books, 2012), 33–60. See also Queer Then and Now: The David R. Kesser Lectures 2002–2020, edited by Debanuj Dasgupta, Joseph V. Donica, and Margot Weiss (New York: The Feminist Press, 2023), 147–82.

105 IT WAS THE BEST OF TIMES, IT WAS THE WORST OF TIMES. Charles Dickens, *A Tale of Two Cities* (Mineola, NY: Dover Publications, 1998), 1.

106 THIRTY-NINE LARGEST LGBT ORGANIZATIONS ANNUALLY SURVEYED BY
MAP Movement Advancement Project, *2010 National LGBT Movement Report*,
https://www.mapresearch.org/2010-national-lgbt-movement-report.

107 REMAIN IN PLACE Lesbian, gay, and bisexual people were allowed to serve in
the military starting in 2011. Transgender people were banned during the Trump
administration in 2016, but the ban was rescinded in 2021. For a brief history of
laws about LGBTQ military service, see https://www.militaryonesource.mil
/relationships/support-community/lgbtq-in-the-military/.

107 IT WILL ADVANCE IF GENDER IDENTITY IS REMOVED The Employment
Non-Discrimination Act would add sexual orientation to federal employment
protections. https://www.aclu.org/documents/fact-sheet-employment-non
-discrimination-act. In 2007, the HRC and then-Congressional Representative
Barney Frank backed a version of the bill that lacked protections for transgender
people. https://www.washingtonblade.com/2017/11/06/10-years-later-firestorm
-over-gay-only-enda-vote-still-remembered/.

111 ARC IDENTIFIED THREE BARRIERS Applied Research Center, *Better Together:
Research Findings on the Relationship between Racial Justice Organizations and
LGBT Communities*, September, 2010. https://www.raceforward.org/sites/default
/files/arcimages/lgbt%20report_091710_final.pdf.

112 AUTHOR AND ANTI-RACIST ACTIVIST TIM WISE Tim Wise, "With Friends like
These, Who Needs Glen Beck? Racism and White Privilege on the Liberal Left,"
Daily KOS, August 18, 2010, https://www.dailykos.com/stories/2010/8/18/894176/-.
Tim Wise proposed three mechanisms that liberals and progressives appear to rely
on to avoid addressing racial justice.

112 COLORMUTENESS Opportunity Agenda, *State of Opportunity 2010*, https://
opportunityagenda.org/messaging_reports/opportunity-in-america/.

112 "I HAVE A DREAM" https://www.brainyquote.com/quotes/martin_luther_king
_jr_115056.

115 HOMONORMATIVITY Roderick Ferguson, "Racing Homo-Normativity: Citizenship, Sociology and Gay Identity," in *Black Queer Studies: A Critical Anthology*
(Durham, NC: Duke University Press, 2005), 52–67.

115 HOMONATIONALISM, Jasbir Puar, *Terrorist Assemblages: Homonationalism in
Queer Times* (Durham, NC: Duke University Press, 2007), 2.

116 2007–2008 SURVEY BY THE HUMAN RIGHTS CAMPAIGN Human Rights
Campaign Foundation, *At the Intersection: Race, Sexual Orientation and Gender*,
August 2009, https://hrc-prod-requests.s3-us-west-2.amazonaws.com/files
/documents/HRC_Equality_Forward_2009.pdf.

116 ISSUES OF COMMON AND OVERLAPPING CONCERN INCLUDE JOBS, HEALTH
CARE ACCESS, AND EDUCATION Donna Victoria and Cornell Belcher, *LGBT
Rights and Advocacy: Messaging to the African American Community*, Arcus Oper-
ating Foundation, December 2009, https://www.arcusfoundation.org/wp-content
/uploads/2009/01/LGBT-Rights-and-Advocacy-Messaging-to-African-American
-Communities-Arcus-Belcher-Victoria-2009.pdf.

116 ZUNA INSTITUTE The Zuna Institute report, "Black Lesbians Matter," is no longer available. A reference to the report in a dissertation by Arianne J. Napier describes it:

> In 2009–2010 Zuna Institute disseminated a National Black Lesbian Needs Assessment that was completed by 1,596 Black lesbian women that helped to identify issues Black lesbian women viewed as important. To complement the quantitative study they conducted multiple focus groups with Black lesbian women in New York, Denver, Atlanta and Chicago with an average of 12 people in each group. These focus groups revealed that Black lesbian women are concerned with issues related to family, health, identity, access to financial and community resources and community activism. The survey revealed that 69.5% of Black lesbian women were interested in creating families and having children, or already have children and 45% were currently raising children or are planning to co-parent.

Arianne J. Napier, "Narratives of Thriving: Black Lesbian and Queer Women Negotiating Racism, Sexism, and Heterosexism" (PhD diss., Smith College, 2015), 22.

116 ALL BEFORE CIVIL RIGHTS ISSUES LIKE MARRIAGE AND PARTNER PROTEC-TION More recent information about lesbians' needs and priorities can be found in the National LGBTQ+ Women's Community Survey, a project initiated by the Vaid Group through its think tank, Justice Work. The executive summary of the first report to come out of the survey, in 2023, *We Never Give Up the Fight*, is available at https://lgbtqwomensurvey.org/.

116 WHITE PRIVILEGE, WRONG ANALYSIS OF THE DEFEAT, IN 2008, OF PROPOSITION 8 The following *Washington Post* article is an example of the conventional wisdom that California's Proposition 8 anti-equal-marriage referendum was passed in part because of support from Black churches; however, it also provides other demographic information about the referendum's support. https://www.washingtonpost.com/news/the-fix/wp/2013/03/26/how-proposition-8-passed-in-california-and-why-it-wouldnt-today/.

117 NAMING OF THE 2009 MATTHEW SHEPARD/JAMES BYRD JR. HATE CRIMES PREVENTION ACT Some history of the Matthew Shepard/James Byrd Jr. Hate Crimes Law can be found at https://www.lawyerscommittee.org/11th-anniversary-of-matthew-shepard-and-james-byrd-hate-crimes-prevention-act/.

117 ABSENCE OF WOMEN OF COLOR The following article details some of the history of persecution of lesbians in the military. https://www.nbcnews.com/id/wbna33230836.

117 MATTHEW SHEPARD Mathew Shepard's parents, the ACLU, the HRC, and the NGLTF opposed the death penalty for Matthew Shepard's killer. https://www.nytimes.com/1999/11/05/us/parents-of-gay-obtain-mercy-for-his-killer.html.

117 SYLVIA RIVERA LAW PROJECT The Sylvia Rivera Law Project (SRLP), https://srlp 117.org/.

117 AUDRE LORDE PROJECT The Audre Lorde Project (ALP), https://alp.org/about.

117 PROJECT FIERCE Project Fierce in Los Angeles is a community organization working on young people's sexual health. https://www.wecanstopstdsla.org/.

117 HOUSING WORKS Housing Works began as an advocate for people with HIV/AIDS and now helps all people obtain affordable housing. https://www.housing works.net/about.

117 QUEERS FOR ECONOMIC JUSTICE Queers for Economic Justice (QEJ), based in New York from 2002 until 2014, folded because of lack of funding. https://www .autostraddle.com/queers-for-economic-justice-closes-its-doors-thanks-to-lack -of-economic-justice-224520/.

119 CLASS REDUCTIONISM, *POVERTY IN THE GLB COMMUNITY*, THE WILLIAMS INSTITUTE The Williams Institute published the report *State Profiles of LGBT Poverty in the United States* in 2019. https://williamsinstitute.law.ucla.edu /publications/state-lgbt-poverty-us/. It published an update, *LGBT Poverty in the United States*, in 2023. https://williamsinstitute.law.ucla.edu/publications /lgbt-poverty-us/.

119 POVERTY IN THE GLB COMMUNITY Randi Feinstein et al., *Justice for All? A Report on LGBT Youth in the New York Juvenile Justice System*, 2001, p. 6. The report is no longer available on the internet, but a summary can be found here: https:// eric.ed.gov/?id=ED471676.

119 MORE DIVERSE BY RACE THAN HETEROSEXUAL COUPLES, GAY AND LESBIAN COUPLES ARE RAISING 4 PERCENT OF ALL ADOPTED CHILDREN, GLB COUPLES ARE ADOPTING AT A HIGHER RATE THAN SINGLE HETEROSEXUALS The 2005 study is no longer available on the internet, but the following is a similar, more recent study from the Williams Institute: https://williamsinstitute .law.ucla.edu/publications/same-sex-parents-us/.

119 THE EVAN DONALDSON INSTITUTE DID A SURVEY OF 307 ADOPTION AGENCIES Before it closed in 2018, the Donaldson Adoption Institute was an important advocate for foster care and adoption by LGBTQ people and its research was cited by the HRC and others. Its 2011 report, *Expanding Resources for Children III*, summarizes the findings of its adoption research. https://www.adoptioninstitute .org/wp-content/uploads/2013/12/2011_10_Expanding_Resources_BestPractices .pdf.

119 MELISSA HARRIS-LACEWELL LABELED IT AT THE APPLIED RESEARCH CENTER'S "FACING RACE" CONFERENCE IN 2010 A summary of Melissa Harris-Lacewell's remarks can be found at https://www.peoplesworld.org/article /facing-race-conference-highlights-hope-vision-and-change/. See the full video of Harris-Lacewell's keynote at the Facing Race Conference at https://www.youtube .com/watch?v=RcAhhcRSsYM.

120 1997 SPEECH TO THE NATIONAL BLACK GAY AND LESBIAN CONFERENCE, THE POET JUNE JORDAN June Jordan, *Affirmative Acts: Political Essays* (New York: Anchor Books, 1998), 177.

122 ROOTS COALITION The ROOTS Coalition of queer and trans people includes at least fourteen progressive organizations and organizes People's Movement Assem-

blies that lead up to US Social Forums. https://rootscoalition.wordpress.com /about-roots/.

123 POET JUNE JORDAN A short biography of June Jordan that includes the quote, "What is the moral meaning of who we are?"—in which she wonders how our definitions of our identities call us to act—can be found at https://bancroft.berkeley .edu/collections/gaybears/jordan/.

9. Assume the Position

125 "PRIVILEGE/SET ME FREE" FROM THE *EASTER* ALBUM Patti Smith, "Privilege (Set Me Free)," *Easter*, Arista Records, 1979.

126 HENRY VAN AMERINGEN Henry van Ameringen (1933–2020) was a donor to LGBTQ organizations large and small before others with his resources were willing to contribute. https://www.nytimes.com/2020/09/24/nyregion/henry-van -ameringen-philanthropist-dead.html.

127 MATTHEW SHEPARD Matthew Shepard (1976–1998) was a student at the University of Wyoming who was tortured and murdered in an anti-gay attack that sparked demonstrations around the country that eventually changed hate-crime laws. https://en.wikipedia.org/wiki/Matthew_Shepard#:~:text=Matthew%20Wayne%20 Shepard%20(December%201,night%20of%20October%206%2C%201998.

128 PUFF DADDY Puff Daddy is one of the stage names of the rapper Sean Combs (1969). https://en.wikipedia.org/wiki/Sean_Combs.

128 MEG WHITMAN Meg Whitman (b. 1956) is a powerful business executive and politician, who first became known as the CEO of eBay. She is currently US ambassador to Kenya. https://en.wikipedia.org/wiki/Meg_Whitman.

128 SHERYL SANDBERG Sheryl Sandberg (b. 1969) is a technology leader, a former COO of Facebook and Meta. Her book *Lean In: Women Work and the Will to Lead* (Knopf, 2013) claimed that women could transcend sexist barriers to career advancement by being more assertive. https://en.wikipedia.org/wiki/Sheryl _Sandberg.

128 NATIONAL ORGANIZATION FOR MARRIAGE Julie Bolcer, "New York State Republicans Thanked for Marriage with $1.2 Million Dollars," *The Advocate*, October 15, 2011.

128 "SLEEPING WITH THE ENEMY" Ed Walsh, "Gay Rights Groups Stir Flap with D'Amato Nod," *Washington Post*, October 23, 1998.

129 THE OUTSPOKEN ENEMIES OF PROGRESSIVE CAUSES Kenyon Farrow, "Gay Marriage in New York: Progressive Victory or GOP Roadmap?," http://www .alternet.org/vision/151444/gay_marriage_in_new_york%3A_progressive _victory_or_gop_roadmap/?page=1.

130 PASSING THE FEDERAL EMPLOYMENT NON-DISCRIMINATION ACT WITH-OUT PROTECTIONS FOR GENDER IDENTITY In 2007, the HRC supported a version of the Employment Non-Discrimination Act that left out protections for transgender people. https://www.washingtonblade.com/2017/11/06/10-years-later -firestorm-over-gay-only-enda-vote-still-remembered/.

131 *POVERTY IN THE GLB COMMUNITY* The Williams Institute 2009 report on poverty in the LGBT community is no longer available. Their website includes a report on poverty from 2013: https://williamsinstitute.law.ucla.edu/publications /lgb-patterns-of-poverty/.

131 *SURVEY OF TRANSGENDER PERSONS* National Center for Transgender Equality and National Gay and Lesbian Task Force, *Injustice at Every Turn*, 2011, https:// www.thetaskforce.org/injustice-every-turn-report-national-transgender -discrimination-survey-lmultiracial-respondents.

131 CENTER FOR AMERICAN PROGRESS ESTIMATED Nico Sifra Quintana, Josh Rosenthal, and Jeff Krehely, *On the Streets: The Federal Response to Gay and Trans- gender Homeless Youth*, Center for American Progress, 2010. https://www .americanprogress.org/article/on-the-streets/.

131 LGBT FAMILIES EXPERIENCE MORE FINANCIAL HARDSHIPS THAN HETERO- SEXUAL FAMILIES Movement Advancement Project, *All Children Matter*, Octo- ber 2011, https://www.lgbtmap.org/all-children-matter-full-report.

132 HRC/HUNTER COLLEGE POLL OF 768 RANDOMLY SELECTED LGBT PEOPLE Patrick Egan, Murray Edelman, and Ken Sherrill, *Findings from the Hunter College Poll of Lesbians, Gays and Bisexuals: New Discoveries about Identities, Political At- titudes and Civic Engagement*, CUNY, Hunter College, 2008. https://mmjccm.org /sites/default/files/2022–05/New_Discoveries_about_Political_Attitudes_Data.pdf.

132 QUEERS FOR ECONOMIC JUSTICE (QEJ) Queers for Economic Justice, *A Fabulous Attitude: Low Income LGBTGNC People Surviving and Thriving on Love, Shelter and Knowledge.* https://search.issuelab.org/resource/a-fabulous-attitude-low-income- lgbtgnc-people-surviving-and-thriving-on-love-shelter-and-knowledge.html.

132 DISPROPORTIONATELY UPPER MIDDLE CLASS Frederick Rose, "Towards a Class-Cultural Theory of Social Movements: Reinterpreting New Social Move- ments," *Sociological Forum* 12, no. 3 (September 1997): 467.

132 2010 MAP REPORT https://www.lgbtmap.org/2010-national-lgbt-movement-report.

133 *POVERTY, PUBLIC ASSISTANCE AND PRIVATIZATION: THE QUEER CASE FOR A NEW COMMITMENT TO ECONOMIC JUSTICE* Queers for Economic Justice, *Poverty, Public Assistance and Privatization: The Queer Case for a New Commitment to Economic Justice*, 2009, https://d3n8a8pro7vhmx.cloudfront.net /q4ej/pages/22/attachments/original/1375202425/poverty-public-assistance-and -privatization.pdf.

134 SYLVIA RIVERA LAW PROJECT Sylvia Rivera Law Project, https://srlp.org/.

134 QUEERS FOR ECONOMIC JUSTICE Queers for Economic Justice closed its doors in 2014. https://www.opendemocracy.net/en/5050/elegy-for-queers-for -economic-justice/.

134 AUDRE LORDE PROJECT (ALP) The Audre Lorde Project https://alp.org/about. CRITICAL RESISTANCE Critical Resistance https://criticalresistance.org /mission-vision/history/.

134 *THE STATE OF WORKING AMERICA* The State of Working America is an ongoing analysis published since 1988 by the Economic Policy Institute. http://stateof workingamerica.org/.

135 2000 MILLENNIUM MARCH https://www.thenation.com/article/archive/whose-millennium-march/.

135 2009 NATIONAL EQUALITY MARCH https://www.washingtonblade.com/2017/06/11/history-marching-washington/.

136 THE CASE BEING HANDLED BY DAVID BOIES AND TED OLSON The unilateral decision of the strange bedfellows, liberal/conservative legal team of David Boies and Ted Olsen to take the case of California's anti-gay Proposition 8 to the Supreme Court was controversial among equal-marriage activists because they feared that the court was not yet ready to support LGBTQ marriage and that losing the case would set back the movement. https://slate.com/human-interest/2014/06/david-boies-and-ted-olsons-new-book-muddles-gay-marriage-history.html.

136 CONTRADICTION IN THE UNITED STATES BETWEEN INCREASED EQUAL RIGHTS AND INCREASED ECONOMIC INEQUALITY Alexander Stille, "Social Inequality and the New Elite," *New York Times*, October 23, 2011, http://www.nytimes.com/2011/10/23/opinion/sunday/social-inequality-and-the-new-elite.html?pagewanted=all.

136 "EQUALITY OF RESULT" https://chicagounbound.uchicago.edu/cgi/viewcontent.cgi?article=3015&context=journal_articles.

137 "IT GETS BETTER" https://philanthropynewsdigest.org/features/on-the-web/it-gets-better-project and https://chicagounbound.uchicago.edu/cgi/viewcontent.cgi?article=3015&context=journal_articles.

139 HOMONORMATIVITY Lisa Duggan, *The Twilight of Equality: Neoliberalism, Cultural Politics and the Attack on Democracy* (Boston: Beacon Press, 2004).

139 HOMONATIONALISM Jasbir Puar, *Terrorist Assemblages: Homonationalism in Queer Times* (Durham, NC: Duke University Press, 2007), 2.

10. After Marriage = Virtual Equality

141 "MISSION ACCOMPLISHED" President George W. Bush famously announced that "Major combat operations have ended" from the deck of the aircraft carrier *Abraham Lincoln* in 2003, in front of a banner declaring "Mission Accomplished." As the Iraq War dragged on for another eight years, it became clear that his announcement was extremely premature and he was widely criticized for it.

141 MASSACHUSETTS SUPREME JUDICIAL COURT'S 2003 DECISION The Massachusetts Supreme Judicial Court's 2003 ruling in *Goodridge et al. v. Department of Public Health* was the first by a state's highest court to establish the right of same-sex couples to marry in that state.

143 FUNDED AT TWENTY-EIGHT CENTS FOR EVERY HUNDRED DOLLARS OF FUNDING FROM US FOUNDATIONS Funders for LGBTQ Issues, *2014 Tracking Report: Lesbian, Gay, Bisexual, and Transgender Grantmaking by US Foundations*, February 25, 2016. https://lgbtfunders.org/research-item/2014-tracking-report/.

148 "NEITHER BENEVOLENT NOR CHARITABLE" https://lambdalegal.org
/history.

149 DOMINATES LARGE PARTS OF QUEER WORK. See Funders for LGBTQ Issues,
2019–2020 Resource Tracking Report: LGBTQ Grantmaking by US Foundations,
2022, https://search.issuelab.org/resource/2019-2020-tracking-report-lgbtq
-grantmaking-by-u-s-foundations.html.

149 PETER DOBKIN HALL Peter Dobkin Hall, "Historical Perspectives on Nonprofit
Organizations," in *The Jossey Bass Handbook of Nonprofit Leadership and Management* (Hoboken, NJ: John Wiley & Sons, 2016), 3–42.

149 LEWIS POWELL Lewis Powell was a justice of the Supreme Court from 1972 to
1987. https://www.washingtonpost.com/wp-srv/national/longterm/supcourt
/stories/powello82698.htm.

149 WILLIAM SIMON William Simon was treasury secretary under Richard Nixon.
https://www.nytimes.com/2000/06/05/us/william-e-simon-ex-treasury-secretary
-and-high-profile-investor-is-dead-at-72.html.

149 HERITAGE FOUNDATION The Heritage Foundation, founded in 1973, is a
conservative think tank that has had a major influence on the policies of Republican presidents from Ronald Reagan to Donald Trump. https://www.nytimes
.com/2018/06/20/magazine/trump-government-heritage-foundation-think-tank
.html.

150 THE TEA PARTY The oil-billionaire brothers Charles G. Koch and David H. Koch
have become known for their extensive political and financial influence in US
politics, advocating a conservative, libertarian, anti-environmental stance.
https://www.theguardian.com/us-news/2018/sep/26/koch-brothers-americans-for
-prosperity-rightwing-political-group.

150 METONYM Miranda Joseph is the author of numerous books about the relationship between culture and capitalism. https://profmirandajoseph.com/.

151 VALUED AT NEARLY $200 BILLION See the Urban Institute, National Center for
Charitable Statistics, *The Nonprofit Sector in Brief,* 2019, https://urbaninstitute
.github.io/nccs-legacy/briefs/sector-brief-2019.

151 THERE WERE 81,777 PRIVATE FOUNDATIONS, WHICH GAVE AWAY MORE
THAN $49 BILLION *Key Facts* is an annual report now published by Candid's
Issue Lab. Their 2013 report, *Key Facts on US Foundations,* can be accessed at
https://search.issuelab.org/resource/key-facts-on-u-s-foundations-2013.html. In-
diana University Lilly Family School of Philanthropy and DataLake Nonprofit Research, LGBTQ+ *Index: Measuring Giving to* LGBTQ+ *Organizations,* 2023, www.
LGBTQIndex.org.

152 "THE NEW LANDSCAPE FOR NONPROFITS" William Ryan, "The New Landscape
for Nonprofits," *Harvard Business Review* (January–February 1999): 129. https://
hbr.org/1999/01/the-new-landscape-for-nonprofits.

152 JUST ANOTHER EMPEROR: THE MYTHS AND REALITIES OF PHILANTHRO-
CAPITALISM Michael Edwards, *Just Another Emperor: The Myths and Realities of
Philanthrocapitalism* (New York: Demos, 2008), 8.

152 MOVEMENT ADVANCEMENT PROJECT (MAP) MAP regularly reports on LGBT organizations and campaigns. https://www.lgbtmap.org/policy-and-issue-analysis /policy-spotlights.

153 FUND SYSTEMIC TRANSFORMATION, NOT JUST PIECEMEAL POLICY CHANGE For a series of video interviews conducted by Dean Spade and Hope Dector with speakers at the Queer Dreams and Nonprofit Blues conference, see https://www.deanspade.net/2016/02/28/queer-dreams-and-nonprofit-blues/.

12. Homo/mentum of the "Status Queer": A Critical Look at the LGBT Movement

155 SUPREME COURT *WINDSOR* DECISION The 2013 *United States v. Windsor* Supreme Court decision overturned the federal Defense of Marriage Act, which recognized only heterosexual marriages as legal, even though some states, like New York and Massachusetts, had legalized same-sex marriages. (It was a precursor to the 2015 *Obergefell v. Hodges* decision, which legalized same-sex marriage in all fifty states.) https://www.nyclu.org/en/cases/united-states-v-windsor-challenging -federal-defense-marriage-act#:~:text=Oral%20argument%20occurred%20 March%2027,determining%20federal%20benefits%20and%20protections.

156 BAYARD RUSTIN Bayard Rustin was an activist in the civil rights movement and organizer of the 1963 March on Washington, who was often ostracized by other leaders because he was openly gay. https://en.wikipedia.org/wiki/Bayard_Rustin. "From Montgomery to Stonewall," https://www.brotheroutsider.org/_files/ugd /4e1f04_a79d9626f6fd4a6e8a13e29846b696f3.pdf?index=true.

157 HOMOSEXUALITY AS A MENTAL ILLNESS One of the first victories of the fledgling gay rights movement was to change the American Psychiatric Association's definition of homosexuality as a mental disorder. https://daily.jstor.org /how-lgbtq-activists-got-homosexuality-out-of-the-dsm/.

157 WORLD HEALTH ORGANIZATION The WHO only completely removed homosexuality from its list of mental disorders in 1990. https://roodepoortrecord.co .za/2018/05/17/today-in-history-who-removed-homosexuality-from-its-list-of -mental-illnesses-web/.

157 LAWS CRIMINALIZING SAME-SEX SEXUAL BEHAVIOR The Supreme Court's 2003 *Lawrence v. Texas* decision overturned its 1986 *Bowers v. Hardwick* decision upholding sodomy laws and invalidated laws against consensual adult sex throughout the United States. https://www.law.cornell.edu/wex/lawrence_v._texas.

157 BAN ON MILITARY SERVICE Congress repealed the Bill Clinton–era "don't ask, don't tell" policy, which banned openly LGBT people from serving in the military, in 2011. https://www.theguardian.com/world/2011/sep/20/us-military-lifts-ban -gay-troops.

157 NOT ELIMINATED FOR TRANS PEOPLE In 2021, the Pentagon announced a policy allowing transgender people to serve in the military, reversing a Trump-era ban. https://www.npr.org/2021/03/31/983118029/pentagon-releases-new-policies -enabling-transgender-people-to-serve-in-the-milit.

159 METROPOLITAN COMMUNITY CHURCH The Metropolitan Community Church, now an international movement, was founded by the Reverend Troy Perry in 1968, to create a religious home for LGBT people. https://visitmccchurch.com/who-is -metropolitan-community-churches-mcc-and-what-do-you-believe/?utm_source =eng&utm_medium=website&utm_campaign=website&utm_term=what-believe -english.

159 PAT BUCHANAN https://voicesofdemocracy.umd.edu/buchanan-culture-war -speech-speech-text/.

159 *BURWELL V. HOBBY LOBBY STORES* https://www.nytimes.com/2014/07/01/us /hobby-lobby-case-supreme-court-contraception.html.

160 GILL ACTION FUND Founded by the gay philanthropist Tim Gill, the Gill Action Fund supported LGBT organizing in the states. The Action Fund stopped operating in 2017, but the Gill Foundation continues to fund LGBT rights. https:// gillfoundation.org/.

160 *VIRTUAL EQUALITY* Urvashi Vaid, *Virtual Equality: The Mainstreaming of Gay and Lesbian Liberation* (New York: Anchor Books, 1995), https://www.penguin randomhouse.com/books/182219/virtual-equality-by-urvashi-vaid/.

161 NOT ALL QUEERS ARE PROGRESSIVE The vast majority of LGBT voters continue to support Democratic candidates. https://thehill.com/homenews/campaign /3740690-lgbtq-voters-overwhelmingly-voted-for-democrats-says-human-rights -campaign/.

162 "CALAMUS" https://whitmanarchive.org/published/LG/1867/poems/21.

162 COMPULSORY HETEROSEXUALITY The poet and essayist Adrienne Rich popularized the term "compulsory heterosexuality" in her 1980 essay, "Compulsory Heterosexuality and Lesbian Existence," *Journal of Women's History* 15, no. 3 (Autumn 2003): 11–48.

13. Irresistible Revolution: Understanding the LGBT Movement

165 BOB JONES UNIVERSITY See Sarah Jones, "Bob Jones University Would Probably Like You to Forget It Once Banned Interracial Dating," *The New Republic*, February 17, 2017.

165 *A BLACK MAN IN THE WHITE HOUSE* Cornell Belcher, *A Black Man in the White House: Barack Obama and the Triggering of America's Racial-Aversion Crisis* (New York: Water Street Press, 2016).

166 JAMES BALDWIN James Baldwin, "Notes on the House of Bondage" in *The Price of the Ticket* (New York: St. Martin's Press, 1985), 673.

166 NATIONAL WOMEN'S MARCH The National Women's March organized the largest protest in US history on January 21, 2017, at multiple sites around the country to protest the election of Donald Trump. The group continues to organize protests and other actions around women's issues. https://www.womensmarch.com/.

166 BREITBART Andrew Breitbart (1969–2012) ran the conservative news site Breitbart. He was known for saying that, "politics is downstream from culture." With his death, the site was taken over by alt-right activist and Donald Trump crony Steve Bannon.

166 GOEBBELS Joseph Goebbels was the Third Reich's minister of propaganda. The idea of the "big lie"—that people will believe a lie if it is repeated often enough—is often attributed to him, although it may have originated with Hitler himself. https://www.jewishvirtuallibrary.org/joseph-goebbels-on-the-quot-big-lie-quot.

168 SUPREME COURT MARRIAGE DECISION The Supreme Court's decision in *Obergefell v. Hodges* made same-sex marriage legal in all fifty states. https://www.npr.org/sections/thetwo-way/2015/06/26/417717613/supreme-court-rules-all-states-must-allow-same-sex-marriages.

168 MICHEL FOUCAULT Michel Foucault (1926–1984) was a French philosopher who studied the workings of power and how it was disseminated throughout society in his many complex works. A gay man, he died of AIDS, one of the first public figures in France to be open about his illness. https://en.wikipedia.org/wiki/Michel_Foucault.

168 JAMES BALDWIN James Baldwin, "Here Be Dragons," in *The Price of the Ticket*, 681.

169 PETER THIEL Peter Thiel (b. 1967) is an openly gay, conservative billionaire, a founder of PayPal, and an investor in Facebook. https://www.newyorker.com/news/letter-from-silicon-valley/what-is-it-about-peter-thiel.

170 PROGRESS ON LGBT RIGHTS Andrew Wallace, *2011 Report on US Philanthropy Foundations Shows 27% Gain in LGBTQ Funding*, Funders for LGBTQ Issues, https://lgbtfunders.org/newsposts/2011-report-on-u-s-foundations-shows-27-gain-in-lgbtq-funding/.

14. The 22nd Century Initiative to Counter Authoritarianism

173 2020 REPORT, THE V-DEM INSTITUTE V-Dem Institute, "Autocratization Surges, Resistance Grows—Democracy Report 2020" (Gothenburg, Sweden: University of Gothenburg, 2020), https://www.v-dem.net/media/filer_public/de/39/de39af54-0bc5-4421-89aefb20dcc53dba/democracy_report.pdf.

173 2021 REPORT, THE V-DEM INSTITUTE V-Dem Institute, "Autocratization Turns Viral—Democracy Report 2021" (Gothenburg, Sweden: University of Gothenburg, 2021), 6. https://www.v-dem.net/media/filer_public/74/8c/748c68ad-f224-4cd7-87f9-8794add5c60f/dr_2021_updated.pdf. According to the 2023 V-Dem Report, 72 percent of the world now lives in autocracies. See https://v-dem.net/documents/29/V-dem_democracyreport2023_lowres.pdf.

176 BETTER CONNECTED NATIONAL INFRASTRUCTURE The inaugural conference of the 22CI was held on July 6–9, 2023, in Minneapolis. The program is available at https://conference.22ci.org/program.

15. Policy as an Act of Faith: Ten Lessons from LGBT Activism

179 HARRY HAY Harry Hay (1912–2002) was a socialist and American gay rights activist who founded the first gay rights organization, the Mattachine Society, in Los Angeles. Ratified in 1951, the Society's mission was to unify homosexuals, educate

others about homosexuality, and lead homosexuals toward unification and education.

179 DEL MARTIN AND PHYLLIS LYON Del Martin (1921–2008) and Phyllis Lyon (1924–2020) were a lesbian activist couple who founded the first US organization for lesbian women, the Daughters of Bilitis. https://www.smithsonianmag.com /smithsonian-institution/incredible-story-lesbian-activists-del-martin-and -phyllis-lyon-180978309/.

182 WE MUST NOT STOP TRYING Samuel Beckett's famous line from his 1983 short story "Worstword Ho!" is relevant here: "Ever tried. Ever failed. No matter. Try again. Fail again. Fail better."

17. It's Time to Re-embrace a Politics of Radical, Queer, Outsider Activism

188 OPENLY GAY MAN FOR PRESIDENT Pete Buttigieg ran for President in 2020 and did well in the Iowa caucuses, but later dropped out of the race. https://www .politico.com/news/2020/03/02/pete-buttigieg-campaign-2020-election-118573.

188 CODIFIED IN FEDERAL LAW The Federal Hate Crimes Statistics Act of 1990 says, "Nothing in this section creates a cause of action or a right to bring an action, including an action based on discrimination due to sexual orientation. As used in this section, the term 'sexual orientation' means consensual homosexuality or heterosexuality." https://ucr.fbi.gov/hate-crime/2017/resource-pages/hate-crime -statistics-act.

188 AUDRE LORDE In "Difference and Survival: An Address to Hunter College." https://bigother.com/2012/04/16/survival-feminist-killjoys-and-the-making-of -transnational-counterpublics-on-watching-audre-lorde-the-berlin-years/.

Fight for $15 movement, 143
Firestone, Shulamith, 23
Flowers, Charles, 15, 39
Ford Foundation, 2, 126, 213
Foster, Jim, 21, 23, 238n7
Foucault, Michel, 168, 259n8
Frank, Barney, 79, 246n45, 250n5
Franke, Katherine, 200
Frankfurt School, 23
fundraising and philanthropy, 2, 11, 15, 25, 35, 36, 38, 102, 108, 117–18, 133, 135, 138–39, 161, 215; nonprofits and, 147–53, 170; Republican, 128–30

Gandhi, Mahatma, 48, 96
gay and lesbian health movement, 71–74
Gay Community News (GCN), 2, 14, 24, 25, 39, 62–63, 148, 212, 242n2
Gay Men's Health Crisis, 74, 245n33
gay rights legal movement, 106
Gessen, Masha, 2, 225
Gill, Tim, 128; Gill Action Fund, 160, 258n10; Gill Foundation, 128, 200, 213
Gingrich, Newt, 61
Ginsberg, Allen, 27
Gleason, Jim, 64
Goebbels, Joseph, 166, 259n6
Goldwater, Barry, 164
good vs. evil, xiv, 13, 48, 104
Gran Fury Collective, 78, 246n43
Green Light Safe-House Project, 29, 148, 212

Hall, Peter Dobkin, 149
Hanssens, Catherine, 64, 243n13
Haring, Keith, 78, 246n42
Hate Crimes Statistics Act, 3, 260n2
Hay, Harry, 179, 259n1
Heckler, Margaret, 76–77
Hellman, Lillian, 29
Helms, Jesse, 42, 64, 70, 240n5, 243n14
Heritage Foundation, 149, 256n6
Hoffman, Amy, 24, 63, 64, 242n8
Holiday, Billie, 249n7
homelessness, 131, 132, 134, 155
homophobia, 7, 42, 55, 88, 93, 95, 113, 130,

142, 148, 156–57, 168, 181, 182, 205; AIDS and, 63, 64–66, 67, 69, 71, 73, 81
"homonormativity" and "homonationalism," 115, 139
Horowitz, Amy, 23, 238n11
Housing Works, 117, 252n21
Hudson, Rock, 68
Human Rights Campaign (HRC), 106, 107, 116, 128, 130, 135, 246n47
Huth, Tom, 24
Hyde, Susan J., 3, 12, 205, 207

identity politics, xiii, 6, 9, 10, 55–57, 85–86, 91–93
immigrant opposition, 90–91, 107, 110, 116, 118, 171, 181
India, 12, 21, 33, 86, 183–85
Indivisible Project, 174
intersectionality, 4, 56, 102, 108, 115, 143, 170, 182, 215

Jagger, Mick, 23, 211
Jordan, June, 120, 123, 212
Joseph, Miranda, 150
Justice Work, 2, 215–16

Kameny, Frank, 23, 238n8
Kennedy, Robert F., 106
King, Martin Luther, Jr., 112, 181–82
Koch, Charles and David, 128, 129, 156, 256n7
Koop, C. Everett, 77
Kowalski, Sharon, 41, 239n2
Kramer, Larry, 75, 80, 245nn33–35
Kristol, William, 48, 240n8

Lacewell, Melissa Harris, 119
Lahiri, Jhumpa, 99
Lambda Legal Defense and Education Fund, 72, 107, 148, 214, 244n30
Left-wing politics, 9, 56–57, 63
Lesbian Avengers, 82, 246n52
Lesbians United in Non-Nuclear Action, 23
Levi, Jeff, 25, 70, 239n17, 244n27
Liguori, Michael, 192

Index · 263